Best Bike Rides
Nashville

Great Recreational Rides
in the Metro Area

JOHN DOSS

FALCON GUIDES

GUILFORD, CONNECTICUT
HELENA, MONTANA

AN IMPRINT OF GLOBE PEQUOT PRESS

To buy books in quantity for corporate use
or incentives, call **(800) 962-0973**
or e-mail **premiums@GlobePequot.com.**

FALCONGUIDES®

FalconGuides is an imprint of Globe Pequot Press.
Falcon, FalconGuides, and Outfit Your Mind are registered trademarks of Morris Book Publishing, LLC.

All photos by John Doss

Text design: Sheryl Kober
Layout artist: Sue Murray
Project editor: Ellen Urban

Maps by Daniel Lloyd © Morris Book Publishing, LLC

Library of Congress Cataloging-in-Publication Data is available on file.

ISBN 978-0-7627-8666-4

Printed in the United States of America

Contents

🏔 Road Bike   🚵 Mountain Bike   🚲 Hybrid

Nashville and Davidson County Rides

Overview

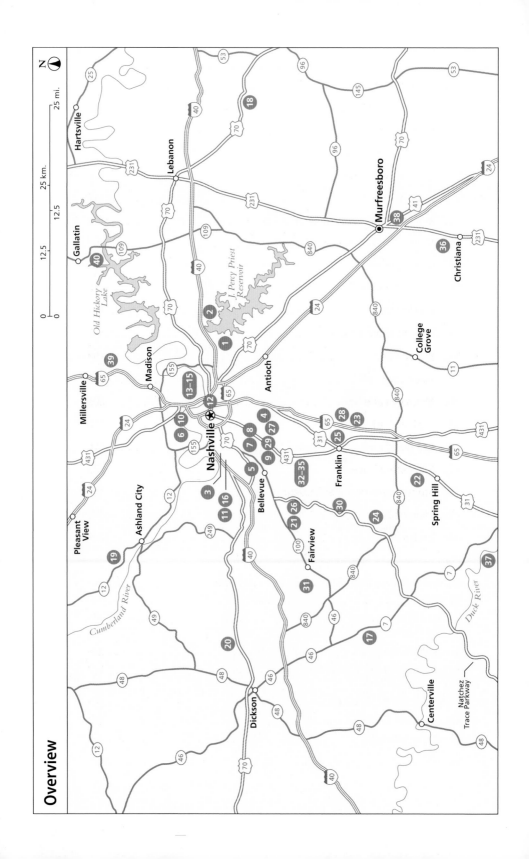

Acknowledgments

Many people contributed to getting this book from idea to print. Thanks to all.

Thanks to everyone in the Harpeth Bike Club, and particularly the "Tuesday/Thursday" bunch. You were more helpful than you know.

If you suggested a ride or a route and helped to pilot one of the rides in this book—THANK YOU.

Thanks to the many people in the cycling community and bike shops in the area who answered questions and facilitated the process in many ways.

Thanks to all at Globe Pequot Press and FalconGuides for their professionalism and assistance.

Thanks to my wife for her interest in this project and encouragement along the way, and her patience and long suffering through all of my biking adventures.

Introduction

Nashville's place in the early history of the United States contributed to its prominence as a city for biking. The Natchez Trace Parkway—The Trace—served as the transportation superhighway between the shipping ports of New Orleans and the interior commerce of the growing US midsection in the early 1800s.

Today, the legacy of The Trace is that it's a great place for biking. It begins about 20 miles from downtown Nashville and is accessible by multiple routes from the downtown area. Two things contribute to its popularity: a 50 mph speed limit tends to calm the auto traffic, and there is no commercial traffic, which absolutely reduces the traffic. Both items are posted and enforced. Moreover, now that it is completed, it is a 440-mile ribbon of mostly rural highway that has rest stops generally at 20- to 50-mile intervals. It is part of the federal national parks system and is well maintained. It has been the place to ride for an hour or a week, or anything in between, and has attracted riders from everywhere as a destination ride, enhancing Nashville's reputation with the cycling community. Several of the rides begin on the Natchez Trace Parkway; other rides include The Trace as part of the route. This book also includes a section on planning multiday rides on The Trace.

The Garrison Creek ride is an excellent introduction to The Trace. Rides like the Trace Loop and Country Store Tour will give you a different perspective on this local treasure. You may want to pack your panniers for a full Trace ride someday.

Within the greater middle Tennessee area around Nashville, the post–World War II construction of hydroelectric dams has produced several freshwater lakes that support vacation destinations and residential development. Growth in communities outside Nashville, such as Franklin and Murfreesboro, has been a boon for two-wheel aficionados. Cycling has contributed to the popularity of these venues. Although many rides in this book are in Nashville, each adjoining county also offers great biking opportunities. Regardless of where you live, if you are in middle Tennessee, there are some great ride venues in your area. Sometimes finding the good ones is a bit of a treasure hunt, and this book can help. Enjoying the rides in this book will allow you to explore the area and identify other good rides.

The Long Hollow ride is one example of an area worth exploring. The Bell Buckle ride will introduce a bit of Tennessee history, and the Arrington ride presents a view of both modern and historic Tennessee, wrapped in some of its most interesting scenery. The Stones River National Battlefield

LP Field Titans Stadium

ride will give you an idea of what it's like to be fully steeped in Civil War history on a bike ride.

In more recent years, Nashville's leaders have embraced progress to make Nashville a more bikeable and walkable city. Various projects have already been completed, bike lanes have been expanded, and more bike paths and trails are continually being developed in the metro area. One source notes that there are 52 miles of completed greenway trails available, with more in development. Some of the in-town rides utilize the greenways as part of the entire route.

These rides invite you to experience some of Nashville's outdoor treasures, including Radnor Lake, Percy Warner Park, Edwin Warner Park, and Bells Bend. You can see the city from one side to the other on the Deep Well to Bicentennial Park and Bicentennial Park to J. Percy Priest Dam rides, and you'll enjoy some of the best in-town greenways on the Richland Creek Greenway, Shelby Bottoms Greenway, and Metro Center Levee Greenway rides. If riding through the woods is more to your liking, you will enjoy Hamilton Creek and Jones Mill at Long Hunter State Park, both single-track rides you can drive to from downtown in 30 minutes or less.

No matter which ride you choose, you're sure to enjoy the adventure along the way, and learn more about the Nashville area in the process. T. S. Eliot reminds us of why we explore in these lines from his poem, "Little Gidding":

We shall not cease from exploration
And the end of all our exploring
Will be to arrive where we started
And know the place for the first time.

Introduction

How to Use This Book

THE RIDES

The rides are listed in numerical order and divided into two groups: Nashville and Davidson County, and Adjoining Counties. The largest number of rides originates in Davidson County, but there are rides in seven other counties that surround Nashville. The presence of three interstates through Nashville makes it easy to reach any of the ride starting points, usually in less than 30 minutes.

There are many great rides in all parts of middle Tennessee; in fact, there are many more rides in each area than there was space for in this book. Hopefully, you can use this book as a jumping-off point; once you're familiar with the area, you can explore other ride venues in the vicinity and develop your own favorites.

All the rides have the same format and information. Each ride has a number, name, a brief summary, and a section that provides more detail about the ride, including:

- **Start:** The location where the ride begins.
- **Length:** The length of the ride in miles (rounded to the nearest mile), including the type of ride (loop, out-and-back, etc.), and the length of both short or long options, if available.
- **Approximate riding time:** An estimate of the time it will take to do the ride, including stops.
- **Best bike:** Suggestions for the type of bike best suited to the ride's terrain.
- **Terrain and trail surface:** The type of terrain you will find on the ride (flat, hilly, etc.) and the trail surface (paved, gravel, single-track, etc.).
- **Traffic and hazards:** A description of the type of traffic you will encounter, both car and pedestrian, as well as other things to look out for along the way.
- **Things to see:** Anything that might be particularly noteworthy on this ride.
- **Maps:** Includes the page number and grid reference for the DeLorme *Tennessee Atlas & Gazetteer*, as well as any other useful maps.
- **Getting there by car:** A set of driving directions that will get you to the starting point.

A detailed description of the ride follows, along with a listing of local bike shops and some of the things you will see on the route. The next section, Miles and Directions, is a turn-by-turn description of the ride, with cumulative mileage. And the last section, Ride Information, includes local attractions, eateries, and restroom locations in the general area of the ride location.

A map of the route that shows an overview of the roads and surrounding area accompanies each ride. The route is clearly marked on the map, including symbols to mark the start and end of the ride, and the miles at each turn. Some of the routes will contain alternate short or long options.

The write-up for each ride should give you enough information to complete each ride if you take some time to prepare. If you are familiar with the area of the ride, then the Miles and Directions section should be all that you need to follow the route. However, the best thing to have on a ride is a person who's familiar with the route riding in front of you, pointing out the hazards and indicating the turns. The next best thing is to have the detailed ride descriptions included in this book. Reading through The Ride section will give you additional details beyond cue sheet data, which should better prepare you for the ride.

If you are unfamiliar with the area, you may wish to spend more time reviewing a map of the ride. The map that is shown for each ride offers a complete depiction of the route. Although it's not a full street map, it does show most of the major roads, and should provide enough information to give you some points of reference.

Bike rides always look different when you are actually riding the route. The ride description will give you an idea of the terrain, climbs, and general topography.

The route directions contain mileage for each turn on the ride. Although the actual miles you have on your bike computer may differ slightly, you should be able to use the route map and route directions to track each turn. If you miss a turn, the best way to get back to the route is to backtrack until you find the missed turn or a previous turn.

The key to having a good ride is to know the route and your abilities. Taking the time to study the route directions and map will make it much easier to follow the route when you do the ride. Having the ride directions clipped on the stem at handlebar level is a good way to keep track of turns on the ride. Sometime, turns are bunched together; urban shortcuts and doglegs can come up quickly, so it's good to know the distances for the next two or three turns so you don't ride by them.

If you're aware of your abilities on the bike, you will be better equipped to determine the distance, terrain, and speed that you can handle, avoiding rides that you will regret. You can use the ride description to assess distance, climbs, and terrain. You may find The Ride section helpful when it comes to selecting the best rides for your desired route and abilities.

Previewing the route and checking out your bike before you start will help you to avoid a lot of problems on the ride, and ensure a safe and enjoyable experience.

Beyond the standard "take a left," or "bear right" directions, the Miles and Directions section always informs you of key intersections. If there is a natural stop in the road, such as a T intersection, traffic light, or stop sign, these are designated so you only have to remember which way to turn. Turns from one street to another are noted with mileages.

PREPARATION

Things to Take with You

Bringing a few key items with you will help you to take care of most issues you may encounter along the way. To address most mechanical problems, you should carry a spare tube, tire levers, bike pump, and a multitool that fits all the screws and nuts on the bike.

You should always do a quick check of your bicycle before beginning a ride. Always make sure your tires are in rideable condition and properly inflated, usually based on manufacturer specs on the outside of the tire. Another easy but important check is to make sure your brakes are working properly. A clean, properly lubricated chain will make shifting easier. A quick test ride can help to determine if everything is tight and functioning properly. You should have a regular bike shop relationship if something needs to be checked or repaired by a professional.

The most frequent mechanical issue encountered on a bike ride is a flat tire. If you have never fixed a flat tire before, there are many resources available to educate yourself on the subject before you take off on that first ride. As of this writing, *Bicycling* magazine offers this training video (www.bicycling .com/video/fix-flat-tire#/video/maintenance/created/d/1). A second opinion is available at eHow (http://www.ehow.com/how_117901_change-bicycle -tire.html). Don't assume you won't have a flat just because you have new tires!

It's a really good idea to have the cue sheet where you can see it while riding. If an alligator clip mounted on your handlebars with a zip tie doesn't work for you, check at your local bike shop for some kind of cue-sheet / map-holder device. There are various devices available online, including Adventure Cycling Association's website (www.adventurecycling.org).

It's a good idea to have water and food with you, especially if you are going to be in rural areas without a lot of stores. You should also have some money to buy snacks and drinks when you do encounter a store. Finally, it is always helpful to have small antibacterial wipes and adhesive bandages with you in case you fall. If all else fails, you should have a cell phone to call for help.

Your Mileage Will Vary

Every effort has been made to make the mileage for the rides as accurate as possible. You will note that for some rides, the point where the mileage counter begins is specifically noted to avoid confusion. For example, the ride counter may begin at a street intersection instead of "in the parking lot," which may be several tenths of a mile away from the intersection, depending on where you are able to park. The distance between each turn should be relatively accurate, but there will be some variation. Two factors cause much of the variation.

First, calibration on a bicycle computer (compared to a car's) is not set at the factory, never to be changed again. To calibrate the odometer on your bicycle computer, you have to accurately enter your wheel circumference or tire size into your computer. This critical piece of data is usually reset each time you change the battery! A small error can make a huge difference in computing mileage.

The other factor is human variation in ride styles. For example, you may turn around to get a dropped water bottle or take in a vista. You may decide to ride or walk farther at rest stops. This can sometimes affect the ride distance by a few tenths of a mile.

The key is to keep an eye on the cues in the Miles and Directions section for the upcoming two or three turns. Of course, there are always road signs and landmarks noted in the ride description, which should assist you in finding your way along the route.

Route Selection

Which street the ride follows is often not an option; sometimes the route determines the streets. But at other times, the routes in this book may make zigzags compared to how you might travel in a car. The primary reason for this is to reduce exposure to traffic whenever possible. This is particularly true of many of the urban rides, some of which include several turns to reduce the amount of traffic you'll encounter along the route.

The ride starts are selected for accessibility and parking. This may cause some of the rides to be a bit longer in some cases, but improved accessibility makes it worthwhile.

There are many good rides in all parts of middle Tennessee. The rides in this book were selected to be a distance of 5 to 35 miles, whenever possible. A second criterion was to select rides that provide an introduction to Nashville and surrounding areas. Another consideration was to minimize climbing; that is, these are meant to be pleasure rides, not training rides. Some areas are easier to ride in, more bike-friendly, and thus offer more possibilities.

If you are including children on your rides, or are just getting into biking, there are six out-and-back rides in this book. Although the length is posted, you can turn around at any time and easily return to the starting point. Furthermore, there are five rides that are very flat and serve as great introductory experiences.

You may be more interested in single-track rides; if so, there are six included in the book. Percy Warner Park mountain bike trail is just being completed, but is not listed in this book. With one exception, all of the single-track rides have more trails in addition to the ones listed in this book. These rides will introduce you to each area and give you a chance to explore on your own.

If you are looking for a more challenging ride, there are rides in this book that are each more than 35 miles long, or have a long option that exceeds 35 miles. You can also combine many rides in this list to make a longer ride. You may find other rides on your own that may combine well with some of the rides found in this book (see Ride Combinations section, below).

Please refer to the Ride Finder section for a breakdown of the rides, identified by city, rural, single-track, climbs, and out and back.

If you would like to expand your options even further, there are several online tools to help search for rides, including Ride with GPS (http://ridewith gps.com). This site has several selection parameters that will help you search for rides in any given area.

Here are several factors you may wish to consider as you begin to build your own ride repertoire:

- Where will the ride start, and in what general area?
- How long will the ride be?
- How hilly will the ride be?
- What types of roads or trails are desired (i.e., rural versus in-town/urban)?
- Are there stores that will be open during the ride?

Ride Combinations

Almost all people who have been cycling for a while experience a certain pattern: At first they take short rides, followed by slightly longer rides; over time, they increase their mileage. Most people getting into the sport find that as their skills improve, they want longer rides, often including the chance to explore different areas.

With this in mind, some of the rides in this book can be extended or combined with another ride to make a longer ride. Here are a few examples; you may find others.

Simply riding further down The Trace and turning around can extend two rides that are on the Natchez Trace Parkway. The Garrison Creek ride is the best example. When you get to the Garrison Creek rest area at Trace mile marker 427, you can just keep riding south for half as many miles as you want to extend your ride, then turn around. Similarly, when the Trace Loop enters The Trace from TN 96, you can turn left and head south down The Trace for half the number of miles you want to add.

Five rides have a common intersection that can serve as the connecting point to combine another ride. You can compare the cue sheets to see which is best for you. The point is the intersection of Del Rio Pike and Cotton Lane. Moran Road, Blazer, Trace Loop, McCrory Lane, and Big East Fork all pass this point. Moran Road, at mile 10.8, and Trace Loop, McCrory Lane, and Big East Fork at mile 1.8 are turning west from this point, while Blazer goes south at mile 1.8.

You can combine Blazer with any of the other four rides and get an approximate 50-mile ride. Another easy combination is to combine Deep Well to Bicentennial Park with Bicentennial Park to J. Percy Priest Dam to get a ride of about 50 miles. You may want to dissect the cue sheets further to discover other combinations.

Extend your riding; the fun is in the discovery. Take some time, get a buddy to go with you, and go for a ride!

SAFETY

Cycling, as with any sport, comes with its own set of risks. Most cycling accidents are related to actions made by the cyclist. Here are some things to consider as general safety recommendations, along with some specific behaviors to remember when riding in traffic.

General Bike Safety

1. **Always wear a helmet.** A helmet is the most important piece of safety gear to wear while riding. If you ride enough miles, eventually you will take a fall, and when you do, you'll have a much better chance of getting up and riding away if you are wearing a helmet. A bruise, cut, or a little road rash should heal in a few days, but injury to your head is always to be avoided. Risks for a serious injury are greatly increased without this single piece of equipment. Also, if your helmet ever takes a hit during an accident, experts recommend replacing it immediately.
2. **Act like a motorist.** You should always signal your intentions well ahead of your actions on the road. Use hand signals to indicate turns. Use your left arm to signal left turns and your right arm to signal right turns; this is less confusing for motorists, and easier for them to see. These same signals should be used if you are biking with a group.
3. **Assist the motorists on the road.** Don't make them guess what you are going to do next. Ride predictably, in a straight line. Don't weave around

parked cars. Don't run traffic lights. Watch for the actions of motorists, especially at intersections where they may turn beside you or in front of you.

4. **Anticipate and call out hazards.** When riding on any road or trail, you will have to navigate around potholes, bumps, tree limbs, and other hazards. Try to constantly scan ahead for hazards so you don't have to make any sudden moves. You want to avoid hitting things with your bike, as you could bend a wheel or, worse, crash. When riding with a group, call out and point to the hazards as you go by them so the bikers behind you are aware of them and can adjust accordingly.

5. **Be aware of other bikers and pedestrians.** When riding in a group, always pay attention to what the group is doing. When riding on greenways and mixed-use trails, always indicate your presence to pedestrians with "On your left" or "On your right" when you overtake them. Never use the greenway or mixed-use trail for high-speed riding.

Riding in Traffic

Every effort has been made to design the rides in this book to use the quietest roads and trails possible, but there will be some traffic on every ride. During these times there are a few things that you can do to reduce your risk of getting in an accident. Riding in traffic improves with practice. By using common sense and some best practices, you can greatly reduce your chances of being in an accident.

Ride defensively. When riding in traffic, it is best to assume that motorists will not see you. This attitude may keep you safe. It will also help you to anticipate problems before they occur and buy you some time to avoid bad situations.

Communicate with traffic. As you are riding, make sure you are communicating your intentions to the cars around you. This includes signaling turns and lane changes, but also moving to the right when you see them coming up behind you, waving them around you when you are stopped, and thanking them for letting you make a left turn. Avoid rudeness, even if you think it is deserved!

Share the road. Sharing the road works both ways. Yes, cars should be courteous to bikers, but bikers should also be polite to cars on a busy road. Stay as far to the right as is safe; ride single file when in a group; and let cars pass when possible. Also, when riding in a group, never ride more than two abreast. If you see a car coming from behind, get into single file so the car can easily pass the group. Demonstrate your courtesy!

Claim the lane (when necessary). There will be times when you need to block a lane of traffic to safely negotiate a turn at an intersection. This is especially true when making a left-hand turn. Remain in the middle of the lane so that you are visible to the traffic traveling in your same direction, as well as to oncoming and cross traffic. To claim a lane, first make sure it is clear, then indicate your intention with a hand signal before slowly moving into the middle of the lane. Stay in the middle of the lane so that no cars can get around you. Once you negotiate the intersection, slowly move back to the right to let cars pass you.

Beware of parked cars. When riding by parked cars, try to keep a door's width away. This will prevent you from being "doored" by someone opening a car door without looking.

Watch all moving cars and their drivers. While riding in traffic, try to look at the driver in a car that may cross your path. Sometimes a driver making a turn in front of you will simply not be expecting a cyclist. You have to be alert at all times. This helps to ensure that drivers can probably see you, and will thus be less likely to hit you.

Focus on riding. It is easy to get distracted when riding in traffic, especially if you are riding through a town. If you are looking at the sights or watching people on the street, you are not focusing on how best to get through traffic, and a moment's distraction may be hazardous. It is better to stop if you want to do some sightseeing instead of slowing down in a way that confuses drivers.

Fido Alert

These routes were developed to avoid "bad dogs." In the city most people keep their dogs penned or leashed. However, this may not be the case in rural areas, and dogs are territorial. If you are riding on streets where dogs live, some may react as if you are an invader. But they may also be friendly; if so, avoid hitting them if they run in front of you. Alternatively, they may be having a bad hair day. Sometimes you can talk to a dog, yell at a dog, or if it gets too close, sling water from your water bottle on it to surprise it. (Don't throw your water bottle.) If all else fails, you may need to get off your bike and walk, possibly putting your bike between yourself and the dog. Once you get past a dog's "territory," it usually stops behaving badly. You may wish to contact local authorities if a condition persists on a favorite route.

If you use these practices when riding in traffic, they will become a habit. This should make riding in traffic safer, easier, and less stressful.

Ride Finder

BEST URBAN RIDES

3 Richland Creek Greenway
5 Deep Well to Bicentennial Park
6 Metro Center Levee Greenway
7 Boulevard Loop

12 Bicentennial Park to J. Percy
   Priest Dam
13 Shelby Bottoms Greenway
14 East Nashville
15 East Nashville Cumberland River

BEST RURAL RIDES

10 Joelton
11 Starbucks to Starbucks
16 Bells Bend
17 Hickman Creek Crossing
18 Watertown
21 Garrison Creek
22 Leiper's Creek
23 Country Church Tour
24 Country Store Tour
25 Factory
26 Kingston Springs Pegram Tour

27 Model Airplane Field to Puckett's
28 Arrington
29 Moran Road
30 Iris City
32 Blazer
33 Trace Loop
34 McCrory Lane
35 Big East Fork
36 Bell Buckle
38 Stones River National Battlefield
39 Long Hollow

BEST OUT-AND-BACK RIDES

3 Richland Creek Greenway
5 Deep Well to Bicentennial Park
6 Metro Center Levee Greenway
12 Bicentennial Park to J. Percy
   Priest Dam

19 Cumberland River Bicentennial
   Trail
21 Garrison Creek

BEST RIDES WITH CLIMBS

8 Percy Warner Park
10 Joelton (long)
16 Bells Bend (long)
21 Garrison Creek
22 Leiper's Creek

23 Country Church Tour
24 Country Store Tour
26 Kingston Springs Pegram Tour
35 Big East Fork (long)

BEST SINGLE-TRACK TRAIL RIDES

1 Hamilton Creek
2 Jones Mill at Long Hunter State
   Park
20 Montgomery Bell

31 Bowie Nature Park
37 Chickasaw Trace
40 Lock 4

Map Legend

Transportation

Interstate/Divided Highway	≡≡≡≡≡
Featured US Highway	=
US Highway	=
Featured State, County, or Local Road	▬▬▬
Primary Highway	——
County/Local Road	——
Featured Bike Route	•••••••••••
Bike Route	•••••••••••
Featured Trail	- - - - - -
Trail/Dirt Road	- - - - - -
Railroad	⊢—⊢—⊢—

Hydrology

Reservoir/Lake	⬭
River/Creek	∿

Land Use

State/Local Park	▢

Symbols

Interstate	(90)
US Highway	(2)
State Highway	(202)
Trailhead (Start)	**10**
Mileage Marker	17.1 ◆—
Capital	✪
Large City	◉
Small City/Town	○
Visitor Center	❷
Point of Interest	■
Parking	🄿
Airport	✈
University/College	🎓
Historic District	🏛
Direction Arrow	→
Other Trailhead	■TH

Nashville and Davidson County Rides

View of J. Percy Priest Lake from East Trail (Hamilton Creek ride)

You can find a little bit of everything in the rides offered in Nashville and Davidson County. One of the nicest things about Nashville is that you can get out of the city into a ride with a true rural feel in just a short time. But Nashville also has a good (and growing) set of bike share lanes to encourage commuting by bicycle.

A combination of greenways and bikeways has created two great rides that will take you from woods to water—Deep Well to Bicentennial Park and Bicentennial Park to J. Percy Priest Dam. By contrast, you can take the Joelton ride to experience some rural riding.

If you are visiting Nashville, there are numerous rides you can take even if you didn't bring your own bike with you; check out the section on Visiting Nashville. You'll find several rides suitable for any skill or fitness level. You can even take a packaged bike tour of the city. During the warmer months, Green Fleet Bicycle Tours and Rentals conduct tours of the downtown area by bicycle (see the Local Bike Shops section in the Appendix).

You can experience some of the best that Nashville has to offer in the way of parks by visiting Shelby Park in east Nashville, Warner Parks in west Nashville, and Radnor Lake in south Nashville. (The latter may make you want to come back and do some hiking.) If you want to work on your fitness while you enjoy the parks, check out the Percy Warner Park ride.

You only have to look across the Cumberland River from the Metro Center Levee Greenway to understand that there will be some hills in the area—you'll definitely get a workout on some of these rides! But rest easy; there are rides in Nashville for every skill level and type of ride.

Hamilton Creek

Hamilton Creek mountain bike trail is part of the Metro Parks System, reputed by the locals to be one of the more technical such trails in the area. Conveniently located on J. Percy Priest Lake, about 12 miles from downtown Nashville, it's accessible from either I-24 or I-40. There are two major trails, the West Trail and the East Trail. The West Trail is recommended as the more advanced of the two, and is also longer—6.74 miles. The easier East Trail is rated as intermediate.

This particular ride covers both parts of the East Trail—Loop A and Loop B. Bell Road is the boundary line between the East and West Trails. There is a subway tunnel on the southern end of the East Trail under Bell Road that connects the East and West Trails. The East Trail is on the Priest Lake side, and offers three views of the lake.

Parking for the West Trail is available on Ned Shelton Road, but this lot (Pinnacle Trail) is usually closed unless there is an event. To access the West Trail, you will have to start from the main trailhead.

Start: The ride begins at the trailhead pavilion, located at the extreme right side of the parking lot as you enter the lot, facing the lake.

Length: 4.5 miles loop ride (East Trail—Loop A and Loop B)

Approximate riding time: 2 hours or less

Best bike: Mountain bike

Terrain and trail surface: This is a good single-track trail, but the terrain is very rolling and rocky.

Traffic and hazards: There will be no traffic on the trail, but there are places where the trail is close to Bell Road (in view at two places); there will be some traffic noise on the trail, especially at those spots. Roots and rocks are the standard on this trail; care is advised.

Maps: DeLorme *Tennessee Atlas & Gazetteer*, page 34, B2. Trail map: http://tennesseemountainbike.com/board/trail_maps/hamilton-creek -trail-map.jpg

Getting there by car: Take I-40 East toward Knoxville. From the I-24 / I-40 split on the east side of Nashville, go 5.6 miles on I-40 and take exit 219, Stewart's Ferry Pike / J. Percy Priest Dam. This is one exit past the airport exit. Make a right turn from the exit ramp and follow Stewart's Ferry Pike, which becomes Bell Road. Continue straight on Bell Road for about 3.5 miles; you will pass the turn for the Elm Hill Marina. You are getting close when you see a sign for Metro Parks—US Army Corp of Engineers. Turn left here onto Hamilton Creek Road and proceed about 0.1 mile. Turn right at the signs for the BMX and mountain bike trails. The trailhead is ahead and to the right. You are on the shores of J. Percy Priest Lake. **GPS:** N36 06.228' / W86 37.470'

THE RIDE

This ride covers the East Trail, both Loop A and Loop B. It goes in a counter-clockwise direction from the trailhead pavilion. This trail may not be as well signed as some of the other single-track trails in the area (some of the signs shown on the website were not in evidence). However, there will be trail riders on weekends and after-work hours. The trail is open from dawn to 11 p.m. according to the sign at the trailhead pavilion.

You can get a copy of the trail map at http://tennesseemountainbike.com/board/trail_maps/hamilton-creek-trail-map.jpg. The map at the trailhead pavilion did not appear to be as current as the one found on the website. You may also consult the Metro Parks site for more information: http://www.nashville.gov/Parks-and-Recreation/Outdoor-Recreation/Mountain-Biking.aspx.

The first part of the trail beginning at the pavilion is graveled. It splits around trees a couple of times. According to the website map, the short connector is 0.11 miles before the East Trail Loop A begins, but it seems to be one continuous trail. You will not be on the trail for long before you discover that one of our major products in middle Tennessee is limestone rock. It will make for some interesting formations along the trail.

You will ride within a few feet of Bell Road the first time at about mile 0.8. Somewhere around mile 1.5, the website shows a cutback trail that returns to the trailhead pavilion. This is the end of Loop A. Loop B seems to blend into the trail without a sign or

Bike Shops

Eastside Cycles: 103 S. 11th St., Nashville; (615) 469-1079; www.eastside-cycles.com
Ride615: 3441 Lebanon Rd. #103, Hermitage; (615) 200-7433; www.ride615.com

Partial view of Priest Lake from East Trail

designation. At about mile 1.8, you may wonder if there is a small cave beside the trail.

At mile 2.6, there is a clear sign for the "#3 Extraction Point." Loop B goes left here. The connector that leads to the West Trail goes right. At mile 2.7, designated on the website as the Rock Garden, you won't be able to miss some impressive limestone outcroppings, marked by signage of two red, downward-facing triangles. You can either go left around the hill, or go straight down the hill and then take the trail to the right.

From this point on, the lake views are ahead of you. The first one is a bit hard to see through the tree cover, but you are getting closer at mile 2.9. The second lake view is at mile 3.4. This segment of the trail is noted on the map as Broken Guitar. The best view of the lake is at mile 3.5. The trail conveniently goes out of the woods to an area that is maintained for lakeside swimming and viewing. You can see the restroom facilities directly ahead of you. This part of the trail is only about 50 yards long, until it retreats back into the woods.

You will intersect the main trail that returns to the trailhead pavilion at mile 4.4. There is no sign. You will reach the trailhead pavilion at mile 4.5. This is the end of the East Trail ride.

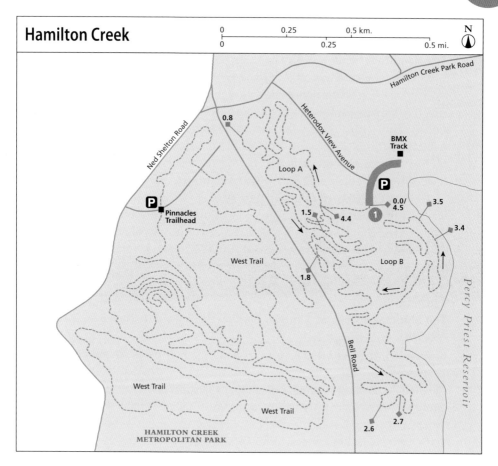

Hamilton Creek

MILES AND DIRECTIONS

0.0 Begin at the trailhead pavilion on the right side of the parking lot when facing the lake.

1.5 This is the end of Loop A. Loop B begins. There is a shortcut return to the trailhead pavilion.

2.6 This is the "#3 Extraction Point." The East Trail Loop B goes left here.

2.7 View the Rock Garden here.

3.4 This is the Broken Guitar trail segment. The lake is in view here.

3.5 The best view of the lake is here at this open area.

4.4 Intersect the main trail that returns to the trailhead pavilion. There is no sign.

4.5 This is the end of the East Trail ride.

RIDE INFORMATION

Local Events/Attractions
The Hermitage: 4580 Rachels Ln., Nashville; www.thehermitage.com. Take I-40 East to exit 221A and follow Old Hickory Boulevard north until you see the entrance sign on the right-hand side of the road.

The Hermitage is the home of Andrew Jackson, seventh president of the United States (1829–37). It is one exit further east on I-40 from the ride route. Built initially in 1819–21, because of fires and other renovations, it was rebuilt on two subsequent occasions, and has been carefully restored and maintained. It is open daily 9:00 a.m. to 4:30 p.m. from October 16 to March 31, and 8:30 a.m. to 5:00 p.m. from April 1 to October 15. Today, original furniture, wallpaper, and personal possessions allow visitors a glimpse into the Jackson family's lives. Some of the farm that was part of the original plantation still exists and is also open for tours, along with the slave quarters, the nearby Tulip Grove, and Hermitage Church.

Local Eateries
The Shipwreck Cove at Elm Hill Marina: 3361 Bell Rd., Nashville; (615) 889-5363.

Restrooms
Mile 0.0: There are portable toilets at the parking lot. There are also permanent restrooms at the parking area, but they may be locked depending on time of year.

Jones Mill at Long Hunter State Park

The US Army Corps of Engineers created J. Percy Priest Dam in 1968, and the impoundment of the Stones River created J. Percy Priest Lake. Although the original objectives behind creating the dam were flood control and hydroelectric power generation, this area has also become a popular recreation area east of Nashville. One of the highlights is Long Hunter State Park.

The Jones Mill mountain bike trail is in the southeast corner of Long Hunter State Park. This one-way single-track trail is mainly situated in the woods, but there are two spots along the trail where the J. Percy Priest Lake is in partial view.

The Tennessee Mountain Bike website calls Jones Mill a beginner trail. It is 3 miles long and winds through some rocky and occasionally rolling terrain. It is mostly flat with no technical areas, but it's still a fun trail with plenty to keep your interest. In the future, according to the Tennessee Mountain Bike website, there will be an intermediate loop and a trials section, with a more-advanced technical loop in the works.

Start: There is a small pavilion at the east end the parking lot. The ride begins there. A sign about 50 feet ahead points to the start of the trail heading left.

Length: 3.5 miles, loop ride

Approximate riding time: About 1 hour

Best bike: Hybrid or mountain bike (mountain bike recommended)

Terrain and trail surface: This is a single-track ride with slightly rolling terrain. The trail is well maintained, with most of the trail in the woods. There are some cedar glade areas where it runs through open areas.

Traffic and hazards: There will be no car traffic on the trail, although there will be plenty of rocky areas to watch for on this ride.

Flowers near Jones Mill mountain bike trail

Maps: DeLorme *Tennessee Atlas & Gazetteer,* page 34, C4. Trail map:
http://tennesseemountainbike.com/board/long-hunter-state-park-bike
-trail.php

Getting there by car: From Nashville, take I-40 East approximately 12
miles from I-440 and I-24/40 intersection to TN 171 S / Mt. Juliet Road,
exit 226A. Turn right (south) and go about 4 miles. Turn left at the brown
Bryant Grove sign and go approximately 1 mile to the end. At the T
intersection, turn left onto Couchville Pike and proceed 1.9 miles; then,
turn right onto the unmarked Barnett Road at the Bryant Grove sign.
Proceed 0.4 mile. The trailhead is on the left, just past the "10 mph and
Jones Mill MBT" sign. There is a large parking lot at the trailhead. **GPS:**
N36 06.710' / W86 47.380'

Long Hunter State Park

Long Hunter State Park is well maintained, with excellent facilities and ranger support. Boaters know about it because of J. Percy Priest Lake, which boasts two public boat-launching ramps. Although it is termed a day park, Long Hunter offers a wide range of community activities, especially kids' camps. In recent years, a volunteer has conducted a weekly Nature Circle designed to "develop a curiosity and love of nature within young children."

Hiking is a special feature at Long Hunter. In addition to Jones Mill mountain bike trail, there are eight hiking trails: Lake Trail, Nature Loop, Inland Trail, Bryant Grove Trail, Day Loop, Volunteer Trail, Deer Trail, and Tyler Sykes Trail. The geographic setting of the park—adjacent to the lake and the woods, and reclaimed open farm terrain—makes for great variety.

The Couchville Cedar Glade State Natural Area is also located in the park, featuring cedar glades, barrens, and edge woodlands. There are some flowers unique to this area; one endangered species found here is the leafy prairie clover. Another variety that seems to grow in the rocks is the limestone fameflower, which has a rose-colored bloom. You may want to check out the 1-mile Tyler Sykes Trail.

The hiking trails vary in length; some can be combined for longer hikes (e.g., the Volunteer Trail / Day Loop Trail). There are 6- and 12-mile options. You can even do overnight hikes to the campgrounds (permit required).

Come check it out! Long Hunter State Park is well worth a visit.

THE RIDE

Begin the trail about 50 feet from the pavilion by making a left turn. If you want to ride the entire trail, follow all signs to Bald Knob. There are two shortcut turnouts on the trail: The first is at mile 0.7, marked by a prominent sign. If you take this shortcut, your total ride will be about 1.5 miles. The park website calls this the "1-mile loop."

The next shortcut is at mile 0.9. There is a prominent sign that directs you to go straight for Bald Knob, or to turn right to return. If you continue on the trail, it is 1.6 miles back to this point. Continuing on the trail, at mile 1.0 you will reach the only bridge on the trail. At mile 1.1, you will reach the start of Bald Knob loop. At mile 1.8, there is a wooded vista of J. Percy Priest Lake. There is a 2.0 mile marker sign just ahead.

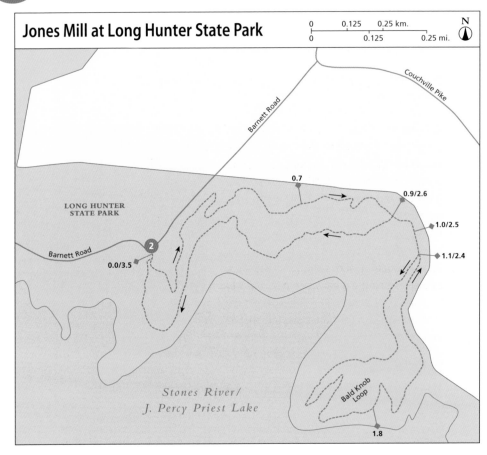

Jones Mill at Long Hunter State Park

Couchville Pike

Barnett Road

0.7

0.9/2.6

LONG HUNTER
STATE PARK

1.0/2.5

Barnett Road

2

1.1/2.4

0.0/3.5

Stones River/
J. Percy Priest Lake

Bald Knob
Loop

1.8

You will cross the bridge again at mile 2.4. At mile 2.6, you will bear left to take the return loop. You are back at the pavilion at mile 3.5. This is the end of the ride—a great opportunity to rest and then do another loop.

MILES AND DIRECTIONS

0.0 Begin at the pavilion and take a left, following the trail sign.

0.7 There is a sign for the shortcut return loop.

0.9 There is a sign for the Bald Knob loop.

1.0 Cross the bridge to continue the ride.

1.1 There is a sign for the Bald Knob loop or return loop branch.

1.8 There is a wooded viewpoint of J. Percy Priest Lake.

2.4 Cross the bridge again on the return loop.

2.6 The trail bears left to return.

3.5 This is the end of ride at the pavilion.

RIDE INFORMATION

Local Events/Attractions

Long Hunter State Park: 2910 Hobson Pike, Hermitage; (615) 885-2422; http://tnstateparks.com/parks/about/long-hunter. Long Hunter State Park is one of Tennessee's state parks located near the Nashville metro area. It has over 20 miles of hiking trails, and is situated on the Stones River / J. Percy Priest Lake impoundment. As such, it supports various boating and swimming activities, as well as being a great place near the city where you can get out into nature. There are various ranger-led activities throughout the year.

Bike Shops

Biker's Choice: 11493 Lebanon Rd., Mt. Juliet; (615) 758-8620; www.thebikerschoice.com
Ride615: 3441 Lebanon Rd., #10, Hermitage; (615) 200-7433; www.ride615.com
Sun & Ski: 501 Opry Mills Dr., Nashville; (615) 886-4854; http://www.sunandski.com

Local Eateries

There are numerous eateries on Mt. Juliet Road on either side of I-40.

Restrooms

There are no restrooms on the trail. There are restrooms at the end of Barnett Road in the area near the picnic shelter. Following the driving directions, instead of turning left into the Jones Mill Trailhead parking lot, continue about 0.9 mile to the restrooms.

Richland Creek Greenway

The Richland Creek Greenway is part of the larger Music City Bikeway system. This ride follows a two-way paved trail on the Richland Creek area of west Nashville. Parts of this ride are included in the Radnor Lake Loop and Deep Well to Bicentennial Park rides. However, it is such an accessible ride from three different points, with easy parking, that it can be a great, stand-alone ride for any occasion. It is almost a circle ride, the turnaround point located at the McCabe Trailhead at mile 2.5.

This area has an interesting transportation history. You will ride by the structure of the first White Bridge Road Bridge, constructed in the 1840s at approximately mile 1.8. Engineer Howard Jones was also the engineer for the Shelby Street Bridge (see Shelby Bottoms Greenway ride). A bit later, in 1852, the railroad you ride by was chartered as the Nashville and Northwestern Railroad. Following the transportation trend, in 1927 the city of Nashville purchased 131 acres to build McConnell Field, the first municipal airport in Nashville. It is now the McCabe Golf Course.

Start: The trailhead is at the Richland Creek Greenway that begins from the parking lot of McCabe Park Community Center, 101 46th Avenue North, Nashville; (615) 862-8457.

Length: 5 miles out and back on the same trail

Approximate riding time: 1 hour or less

Best bike: Any bike

Terrain and trail surface: Flat ride on a paved asphalt bike path or on elevated boardwalk platform, except for two short climbs

Traffic and hazards: The ride is entirely on closed bike paths. There will be no car traffic, but the trail may be crowded with other bikers, runners, walkers, and in-line skaters. The elevated boardwalk trail structures narrow the trail and may be slick if there has been any rain or heavy fog.

Maps: DeLorme *Tennessee Atlas & Gazetteer*, page 33, B8. Trail map: Nashville.gov website, Richland Creek Greenway (dated); https://maps .google.com/maps/ms?ie=UTF8&hl=en&msa=0&msid=1143513168912 71919778.000435dbb9a2b71037ed1&t=h&z=15

Getting there by car: From downtown Nashville, proceed west and follow US 70 / Broadway / West End Avenue until you get to Murphy Road in the 3300 block of West End Avenue, at the traffic light. Turn right onto Murphy Road for 1.2 miles, and turn left beside the McCabe Park Community Center. Bear right into the parking lot behind the community center, adjacent to the driving range. **GPS:** N36 7.5756' / W86 50.8776'

THE RIDE

The ride follows the bike path, well-marked once you get started. The path begins at the back right corner of the McCabe Park Community Center parking lot as you face away from Murphy Road. The driving range will be adjacent on your left side. Murphy Road becomes 46th Avenue North at the sharp turn just at the community center.

You will first encounter the Wyoming Trailhead. This point also picks up the Music City Bikeway. As you leave this point, you will notice that this is one of the places where the trail is not flat. There is a short downhill and a 90-degree right turn at the bottom. The trail runs beside the McCabe Golf Course, but don't worry—there is a very tall fence that will protect you from any stray golf balls. The trail will run beside Richland Creek; at each of the two creek crossings, the trail surface changes to a boardwalk structure. As you proceed over Richland Creek, there is an access point at mile 1.4 at the Nashville State Community College, but stay on the Greenway.

Bike Shops

Cumberland Transit: 2807 West End Ave., Nashville; (615) 321-4069; http://cumberlandtransit.com/cycling/
Gran Fondo: 5133 Harding Rd., Suite A6, Nashville; (615) 354-1090; http://www.granfondocycles.com/
Gran Fondo Trail & Fitness: 5133 Harding Rd., Suite B-1, Nashville; (615) 499-4634; http://www.granfondotrail.com/
Green Fleet Bicycle Shop: 1579 Edgehill Ave., Nashville; (615) 379-8687; http://greenfleetbikes.com
Halcyon Bike Shop: 1119 Halcyon Ave., Corner of 12th Ave. S. and Halcyon Ave., Nashville; (615) 730-9344; www.halcyon bike.com

Early trestle foundation

You will again cross over Richland Creek on the boardwalk surface. Immediately before crossing over Richland Creek at mile 1.8, there is an access to the right. This is the Lion's Head Trailhead, and the cutoff point for the Music City Bikeway. Continue on the Greenway. You will pass by the NES Trailhead after crossing over Richland Creek at mile 2.0. The original White Bridge Road bridge structure is on your right. Proceed past this and turn left just before the trail ends at Cherokee Avenue. Go up the hill to the McCabe Trailhead shelter. This is the turnaround point for the ride at mile 2.5. You will return back on the same path.

MILES AND DIRECTIONS

0.0 Begin at the McCabe Driving Range and follow the bike path.

1.4 Nashville State Community College access point. Continue on the bike path.

1.8 Lion's Head Trailhead access point. Continue on the bike path.

2.0 NES Traillead access point. Continue on the bike path.

2.5 This is the turnaround point at the McCabe Trailhead.

5.0 This is the end of the ride.

Best Bike Rides Nashville

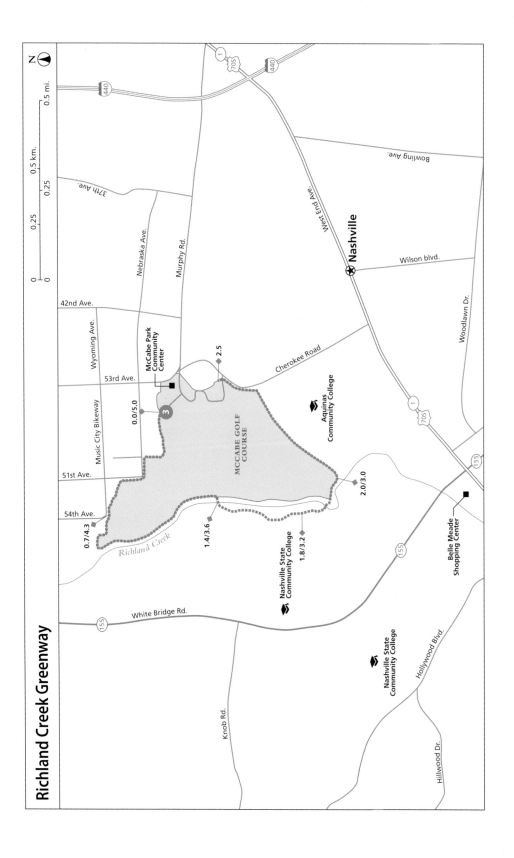

Richland Creek Greenway

Local Events/Attractions

Nashville is sometimes referred to as the Athens of the South because of the number of institutions of higher learning in the area. Two local universities nearby with prestigious schools of music are Belmont University and Vanderbilt University Blair School of Music. They offer various concerts featuring both faculty and students. Each has a calendar of events page on its website. Following is contact information for each one:

Belmont School of Music: 1900 Belmont Blvd., Nashville; (615) 460-6408; http://www.belmont.edu/music/calendarevents/index.html

Vanderbilt University Blair School of Music: 2400 Blakemore Ave., Nashville; (615) 322-7651; http://blair.vanderbilt.edu/events/

Local Eateries

There are various restaurants in the area. It is easiest to exit at the NES Trailhead access. The Belle Meade Shopping Center and the Hill Center are just around the corner after you cross the White Bridge Road Pedestrian Bridge on your left, once you get to the trailhead. There are several restaurants and a Starbucks.

From the NES Trailhead, to the right from this point, if you go about 0.25 mile, you will find various shops and restaurants on White Bridge Road at the intersection of Post Road (the first street) and White Bridge Road. You also get to the same area if you take the Lion's Head Trailhead access at mile 1.8. It is about 0.3 mile to White Bridge Road from this trailhead.

Also, at the beginning of the ride, there are several restaurants on either side of Murphy Road. A local restaurant and coffee shop, Star Bagel, is directly across the street from the start of the ride.

Nashville's Municipal Airfields

McConnell Field was the first true municipal airport for the city of Nashville, located along Murphy Road, Richland Creek, the railroad, and Colorado Avenue. In 1927 the city bought 131 acres from Warren Sloan and made this the Nashville airport.

Technology and flight demands soon caused the site to become obsolete in the 1930s, so a new municipal airport was built at Berry Field, still the site of Nashville International Airport. Progress came quickly when American Airlines landed the first plane at the new airport in 1937.

Dutchman's Curve

There are old limestone trestle foundations standing at approximately mile 1.8 of this ride. This is Dutchman's Curve, the site of the deadliest train wreck in US history. On July 9, 1918, two crowded trains collided head-on at this location. The impact caused passenger cars to derail into the surrounding cornfields, and fires broke out in the wreckage. Over a hundred people died, including many African-American workers journeying to work at the munitions plant near Old Hickory.

Train No. 4 was coming from Memphis, and Train No. 1 was coming from Nashville. By convention, Train No. 1 waited for the express from Memphis to pass at the double tracks at Centennial Park, about 2 miles east from the point of the collision. Because both engineers were on the right side, they were unable to see ahead due to the curve. Fourteen crew members from both trains were killed. The engineer from the Memphis express, Mr. Lloyd, was killed. He was scheduled to retire the next day.

It is speculated that this limestone foundation may be part of the initial construction of the railroad dating back to before the Civil War.

Restrooms

Mile 2.0: There is a portable restroom as you cross Richland Creek.

Mile 2.0: This is off the ride, but if you exit at the NES Trailhead, there is a portable restroom facility at the entrance to Richland Creek Greenway in 0.6 mile.

Radnor Lake

Radnor Lake is one of the Nashville gems in the southern part of Davidson County, 8 miles from downtown. The 85-acre lake is situated in the state's first Natural Area, which measures 1,118 acres. It is designated for day use only. Visitors are able to view an assortment of migratory waterfowl and songbirds, reptiles, amphibians, and white-tailed deer. There is also a diversity of wildflowers, trees, shrubs, vines, mosses, and fungi. The road beside Radnor Lake is only 1.2 miles long, and there is no biking allowed on the trails in the park; this is a bike, then hike, or a larger bike in a loop trip. But the scenery of Radnor Lake is not to be missed!

Radnor Lake was constructed in 1914 by the Louisville and Nashville Railroad as a source of water for their steam engines, and for the cattle housed at nearby Radnor Railroad Yards. As the steam engine disappeared, the need for such large quantities of water also disappeared, and the property was put up for sale. It was originally purchased by the Oman Company as a residential development site. However, it had already become a well-known natural site. A combination of public and private efforts saved Radnor Lake, and it became the State of Tennessee's first Natural Area open to the general public. It has continued to be supported by this public/private partnership to become the 1,118-acre area, with a recent acquisition just completed.

Start: The start of the ride is the Radnor Lake State Natural Area visitor center: 1160 Otter Creek Rd., Nashville; (615) 373-3467.

Length: 21 miles, loop ride

Approximate riding time: 2 hours

Best bike: Any bike

Terrain and trail surface: This is "Nashville rolling" terrain, with a climb near the end of the ride. The entire ride is on paved streets or bike paths, except for the paved surface around Radnor Lake, which is very uneven, especially on the lakeside.

Traffic and hazards: Although the route was designed to avoid places with heavy traffic, there are short sections where you will encounter some. Part of the ride is on busy streets with a bike lane. The road surface around Radnor Lake is uneven, and you're also sharing this road with pedestrians; ride slowly and announce when you pass. Watch for surfaces that may be dangerous and for barriers around the lake.

Things to see: Radnor Lake, waterfowl and songbirds, reptiles, amphibians, and white-tailed deer

Maps: DeLorme *Tennessee Atlas & Gazetteer*, page 34, C1

Getting there by car: Radnor Lake is south of Nashville on Otter Creek Road. It is accessible from either 21st Avenue South / US 431 / Hillsboro Pike / TN 106 or 8th Avenue South / US 31 / Franklin Pike. In either case proceed south out of Nashville until you get to Otter Creek Road. It will only turn one way. Follow the signs to Radnor Lake. The ride is based on access from the 21st Avenue South / Hillsboro Pike side, but you can do the ride from either way. If you approach from the Franklin Pike entrance, you will follow the access road around the lake until you reach the visitor center to begin the ride. **GPS:** N36 03.800' / W86 48.600'

THE RIDE

This ride begins at the Radnor Lake State Natural Area visitor center, on the west side of the park. It is a loop ride. The loop will go generally west and circle to Belmont University through west Nashville via part of the Music City Bikeway and Greenway; then, you'll use bike lanes and a couple of neighborhood shortcuts around the southern part of town and return back to Radnor Lake.

From the parking lot, turn right to get onto Otter Creek. Cross Granny White Pike, then proceed to Hillsboro Pike at mile 2.3. Hillsboro Pike is busy, but there is a bike lane. Proceed right, heading north until you reach Tyne Boulevard at mile 3.2. There is a large church on the corner. There is a turn lane to ease the left turn on Tyne Boulevard. Follow Tyne until you reach Belle Meade Boulevard.

Turn right on Belle Meade Boulevard and proceed until you reach US 70 / Harding Road. Turn right for this short leg on a busy street. After you go through the first traffic light at the intersection of Harding Road and Hillwood Boulevard, turn left into the Kroger parking lot at mile 7.2 and proceed through the Belle Meade Shopping Center. Go under the White Bridge Road overpass at mile 7.4, then immediately turn left onto the pedestrian and bike bridge over the railroad tracks and follow the signs onto the Greenway. The Publix store will be on your right as you get on the bridge.

You will go 0.4 mile to a trail intersection; take a right. Be cautious on the wooden bridges; they narrow the trail, and are slick if there has been any rain. Follow the Richland Creek Greenway and go straight to the end of the bike path to the street at mile 8.5 (do not take the left turn in the bike path).

The route skirts traffic as much as possible for about the next 3 miles to get over to the Belmont Campus area. Take a right onto Cherokee and follow it to the next intersection; turn left onto Aberdeen, also at mile 8.5. At the intersection at mile 9.0, Aberdeen becomes Princeton. Follow Aberdeen/Princeton to Craighead at mile 9.3, and turn right onto Craighead. Take a left at the intersection onto Central at mile 9.3, and follow it to Bowling Avenue at mile 9.5. As you approach the traffic light intersection at West End Avenue, at mile 9.7, get into the right lane at the intersection.

Make a left turn onto West End (from the right lane) and turn right at the first street, Elmington, at mile 9.8. Follow Elmington to the three-way stop in front of West End Middle School, at mile 10.0, and turn left at Ransom. You will ride over I-440 as you follow Ransom to Fairfax, and turn right at mile 10.3. This is one of the Bike Lane sections of the ride. Follow Fairfax through the stops and traffic light until you reach 21st Avenue South at mile 11.2. Turn right onto 21st Avenue South. Be very cautious at this busy intersection; watch the oncoming traffic as you make the turn. Turn left onto Portland Avenue, the first street in about 260 feet. The turn will be at the end of the traffic island.

There are a few more quick turns. At mile 12.0, turn left on Elmwood, then right onto 12th Avenue South at mile 12.3. In the same block, turn left onto Caruthers at mile 12.4, then right at the next block onto Lealand Lane / 10th Avenue South at mile 12.5.

Enjoy the ride through this residential neighborhood. At the turn onto Robertson Academy Road, don't be confused by the names change: it is Robertson Academy Road to the left and Grassland Lane

Bike Shops

Cumberland Transit: 2807 West End Ave., Nashville; (615) 321-4069; http://cumberlandtransit.com/cycling/
Gran Fondo: 5133 Harding Rd., Suite A6, Nashville; (615) 354-1090; http://www.granfondocycles.com/
Gran Fondo Trail & Fitness: 5133 Harding Rd., Suite B-1, Nashville; (615) 499-4634; http://www.granfondotrail.com/
Green Fleet Bicycle Shop: 1579 Edgehill Ave., Nashville; (615) 379-8687; http://greenfleetbikes.com
Halcyon Bike Shop: 1119 Halcyon Ave., Corner of 12th Ave. S. and Halcyon Ave., Nashville; (615) 730-9344; www.halcyonbike.com

Radnor Lake

to the right. Be aware of the traffic on Franklin Pike. It can be busy at times, and the traffic may be moving fast.

The next 2 miles will skirt around as much of the busy Franklin Pike traffic as possible. Turn right onto Franklin Pike. You will pass the John Overton High School campus and turn left on Lambert Drive.

You will go under I-65 South before the turn onto Regents Drive. Another name change; Hogan Road becomes Otter Creek Road when you cross over Franklin Pike.

This part of the ride will involve a 200-foot elevation-gain climb. Proceed to Radnor Lake. The park boundary is at mile 19.3. If you parked at the west parking lot on the visitor center side, prepare to be awed by the view. You will follow this park road until you make a turn at the visitor center at mile 21.0. This is the end of the ride.

Travellers Rest Plantation & Museum

636 Farrell Pkwy., Nashville; 615-832-8197; travellersrestplantation.org

Travellers Rest is listed in the National Register of Historic Places, and open for historic tours, specialty tours, and events hosting. It was the Nashville home of Judge John (1766–1833) and Mary Overton and their descendants for 150 years.

Judge Overton was one of the wealthiest and most learned men of his time. He was also a close friend and adviser of Andrew Jackson; in fact, the two men cofounded Memphis. Travellers Rest was the name Judge Overton gave to the house, reflecting how he would rest there after long horseback trips as a circuit judge.

Late in the 1790s, Judge Overton purchased a Revolutionary War grant from the heirs of David Maxwell. He and Mrs. Overton began building a popular style house of the time—a vernacular Federal style house. The original structure was a two-story house with four rooms.

There's an interesting story related to the house's construction, which has continued to this day. In 1798 while a cellar was being dug, artifacts of a prehistoric Native American village were discovered. They included arrowheads, pottery, animal bones, and human remains. Originally, Colonel Overton named the house Golgotha, meaning "hill of skulls." Beginning in the 1800s, various professional archaeologists have examined these artifacts. The conclusion: The remains are those of a Mississippian village of about two hundred to three hundred people who inhabited the area around AD 1000–1400.

After the death of Mrs. Overton in 1862, her son John and his wife, Harriet, occupied the house. At that time, the plantation farm covered 1,050 acres and was worked by eighty slaves.

The house has undergone numerous renovations over the years. Initially completed in 1799, it was refurbished in 1808, 1828, and after the Civil War. Artifacts from both white and black cultures reveal many stories from these years. The 1833 death inventory of Judge Overton was a particularly useful part of that story.

The house's near demise was related to the railroads. The National Society of Colonial Dames of America in Tennessee rescued it in 1954 from a planned demolition by the L & N Railroad. Radnor Yards and mixed twentieth-century growth had encircled the house.

Beginning with the late eighteenth century and continuing with a significant role in Nashville's Civil War history, Travellers Rest is an interesting place to visit.

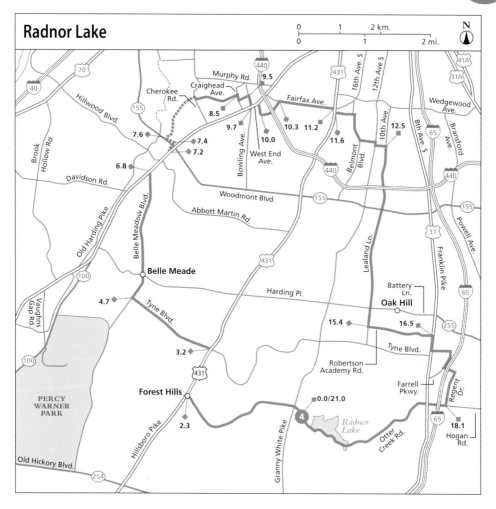

MILES AND DIRECTIONS

0.0 Begin the ride from the visitor center. Turn right to begin the ride.

2.3 Turn right onto US 431 / Hillsboro Pike / TN 106.

3.2 Turn left onto Tyne Boulevard.

4.7 Turn right on Belle Meade Boulevard.

6.8 Turn right on US 70 / Harding Road.

7.2 Turn left into the Belle Meade Shopping Center at the Kroger store.

7.4 Turn left onto the White Bridge Road pedestrian overpass.

7.6   Bear right to enter the Richland Creek Greenway.

8.0   Follow the Greenway to the intersection and turn right.

8.5   Turn right onto Cherokee Avenue. Take an immediate left onto Aberdeen Avenue.

9.0   Aberdeen Avenue becomes Princeton Avenue.

9.3   Turn right onto Craighead Avenue. Turn left onto Central Avenue.

9.5   Turn right onto Bowling Avenue.

9.7   Turn left onto West End Avenue.

9.8   Turn right onto Elmington Avenue.

10.0 Turn left onto Ransom Avenue.

10.3 Turn right onto Fairfax Avenue.

11.2 Turn right onto 21st Avenue South.

11.3 Turn left onto Portland Avenue. Watch for oncoming traffic as you make the turn.

11.6 Portland Avenue becomes Belmont Boulevard.

12.0 Turn left on Elmwood Avenue.

12.3 Turn right onto 12th Avenue South.

12.4 Turn left onto Caruthers.

12.5 Turn right onto 10th Avenue South / Lealand Lane.

15.4 Turn left onto Robertson Academy Road.

16.5 Turn right onto Franklin Pike.

16.8 Turn left onto Lambert Drive.

17.4 Turn left onto Farrell Parkway.

17.6 Turn right onto Regent Drive.

18.1 Turn right onto Hogan Road.

18.4 Stay on Hogan Road and cross Franklin Pike; it becomes Otter Creek Road.

19.3 Enter the Radnor Lake Park.

21.0 This is the end of the ride at the visitor center.

RIDE INFORMATION

Local Events/Attractions

Radnor Lake State Natural Area: 1160 Otter Creek Rd., Nashville; (615) 373-3467; www.radnorlake.org. This area features 6 miles of easy to strenuous walking trails and scheduled interpretive programs. It is a day-use-only area. The Tennessee State Parks System staffs and manages it. Activities at Radnor Lake include hiking, wildlife observation, photography, and interpretive programs. Park ranger–led environmental educational programs ranging from wildflower hikes to reptile programs are available. A schedule is available at the visitor center or online.

Travellers Rest Plantation & Museum: 636 Farrell Pkwy., Nashville; (615) 832-8197; travellersrestplantation.org. At mile 17.4 on the ride is the preserved home of Revolutionary War soldier Judge John Overton. It was constructed in 1799 and remained in the family until the 1950s. It is now preserved on the National Register of Historic Places. It offers tours and other events throughout the year that describe life from the early 1800s until the days of Civil War battles in Nashville.

Local Eateries

There are various restaurants in the area. You ride by the Belle Meade Shopping Center and the Hill Center beginning at mile 7.2. There are several restaurants and a Starbucks. Also, at mile 7.6, if you go about 0.25 mile past the turn to the Greenway, there are various shops and restaurants on White Bridge Road at the intersection of Post Road (the first street) and White Bridge Road.

Restrooms

Mile 0.0: The visitor center has restroom facilities. It is open when the park is open.

Mile 7.6: There is a portable restroom facility at the entrance to Richland Creek Greenway.

Granny White Pike

Granny White Pike, or 12th Avenue South, was named for Lucinda White. She was an innkeeper in the early 1800s. Granny White Tavern was near the 5100 block of Granny White Pike, about 4 miles south of the turn on this ride onto 12th Avenue South at mile 12.3. Travelers along the Natchez Trace, 4 miles west of the tavern, were attracted to the inn, famous for its food, brandy, and comfortable beds.

Deep Well to Bicentennial Park

The Deep Well to Bicentennial Park loop is based on the Metro Nashville's Music City Bikeway system. It's an interesting to ride from the woods of Percy Warner Park to the foot of the Tennessee State Capitol in downtown Nashville. The key to this ride is to watch for the Music City Bikeway signs along the route.

This is an out-and-back ride. With less than a 1-mile exception, you cover the same route on the return as you do on the outgoing ride.

Start: The ride begins at the Deep Well parking lot in Percy Warner Park off TN 100.

Length: 22 miles, out-and-back ride

Approximate riding time: 2 hours

Best bike: Any bike

Terrain and trail surface: The terrain on the ride is flat to rolling. The surface is mostly city streets with a bike lane. There is a short section on the paved bike trail of the Richland Creek Greenway.

Traffic and hazards: There could be some traffic on this ride at any time. The busiest section is on Charlotte Pike. This ride is a good weekend or off-peak-hours ride. There are some places on Charlotte Pike where the bike lane will disappear, but it's still part of the Music City Bikeway, and there is shared-road bike signage.

Things to see: Tennessee State Capitol

Maps: DeLorme *Tennessee Atlas & Gazetteer*, page 33, C8

Getting there by car: From Nashville, proceed west. Follow US 70 / Broadway / West End Avenue / Harding Road through the Belle Meade area. At the Y intersection of US 70 and TN 100, get in the left lane and follow TN 100 for 1.6 miles. Turn left through the large limestone entrance into the Deep Well Entrance to Percy Warner Park. The parking lot is about 0.5 mile from TN 100. **GPS:** N36 04.530' / W86 52.730'

THE RIDE

Begin the ride from the parking lot at the Deep Well Trailhead at Percy Warner Park. There are outdoor restrooms here. Ride toward TN 100 to begin the ride. TN 100 is busy, so look carefully, and then turn right; you will need to get into the left lane immediately. Turn left onto Vaughn's Gap Road at mile 0.7 and cross the tracks. Turn right onto Percy Warner Boulevard at mile 0.9. At mile 2.0, you will turn right onto busy US 70 and make an immediate left turn at the traffic light onto Old Harding Pike. You will be on this road for almost 3 miles; it will have a bike lane most of the way. The name of the road changes to Post Road at mile 2.6. As you approach White Bridge Road at mile 4.7, stay in the right lane.

Cross White Bridge Road, mile 4.7, at the light and take a dogleg—first left, then right—and proceed behind the stores following the Music City Bikeway. The route continues behind the stores for the next 0.3 mile. As you get to the back of the shopping center there is a larger parking lot; the access road to Richland Creek Greenway is on your right.

Follow this access bike path behind Nashville State Community College; when you reach the Greenway at mile 5.2, go left toward the Wyoming Avenue Trailhead. As you approach this trailhead at mile 6.5, you will dogleg left, then right, onto Wyoming Avenue.

Follow Wyoming Avenue to 46th Avenue North then to Charlotte Pike at mile 7.4, turn right. Although it is a busy street, you will have a bike lane most of the way on Charlotte Pike. There are Music City Bikeway signs at multiple streets, but this ride turns left at 16th Avenue North at mile 10.1.

Bike Shops

Cumberland Transit: 2807 West End Ave., Nashville; (615) 321-4069; http://cumberlandtransit.com/cycling/
Gran Fondo: 5133 Harding Rd., Suite A6, Nashville; (615) 354-1090; http://www.granfondocycles.com/
Gran Fondo Trail & Fitness: 5133 Harding Rd., Suite B-1, Nashville; (615) 499-4634; http://www.granfondotrail.com/
Green Fleet Bicycle Shop: 1579 Edgehill Ave., Nashville; (615) 379-8687; http://greenfleetbikes.com
Halcyon Bike Shop: 1119 Halcyon Ave., Corner of 12th Ave. S. and Halcyon Ave., Nashville; (615) 730-9344; www.halcyonbike.com

Turn left on Jo Johnston Avenue at the top of the hill. Turn left onto 10th Avenue North at mile 10.7. You will cross over the tracks once more and turn right onto Harrison Avenue. You will stay on this street until you get to the roundabout at 7th Avenue North at mile 11.2. Bicentennial Park is on your right; this is the turn point for the ride.

Bicentennial Park gateway

The buildings on the left about 100 yards away on 7th Avenue North make up the farmers' market area. You'll find restrooms and restaurants here. Facing south toward the trestle, you will see the Tennessee State Capitol on the hill.

The return ride begins from the roundabout as you retrace the ride back on Harrison Street. Turn left onto 10th Avenue North and cross the tracks. (If you are counting, you cross the tracks three times on each leg of the ride.) Turn right onto Jo Johnston Avenue. This time you will stay on Jo Johnston Avenue until the T intersection with Dr. D. B. Todd Jr. Boulevard, at mile 12.3; turn left here.

There is a traffic light with a right-turn lane around the island at Charlotte Pike. Take the right lane and turn right onto Charlotte Pike. The bike lane disappears twice on the return leg, but the road has shared-road bike signage. As you approach the light at 46th Avenue North at mile 14.9, get in the left-turn lane and turn left on 46th Avenue N.

Proceed until you reach Wyoming Avenue at mile 15.4 and turn right. As you pass a church on your right and notice the upcoming turn in the street, turn left onto the Richland Creek Greenway at mile 15.8. After you cross the boardwalk bridge over Richland Creek, turn right on the first access road at mile 17.0. Proceed down the access path behind Nashville State Community College and turn left when you get to the parking lot. As you get to White Bridge Road, this may be a good place to look for a snack.

Cross White Bridge Road and follow Post Road, which becomes Old Harding Pike, and turn right at the traffic light at US 70 South at mile 20.2. Get into the center lane to turn left at Percy Warner Boulevard, the next street at mile 20.3. You will intersect Vaughn's Gap Road and make a left turn. Cross the tracks for the last time and turn right onto TN 100. Watch for fast-moving traffic, and turn left at the Deep Well entrance at mile 21.7. Proceed to the parking lot; this is the end of the ride.

MILES AND DIRECTIONS

0.0 Begin at the Deep Well parking lot of Percy Warner Park on TN 100; ride toward TN 100.

0.6 Turn right onto TN 100.

0.7 Turn left onto Vaughn's Gap Road.

0.9 Turn right onto Percy Warner Boulevard.

2.0 Turn right onto US 70 South / Harding Road and get into the left-turn lane.

2.1 Turn left onto Old Harding Pike at the traffic light.

West Meade

Just as you make the turn onto Old Harding Pike at mile 2.1, there is a large redbrick house sitting back from the road. Judge Howell Jackson completed West Meade, this two-story Victorian house, in 1886. The contract price for the house was $12,900. Judge Jackson was married to Mary Elizabeth Harding in 1874. Mary Elizabeth's sister Selene Harding was the wife of General William Hicks Jackson. General Jackson and Selene were the last owners of the Belle Meade Plantation, on Harding Road, about 1 mile down the road from West Meade. The two farms had a special sister relationship.

Originally the West Meade farm included about 3,000 acres. Most of the area covered by the ride from TN 100 to the present house was part of the original farm. West Meade was a noteworthy place in its time. The Howell Jacksons hosted President Cleveland for a luncheon in 1887.

There was one significant difference between Belle Meade and West Meade. Belle Meade was sold by Selene Harding Jackson to pay off debts to creditors, while West Meade was inherited, debt-free, along with other property at the death of Mary Harding Jackson in 1913.

Today, West Meade is privately owned.

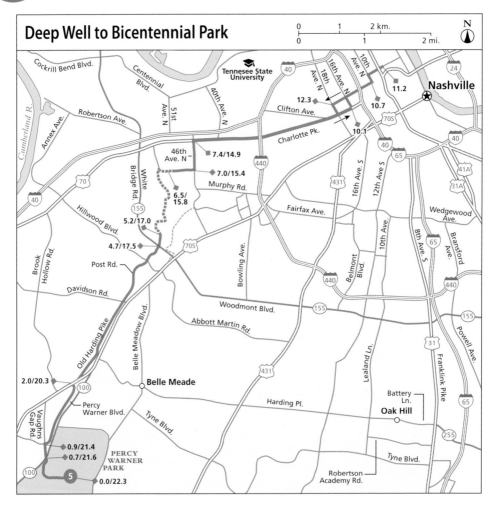

Deep Well to Bicentennial Park

2.6 Old Harding Pike becomes Post Road. Continue on Post Road to White Bridge Road.

4.7 Cross White Bridge Road and enter Lion's Head Shopping Center.

4.8 Dogleg left, then right, and continue through Lion's Head Shopping Center behind the stores.

5.2 Turn left; follow the Richland Creek Greenway toward the Wyoming Avenue Trailhead.

6.5 Turn right and follow Wyoming Avenue to 46th Avenue North.

7.0 Turn left onto 46th Avenue North.

7.4	Turn right onto Charlotte Pike.
10.1	Turn left onto 16th Avenue North.
10.3	Turn right onto Jo Johnston Avenue.
10.7	Turn left onto 10th Avenue North.
10.9	Turn right onto Harrison Street.
11.2	Turn left onto 7th Avenue North; Bicentennial Park is on the right. Turn around to return to Deep Well.
11.2	Turn right onto Harrison Street.
11.5	Turn left onto 10th Avenue North.
11.6	Turn right onto Jo Johnston Avenue.
12.3	Turn left onto Dr. D. B. Todd Jr. Boulevard.
12.5	Turn right onto Charlotte Pike.
14.9	Turn left onto 46th Avenue North.
15.4	Turn right on Wyoming Avenue.
15.8	Turn left to access Richland Creek Greenway at the Wyoming Avenue Trailhead.
17.0	Exit the Richland Creek Greenway at Nashville State Community College / Music City Bikeway.
17.2	At the parking lot, bear left and ride through the Lion's Head Shopping Center behind the stores; take the dogleg left, then right, onto Post Road.
17.5	Cross White Bridge Road and continue on Post Road.
19.6	Post Road becomes Old Harding Pike. Continue on Old Harding Pike.
20.2	Turn right onto US 70 South / Harding Road at the traffic light.
20.3	Turn left at Percy Warner Boulevard, the next street.
21.4	Turn left onto Vaughn's Gap Road.

Richland Creek Library

Just before you turn on Charlotte Pike at mile 7.4, you may notice the Richland Creek Library on your left. The public radio station in Nashville, WPLN-FM, celebrated its fiftieth anniversary in December 2011. The station began in the basement of this library in 1961, when it was an entity of the Metropolitan Government of Nashville.

21.6 Turn right onto TN 100 just as you cross over the tracks.

21.7 Turn left off TN 100 at the Deep Well entrance to Percy Warner Park. The parking lot is just ahead.

22.3 This is the end of the ride.

RIDE INFORMATION

Local Events/Attractions

The Bicentennial Capitol Mall State Park: 600 James Robertson Pkwy., Nashville; (615) 532-0001; http://www.tn.gov/environment/parks/Bicentennial/. This is the official name for Bicentennial Park at mile 11.2. The 19-acre park, managed by the State of Tennessee Parks system, is designed to complement the Tennessee Capitol Building, give visitors a taste of Tennessee's history and natural wonders, and serve as a lasting monument to Tennessee's bicentennial celebration (1776–1996). Park rangers provide interpretive tours of the park, historical presentations in period dress, and off-site programs by reservation. The Nashville farmers' market is located next to the park and houses a selection of locally owned and operated restaurants and shops inside its Market House, open year-round. Restrooms are available under the train trestle. Their website provides more information, including a calendar of events.

The Frist Center for the Visual Arts: 919 Broadway, Nashville; (615) 244-3340; http://fristcenter.org/. The Frist Center is a relatively new and exciting downtown destination. It opened in April 2001, and since then has hosted a spectacular array of art from the region, the country, and around the world. The vision of the Frist Center is to inspire people through art to look at their world in new ways. Their mission is to present and originate high-quality exhibitions with related educational programs and community outreach activities. The center is privileged to occupy one of Nashville's great historic landmarks—the former main post office, built during 1933–34. The Frist has on on-site cafe and gift shop. Check out their website for more information and a calendar of events and exhibitions.

Local Eateries

When you intersect White Bridge Road at mile 4.7 and mile 17.5, there will be several restaurants on either side of the road. Also, there are various eating places in the farmers' market area when you get to Bicentennial Park at mile 11.2.

Restrooms

Mile 0.0: Portable restrooms only are available at the Deep Well Trailhead.
Mile 11.2: The farmers' market building to the left has restrooms.

Metro Center Levee Greenway

The Metro Center Levee Greenway was one of the earlier greenways in Nashville. This is a good ride in the downtown area. The scenery is interesting beside the Cumberland River, and the route is flat, recently repaved, and relatively short. If you are looking for an easy 1-hour ride, this is it; and if you want a few more miles, you can do the ride again!

Start: The ride begins at the Great Circle Road Trailhead of the Metro Center Levee Greenway.

Length: 8 miles, out-and-back ride

Approximate riding time: About 1 hour

Best bike: Any bike

Terrain and trail surface: The ride is flat along the levee. The trail has been recently repaved.

Traffic and hazards: There will be no car traffic, but the trail may be crowded with other bikers, runners, walkers, and in-line skaters, especially on weekends. Also, during the week, this is a great place for a walk for people working in the Metro Center. It is best to announce when passing someone.

Maps: DeLorme *Tennessee Atlas & Gazetteer*, page 34, A1. Nashville Metro Government website: http://www.nashville.gov/Portals/0/SiteContent/Parks/images/greenways/small-metrocenter%20levee.jpg

Getting there by car: The ride begins at the end of Great Circle Road in Metro Center. From I-65, take the Rosa L. Parks Boulevard / 8th Avenue / US 41A exit and proceed north. Turn right at the second light onto Vantage Way. Turn right at the intersection of Vantage Way and Great Circle Road. It is 1.2 miles from the I-65 exit to the Metro Center Levee Greenway at the end of Great Circle Road. There is a small parking lot at the trailhead. **GPS:** N36 11.32' / W86 47.08'

6

THE RIDE

The ride is very easy to follow. Get on the Greenway and head west. You are following the current of the Cumberland. When you intersect Ed Temple Boulevard, this is the turnaround point at mile 3.8. Then, retrace the path. It may be a bit confusing when you get to the Ted Rhodes Golf Course, because the path is adjacent to the golf cart path, but just watch the signs. You'll reach the end of the ride at mile 7.6, back at the Great Circle Road Trailhead.

Ted Rhodes (1913–69) was born and raised in Nashville, and is credited as the first African-American professional golfer. He played the US Open in 1948. Originally called the Cumberland Golf Course, the course was renamed the Ted Rhodes Golf Course in 1969.

MILES AND DIRECTIONS

0.0 Begin at the Great Circle Road Trailhead of the Metro Center Levee Greenway and head west.

3.8 At the intersection with Ed Temple Boulevard, turn around and retrace the route to return to the Great Circle Road Trailhead.

7.6 This is the end of the ride at the Great Circle Road Trailhead.

Dominican Sisters of Nashville

The first street you pass as you exit I-65 headed toward the ride start is Dominican Drive. The Congregation of St. Cecilia that began in 1860 is located here. The initial vision was to provide education for "girls and young ladies." The realities of the Civil War greatly affected initial efforts, but a building was completed in 1862. The sisters and students watched as the Union Army took control of the Tennessee state house on Capitol Hill.

Although the Civil War continued to affect the school, the sisters nursed the sick during Nashville's cholera outbreak in 1866. The school was rescued from the auction block in 1867 by the bishop of the time, and the Dominican Sisters of Nashville survived. Their website notes: "They expanded in numbers of sisters and reached thousands of students with the opening of numerous schools. Simplicity, hospitality and devotion were the hallmarks of this small southern community. Next to her larger northern counterparts, the Congregation was outside of the mainstream, diminutive and not well-known."

The Dominican Sisters continue to thrive today, supporting several schools in the area, including Aquinas College.

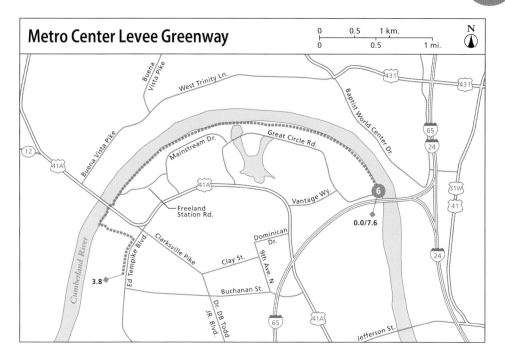

Metro Center Levee Greenway

0   0.5   1 km.
0   0.5   1 mi.

N

RIDE INFORMATION

Local Events/Attractions

The Country Music Hall of Fame and Museum: 222 5th Ave. S., Nashville; (615) 416-2001; http://countrymusichall offame.org. A local gem in the country music scene, this museum, operated by the Country Music Foundation, illustrates much of the local history. Its mission is "to identify and preserve the evolving history and traditions of country music and to educate its audiences." The Hall of Fame continuously offers various exhibits and collections of country music memorabilia, along with various programs for schools. The museum is open daily from 9 a.m. to 5 p.m., and can be accessed directly from the Music City convention center.

Bike Shops

Cumberland Transit: 2807 West End Ave., Nashville; (615) 321-4069; http://cumberlandtransit.com/cycling/

Eastside Cycles: 103 South 11th St., Nashville; (615) 469-1079; http://www.eastside-cycles.com/

Green Fleet Bicycle Shop: 1579 Edgehill Ave., Nashville; (615) 379-8687; http://greenfleetbikes.com

Halcyon Bike Shop: 1119 Halcyon Ave., Corner of 12th Ave. S. & Halcyon Ave., Nashville; (615) 730-9344; www.halcyonbike.com

American Baptist College

American Baptist College

Up on the bluffs on the other side of the Cumberland River is American Baptist College, a private, historically black college where, since 1924, students have received a world-class Christian education and preparation for leadership, ministry, and social justice. ABC offers undergraduate and graduate degree programs at its Nashville, Tennessee, campus and globally, online. The present site of 53 acres was purchased with the help of the National Baptists in 1921. The first building, Griggs Hall, was erected in 1923 and housed dormitory rooms, dining hall, library, and classrooms.

Local Eateries

When you exit I-65 and travel to the start of the ride, you'll find several places to eat on Rosa L. Parks Boulevard, on both sides of the road. The Germantown community is also nearby—in the northeast corner of the quadrant formed by the intersection of Rosa L. Parks Boulevard / 8th Avenue / US 41A and Jefferson Street—and offers a variety of eating and shopping opportunities.

Restrooms

There are no facilities of any kind on this ride.

Boulevard Loop

Belle Meade Boulevard off Harding Road / US 70 South in west Nashville is a great short ride, and goes all the way to Percy Warner Park. It's interesting to see this subdivision, established in the early part of the twentieth century; I dare you to find two houses that are alike! It's best to drive down the boulevard and park in the Percy Warner Park parking area and then ride from that point. This four-lane road offers a very biker-, runner-, and walker-friendly ride. The 5-mile trek is short, so you can make several loops, or ride up into Percy Warner Park if you want to add some more miles.

Belle Meade, the city, is only 3 square miles in area. Most of the land came directly from the dissolution of Belle Meade Plantation. John Harding, its founder, acquired the first parcel in 1807. He and his son, William Giles Harding, added substantially to the plantation. William Giles Harding's son-in-law William Hicks Jackson furthered Belle Meade's reputation and standing as a horse-breeding farm. But after three generations, Belle Meade Plantation was sold in 1906. The Belle Meade Golf Links, platted in 1915, was one of the early subdivisions that originated from the former Belle Meade Plantation.

Start: The ride starts at the entrance to Percy Warner Park. The Park is at the intersection of Page Road and Belle Meade Boulevard.

Length: 7 miles (5-mile short option), loop ride

Approximate riding time: About 1 hour

Best bike: Any bike

Terrain and trail surface: The terrain is flat to gently rolling on a paved, four-lane road.

Traffic and hazards: This street is very biker-, walker-, and runner-friendly, but it is a local street that supports traffic flow from several major thoroughfares. There is one four-way stop and one traffic light on the ride. The traffic light at the intersection with Harding Place is busy. Ride in the right lane. Walkers and runners are advised to use the left lanes.

Maps: DeLorme *Tennessee Atlas & Gazetteer*, page 33, C8

Getting there by car: From Nashville, proceed west. Follow US 70 South / Broadway / West End Avenue / Harding Road through the Belle Meade area. At Belle Meade Boulevard, turn left and head south on Belle Meade Boulevard 2.7 miles to the park entrance. **GPS:** N36 04.58' / W86 52.01'

THE RIDE

The ride begins at the Percy Warner Park entrance gate. There is a traffic light at mile 1.0 at the intersection of Harding Place. There is a four-way stop at mile 2.0 at Jackson Boulevard. As you proceed you will pass the Emanuel Baptist Church and begin a gentle descent to Harding Road / US 70 South. As you approach Harding Road, get into the left lane to prepare for the turn. There is a cut-through at mile 2.7; turn around here and head back to Percy Warner Park.

You may want to stop at the turn and take a look at the bronze horse and colt statue at the entrance to Belle Meade Subdivision. At this point you head back to Percy Warner Park. You can end the ride at mile 5.4, when you reach the park parking lot.

An optional part of the ride from here is to continue up the hill to the right into Percy Warner Park. Just past the top of the hill, take the left fork. The top of the allée is an interesting viewpoint at mile 6.2. An allée is an alley in a park or garden that is bordered by bushes or trees. You will get an interesting

Bike Shops

Cumberland Transit: 2807 West End Ave., Nashville; (615) 321-4069; http://cumberlandtransit.com/cycling/
Eastside Cycles: 103 South 11th St., Nashville; (615) 469-1079; http://www.eastside-cycles.com/
Gran Fondo: 5133 Harding Rd., Suite A6, Nashville; (615) 354-1090; http://www.granfondocycles.com/
Gran Fondo Trail & Fitness: 5133 Harding Rd., Suite B-1, Nashville; (615) 499-4634; http://www.granfondotrail.com/
Green Fleet Bicycle Shop: 1579 Edgehill Ave., Nashville; (615) 379-8687; http://greenfleetbikes.com
Halcyon Bike Shop: 1119 Halcyon Ave., Corner of 12th Ave. S. & Halcyon Ave., Nashville; (615) 730-9344; www.halcyonbike.com

Belle Meade Boulevard from allée

perspective of the route. Proceed from here on the one-way road back to the parking lot. This is the end of the ride, at mile 7.0.

MILES AND DIRECTIONS

0.0   Begin the ride at the entrance gate to Percy Warner Park. Head back down Belle Meade Boulevard.

1.0   Traffic signal at the intersection with Harding Place.

2.0   Four-way stop at Jackson Boulevard.

2.7   Turn around and retrace the route back to Percy Warner Park.

5.4   Proceed through the parking lot and bear right, heading up the hill into Percy Warner Park. This is the optional end of ride.

6.0   Take the left fork here to do this short loop.

6.2   This is the viewpoint from the top of the allée.

7.0   This is the end of the ride at the parking lot.

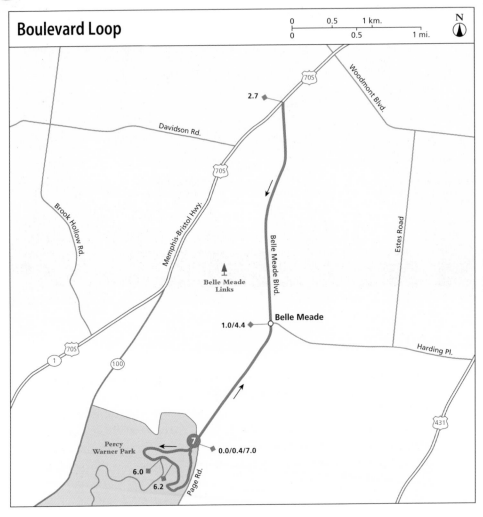

RIDE INFORMATION

Local Events/Attractions

Belle Meade Plantation: http://bellemeadeplantation.com/. This plantation is about 1 mile south of Belle Meade Boulevard on US 70 / Harding Road. Tours of this Greek Revival mansion are available daily. There is also a restaurant and gift shop. In addition to its attraction as a tourist destination, the large "barn" is used to host weddings and corporate events.

Cheekwood Botanical Garden & Museum of Art: 1200 Forrest Park Dr., Nashville; (615) 356-8000; www.cheekwood.org/. Located about 3 miles west

Bronze horse and colt

of Belle Meade Boulevard, off Harding Road, this 55-acre site includes an art museum, botanical gardens, a restaurant, gift shop, sculpture trail, changing art exhibits, and the Botanic Hall. Saturday-morning art activities for families take place 10 a.m.–noon in the Learning Center. For current exhibits, see Art Listings. Garden and museum hours are 9:30 a.m.–4:30 p.m. Tues–Sat; 11:00 a.m.–4:30 p.m. Sun; closed Mon, except for federal holidays. There is a gate fee.

Local Eateries

There are various restaurants in the area. About a mile before you get to Belle Meade Boulevard, at the Belle Meade Shopping Center and the Hill Center, there are several restaurants, including coffee shops. There are also various shops and restaurants on White Bridge, less than 0.5 mile from the intersection of White Bridge Road and Harding Road. Another shopping area is located past Belle Meade Boulevard, about 0.5 mile west on US 70 / Harding Road. Several restaurants and shops are located on either side of the road.

Restrooms

There are no restrooms on this ride.

Percy Warner Park

Percy Warner Park is a popular park in the southwest part of Nashville covering 2,058 acres. The grand sandstone entrance was donated by the wife and daughter of Percy Warner, dedicated in 1932.

The park is generally wooded, with hiking trails and bridle paths running through the woods. The area is alive with wildlife, including deer, turkey, and smaller animals. The road is mostly a one-way paved trail through the park, and is completely open to car traffic. The park is so popular with runners that you will notice running route designations on signage. This is a great practice ride with two notable climbs, called "climbs at 3 and 9" by the locals. Parking is sometimes a challenge in busy times; there's an overflow parking lot across the street from the entrance. But it may not be open at all times.

This is a great after-work, near-downtown ride. If you want a longer ride, take a right out to Old Hickory Boulevard at mile 5.0 and head south toward Williamson County and Franklin, or just do the loop again. In summer when leaves are on the trees, it's a pleasant, shaded ride through the woods, and on windy spring and fall days, the hills break the wind during much of this ride. Numerous benches are installed along the roadway; you may wish to stop and take in a bit of nature on one of them. If you are so inclined, bring a picnic lunch and spread it out on one of the picnic tables along the route! The shelter picnic areas you see along the way are available by reservation at (615) 862-8408. There are plenty of roads in the park to explore in addition to the ones designated in this ride. Enjoy!

Start: The ride begins at the Percy Warner Park entrance.

Length: 11 miles, loop ride

Approximate riding time: About 1 hour

Best bike: Any bike

Terrain and trail surface: This is a paved road. The terrain is rolling, with two climbs of about 0.5 mile each, approximately at miles 3.0 and 9.0 on the ride. The trail is signed. Usually the road is signed "Main Drive," although sometimes it is signed "Scenic Drive."

Traffic and hazards: This is a relatively busy park especially on weekends and during the warmer months. The road is mainly one-way, but it's only a bit wider than a one-lane road, and there is no shoulder. The road follows the terrain up, around, and down the hills. There is one hairpin turn at the bottom of a steep descent and several sharp turns. The visibility on some of the turns on the descents is limited. Be aware of walkers, joggers, runners, baby strollers, other bikers, and cars. Also, the bridle paths cross this road, so be aware of the horses. The hiking trail through the woods crosses the road; sometimes hikers may not hear or look for approaching bicycles.

Things to see: Woodsy road, wildlife

Maps: DeLorme *Tennessee Atlas & Gazetteer*, page 33, C8. Park map: http://www.nashville.gov/Portals/0/SiteContent/Parks/docs/outdoor/ Hiking%20Trails/Percy%20Warner%20Park%20Map_Updated%202011- 9-27.pdf

Getting there by car: From Nashville, proceed west. Follow US 70 South / Broadway / West End Avenue / Harding Road through the Belle Meade area. At Belle Meade Boulevard, turn left and head south on Belle Meade Boulevard 2.7 miles to the park entrance. **GPS:** N36 04.58' / W86 52.01'

THE RIDE

This ride is very easy to negotiate: Begin at the parking lot and follow the road in a big loop until you return back to the parking lot. But do not take any of the side loops or shorter paths! There are multiple entrances and exits from the park, as well as interior loops. This route is generally the loop around the park perimeter.

The Percy Warner Golf Course is on the right as you begin the ride. You will be greeted by a short climb when you begin. Shortly after, at mile 0.6, bear right to stay on the Main Drive. However, if you want a short ride, you can go straight here and loop back to the parking lot; the distance is about

Bike Shops

Cumberland Transit: 2807 West End Ave., Nashville; (615) 321-4069; http:// cumberlandtransit.com/cycling/

Gran Fondo: 5133 Harding Rd., Suite A6, Nashville; (615) 354-1090; http://www .granfondocycles.com/

Gran Fondo Trail & Fitness: 5133 Harding Rd., Suite B-1, Nashville; (615) 499- 4634; http://www.granfondotrail.com/

Percy Warner Park allée

1.2 miles. This short loop connects to the allée you rode by at the beginning of the ride.

Immediately as you round that turn at 0.6 mile, the Warner Woods hiking trail crosses the road. Watch for hikers here. Continuing on, you will have a short downhill and another short climb. The road is rough due to much patching at mile 1.4, especially in the curve. There is a sign for the Deep Well Picnic Area, but you will bear left on the Main Drive at mile 1.7. There is a secondary parking lot accessed from TN 100 at mile 2.0; continue straight at this point. There is a portable restroom here. This is another access to the Deep Well Picnic Area, and the intersecting road with the Music City Bikeway.

The Larkspur Hill climb begins at mile 2.7 and continues along rolling terrain until mile 3.3. Just as the hill levels out at Gum Ridge, continue straight to stay on the Main Drive. There is an interesting viewpoint to the southwest on the right as you go up a short rise. The downhill that follows this climb will be your reward, but be aware of the curves—first right, then left, then right again as the road winds down around the hill. There is another loop road at mile 4.2 where you will bear right, but you will be enjoying the downhill and it's likely you won't notice the road!

Best Bike Rides Nashville

Make a hard left at mile 4.7 to follow the Main Drive. At mile 5.0, continue straight. An access road intersects Old Hickory Boulevard at Vaughn Road. This is the best place to exit if you want to add some miles to the ride.

After you go up a short ascent at about mile 5.2, you will see a large open area and a horse track on the right. This is the site of the steeplechase track. The Iroquois Steeplechase is an annual fund-raising event for Vanderbilt Children's Hospital on the second Saturday in May. It's a great spring outdoor event that attracts thousands. (**Note:** Some of the park roads are closed for this event.)

The Harpeth Hills Golf Course is on your right at mile 6.5. This is the beginning of the two-way road section of the ride that allows golfers to enter the park. You will continue on the Main Drive at mile 7.2. This intersection to Chickering Road ends the two-way road.

The second climb begins at mile 8.8. You will see one of those tantalizing benches just as the climb begins. Shortly after, on one of the nice descents, the Mossy Ridge hiking trail crosses the road. Caution here; you are on a downhill at a place where hikers might not be expecting a bike as they cross the road.

At about mile 10.3, as you make a right turn and begin a sharp descent, begin braking to prepare for Hairpin Curve at mile 10.5. There is a very bucolic limestone fence that defines the curve. The road is a bit rough around this and some of the other curves as you descend. It's all downhill from here! You will get a full view of the entrance area as you make the last descent into the parking lot to the end of the ride, at mile 11.2. Watch for extra traffic that may have stopped or is blocking the road waiting to access a parking spot.

MILES AND DIRECTIONS

0.0   Begin at the park entrance sign.

0.6   Bear right to continue on the Main Drive.

1.7   Bear left to continue on the Main Drive.

2.0   Hwy 100 parking access, continue straight.

3.3   Go straight to continue on the Main Drive.

4.2   Bear right to continue on the Main Drive.

4.7   Make a hard left to continue on the Main Drive.

5.0   Continue straight on the Main Drive.

5.2   Iroquois Steeplechase is on the right.

6.5   Harpeth Hills Golf Course is on the right.

7.2   Continue straight on the Main Drive.

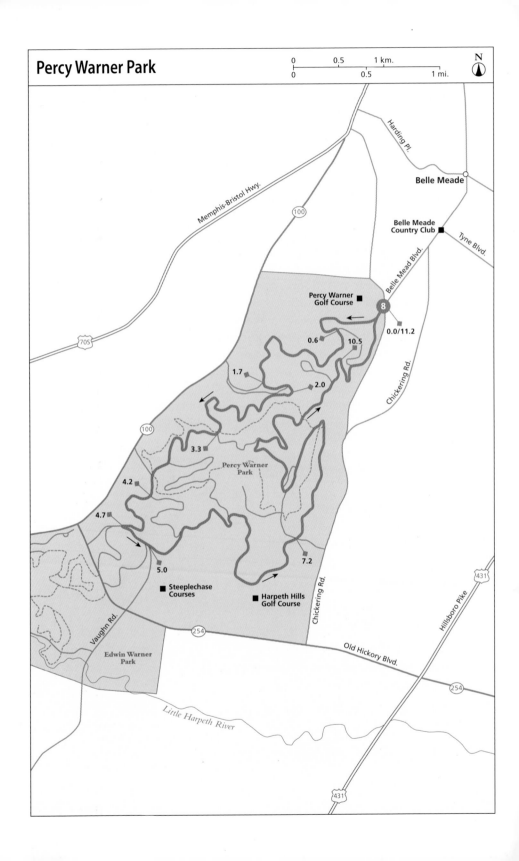

8.8 Half mile climb begins here.

10.3 Caution, sharp descent begins.

10.5 Caution, hairpin curve is here.

11.2 This is the end of the ride.

RIDE INFORMATION

Local Events/Attractions

The Belle Meade Plantation: http://bellemeadeplantation.com/. Located about 1 mile south of Belle Meade Boulevard on US 70 / Harding Road, tours of this Greek Revival mansion are available daily. There is also a restaurant and gift shop. In addition to its attraction as a tourist destination, the large "barn" is used to host weddings and corporate events.

Warner Park Nature Center: 7311 TN 100, Nashville; (615) 352-6299; www .nashville.gov/parks/nature/wpnc. This visitor center, managed by the Metro Parks and Recreation Department and located south of Percy Warner Park, is worth a visit. As the name implies, this is a place for learning about nature. There are various displays, events, and many programs for schoolchildren.

Local Eateries

There are various restaurants in the area. About a mile before you get to Belle Meade Boulevard, at the Belle Meade Shopping Center and the Hill Center, there several restaurants, including coffee shops. There are also various shops and restaurants on White Bridge, less than 0.5 mile from the intersection of White Bridge Road and Harding Road. Another shopping area is located past Belle Meade Boulevard, about 0.5 mile west on US 70 / Harding Road. Several restaurants and shops are located on either side of the road.

Restrooms

Mile 2.0: Portable restrooms only are available here.

Edwin Warner Park

Edwin Warner Park (EWP) is a 606-acre park adjacent to Percy Warner Park. The two parks are separated by Old Hickory Boulevard. Edwin Warner succeeded his brother Percy on the Park Board in 1927. He is credited with the major land acquisitions to create both parks. The Works Progress Administration (WPA) was responsible for developing much of the land for the Warner Parks. Percy is also credited with direct supervision of these efforts. The park area south of Old Hickory Boulevard was named in his honor in 1937.

Until 1989, auto traffic was allowed in both Percy Warner Park and Edwin Warner Park. The drive route intersected and crossed Old Hickory Boulevard going from Percy Warner Park into Edwin Warner Park. This ride combines some of the closed road of EWP with the Metropolitan Nashville Music City Bikeway. There are several large picnic sites in EWP, along with ball fields.

This ride is an introduction to this area, but leaves many trails you may want to explore on your own. The good news is that the park is accessible from downtown Nashville and Bellevue, and you are always near the Warner Park Nature Center.

Start: The ride begins at the Natchez Trace Trailhead adjacent to the parking lot. There is a covered shelter displaying a large trail map.

Length: 7 miles, loop ride

Approximate riding time: 1 hour

Best bike: Any bike

Terrain and trail surface: The terrain is mixed hills and flat bike paths. All surfaces are paved roads or bike paths.

Traffic and hazards: Except for a short 0.1 mile stretch on Old Hickory Boulevard, and a bit of interior park road, the entire ride is closed to auto traffic. Be cautious on Old Hickory Boulevard, as it's very busy, and there is a narrow shoulder. This is a busy park especially on weekends and during the warm months. The road follows the terrain up, around, and down the hills. The visibility on some of the turns on the descents is limited. Be aware of walkers, joggers, runners, baby strollers, and other bikers.

Things to see: Deer, turkeys, and other wildlife (especially in the early mornings and late afternoons)

Maps: DeLorme *Tennessee Atlas & Gazetteer*, page 33, C8. Park map: http://www.nashville.gov/Portals/0/SiteContent/Parks/docs/outdoor/ Hiking%20Trails/Edwin%20Warner%20Park%20Map_Updated%20 2011-9-27.pdf

Getting there by car: From Nashville, proceed west. Follow US 70 / Broadway / West End Avenue / Harding Road through the Belle Meade area. At the Y intersection of US 70 and TN 100, get in the left lane and follow TN 100 for 3.6 miles. The park entrance is south of the major intersection at Old Hickory Boulevard. Turn left through the large limestone entrance into the Percy Warner Park. The Natchez Trace Trailhead is directly in front of you, and the main parking lot is ahead and right; the Warner Park Nature Center is ahead and left 0.3 mile. If the parking lot is full, head toward the Nature Center and watch for overflow parking areas. **GPS:** N36 4.53' / W86 52.7046'

THE RIDE

The ride begins at the Natchez Trace Trailhead shelter, where you'll find a descriptive map of the park. The road is closed to traffic, with an auto barrier and a walk lane next to it. Negotiate through the road barrier. At the top of this rise turn left at 0.1 mile. As you ascend a short climb and reach an intersection at 0.5 mile, take the left fork.

At 0.9 mile you will see a road-closure gate. Walk your bike around this gate. You are at the top of a hill at Old Hickory Boulevard. Look carefully to the left. Turn right and head down the hill on Old Hickory Boulevard only 0.1 mile. Take the first right, go around the road-closure gate, and you're back on the closed trail at mile 1.0. As you made the turn onto Old Hickory Boulevard you may have noticed a road that seemed to be coming from across the street. This

Bike Shops

Cumberland Transit: 2807 West End Ave., Nashville; (615) 321-4069; http:// cumberlandtransit.com/cycling/
Gran Fondo: 5133 Harding Rd., Suite A6, Nashville; (615) 354-1090; http:// www.granfondocycles.com/
Gran Fondo Trail & Fitness: 5133 Harding Rd., Suite B-1, Nashville; (615) 499-4634; http://www.granfondotrail.com/
Trace Bikes: 8080B TN 100, Nashville; (615) 646-2485; http://tracebikes.com/

View of picnic area, Edwin Warner Park

was where the old road crossed over Old Hickory Boulevard before the 1989 closing of this park to car traffic.

Turn right at the first intersection at mile 1.4. This is a short loop road with some good viewing points at mile 1.6 and 1.9. At mile 2.0, you will proceed straight onto the main road. Bear left at 2.1 miles to continue on the loop road. After a climb, turn right at the main loop road at mile 2.3. You will follow the contour of the hill and begin to make a slight descent. At mile 2.6, you are approaching one leg of a Y intersection. Make a hard left to take the other fork of this Y intersection. You will be rewarded with a downhill.

You will approach another road-closure gate at mile 3.1. You may have to walk your bike around it. You will go about 0.1 mile to the main road. At mile 3.2, bear right, then take an immediate left. There is a restroom facility on the left (closed during the winter months). At mile 3.4, turn right onto the first road, which leads to a large sign, "Metro Parks Music Bikeway." The Harpeth River Greenway begins here. Follow the bike path as it winds around and under TN 100 at mile 4.5. The Ensworth High School campus will be on the right until you reach TN 100. Stay straight on the path (do not take the left fork); the trail ends at mile 4.8. This is the turnaround point for the ride.

You will retrace the route, proceeding back under TN 100 and following the bike path. At mile 6.1, turn left just as you pass a wooden marker post. You will proceed by athletic fields on your right and the Ensworth High School campus on the left. Part of this road is a now-closed public road. You may notice the back of the original house for Devon Farm. Established in 1795, this farm was owned by the Davis-Hicks family for seven generations and originally contained thousands of acres, until it was sold to become the Ensworth High School campus. Some of Devon Farm became part of Percy Warner Park.

Turn right at the intersection at mile 6.6 to stay on the path headed back to the Natchez Trace Trailhead. You are back at the trailhead at mile 7.1; this is the end of the ride.

MILES AND DIRECTIONS

0.0   Begin the ride at the Natchez Trace Trailhead.

0.1   Turn left to stay on the main road.

Warner Parks History

Percy Warner Park began in 1807 with a 250-acre land purchase by pioneer John Harding. The Belle Meade Plantation, named by its owner, experienced its rise and fall in later years based on the race-horse industry. Luke Lea, former senator and real estate developer, purchased the "high pasture" in its waning days in 1911. In 1927, Colonel Lea and his wife donated this property along with additional acreage, totaling 868 acres, to the city of Nashville for use as a public park. Percy Warner Park was named in 1927 after the death of Percy Warner, president of the park board and Lea's father-in-law.

Percy's brother, Edwin, then became the park board president. It was under Edwin Warner's leadership that the total 2,681 acres of Warner Parks were developed. It was very attractive to the city as a Works Progress Administration project. WPA developed the roads and entrances through the park. The stone entrance to Edwin Warner Park is one example of the fine craftsmanship found here. The part of the park south of Old Hickory Boulevard was renamed Edwin Warner Park in 1937 in recognition of his contributions.

WPA also built the steeplechase horse-racing course. Saturday, May 10, 1941, was the inaugural race for this event, called the Iroquois Steeplechase. This event has taken place every year since that time, except for 1945, the oldest continuously run amateur steeplechase in the United States. The event was named by designer William du Pont Jr. in honor of Iroquois, an American-bred horse that won the 1881 English Derby. In addition to its charm as a great springtime event, Iroquois Steeplechase also raises funds for Vanderbilt Children's Hospital.

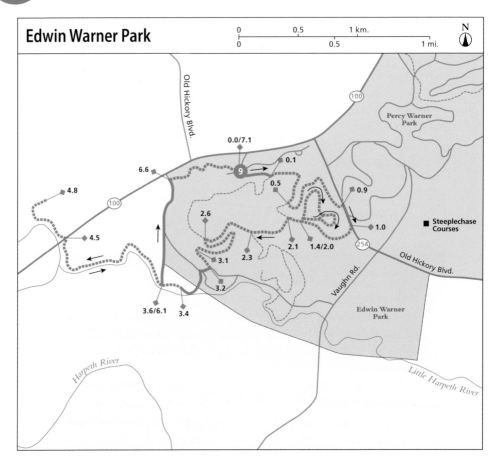

Edwin Warner Park

0 0.5 1 km.
0 0.5 1 mi.

N

0.5 Bear left at the Y intersection.

0.9 The road is blocked by the auto-barrier gate. Walk your bike around the gate and carefully turn right onto Old Hickory Boulevard for 0.1 mile.

1.0 Turn right and negotiate around the closed barrier gate to return back onto the closed trail.

1.4 Proceed right at the first intersecting road.

1.6 Viewpoint.

1.9 Viewpoint.

2.0 Proceed straight to continue on the main loop road.

2.1 Bear left to continue on the loop road.

2.3 Turn right onto the main loop road.

2.6 Turn left to take the other fork at this intersection.

3.1 Negotiate around the auto-barrier gate.

3.2 Bear right onto the main road. Take an immediate left after about 50 yards. There is a restroom on your left.

3.4 Turn right on the first road. Harpeth River Greenway begins at the sign.

4.5 Follow the bike path as you proceed under TN 100.

4.8 The bike path ends at a parking lot; this is the turnaround point for the ride.

6.1 Turn left after you pass the wooden post on the bike path to return to the parking lot.

6.6 Turn right on the bike path to return to the parking lot.

7.1 This is the end of the ride as you return to the Natchez Trace Trail-head shelter.

RIDE INFORMATION

Local Events/Attractions

The Belle Meade Plantation: http://bellemeadeplantation.com/. Located about 4 miles east on US 70 / Harding Road, tours of this Greek Revival mansion are available daily. There is also a restaurant and gift shop. In addition to its attraction as a tourist destination, the large "barn" is used to host weddings and corporate events.

Warner Park Nature Center: 7311 TN 100, Nashville; (615) 352-6299; www .nashville.gov/parks/nature/wpnc. This visitor center, managed by the Metro Parks and Recreation Department and located south of Percy Warner Park, is worth a visit. As the name implies, this is a place for learning about nature. There are various displays, events, and many programs for schoolchildren.

Local Eateries

There is a shopping area at the intersection of US 70 / Harding Road and TN 100. Several restaurants and other shops are located on either side of the road for about 0.5 mile. Gran Fondo Bike Shop is also in this area. There is another shopping area on TN 100 approximately 0.9 mile past the entrance of Percy Warner Park, offering various restaurants (including a coffee shop) and stores.

Restrooms

Mile 0.0: There are restroom facilities at the Warner Park Nature Center 0.3 mile from the ride start.

Mile 3.2: There are permanent restrooms here (although they are closed during the winter months).

Joelton

This loop ride takes you from the Metro Center Levee Greenway to Joelton and back. Most of the ride miles are in more rural parts of northern Davidson County.

Joelton is a semirural, northern suburb of Nashville, part of the Nashville Metropolitan government system. It is accessed from I-24 North from Nashville at exit 35. It was the site of Miranda Lambert's music video for her song, "Only Prettier," filmed in June 2010. The video also featured appearances by Kellie Pickler, Laura Bell Bundy, and Hillary Scott of Lady Antebellum. You will also ride by Fontanel, the former residence of Barbara Mandrell.

Start: The ride begins at the Great Circle Road Trailhead of the Metro Center Levee Greenway.

Length: 38 miles (20-mile short option), loop ride

Approximate riding time: About 3 hours, short option about 2 hours

Best bike: Any bike

Terrain and trail surface: The terrain varies on the ride, but is generally rolling. There are two climbs, which are not steep but may seem a bit long. The ride is mainly on rural roads, but there is a little bit of bike greenway at the start.

Traffic and hazards: The traffic depends on your proximity to Nashville. The Clarksville Highway / US 41A / Rosa L. Parks Boulevard is busy. The part of the ride over the Cumberland River does not have a bike lane designated, but it is short. The relatively short segment on Old Hickory Boulevard can be busy based on time of day.

Things to see: Fontanel

Maps: DeLorme *Tennessee Atlas & Gazetteer*, page 34, A1

Getting there by car: The ride begins at the end of Great Circle Road in Metro Center. From I-65, take the Rosa L. Parks / 8th Avenue / US 41A exit and proceed north. Turn right at the second light onto Vantage Way. Turn right at the intersection of Vantage Way and Great Circle Road. It is 1.2 miles from the I-65 exit to the Metro Center Levee Greenway at the end of Great Circle Road. There is a small parking lot at the trailhead. **GPS:** N36 11.32' / W86 47.08'

THE RIDE

You will begin the ride by following the Metro Center Levee Greenway west to the first exit at the Freelands Station Road Trailhead. In 1769, James Robertson and John Donelson founded Fort Nashborough on the Cumberland River. This became the first of a series of settlements known as the Cumberland Settlements. Sometime around 1780, Freelands Station, one of the principal stations of the Cumberland Settlements, was constructed. One of the founders was James Robertson. On January 11, 1781, his son Felix was born at Freelands Station, about 2 miles south of the trailhead.

The first part of the ride will exit Metro Center, cross the Cumberland River, and exit the city. You will see some of the same streets more than once as the route will stick to roads with less car traffic. As you exit the Levee at mile 2.8 you are on Freelands Station Road. Follow it to the intersection with Mainstream Drive and turn right at mile 3.2. At the next street, turn right onto Rosa L. Parks Boulevard, at mile 3.4. You will have a bike lane when you make this turn.

As you approach Clarksville Pike / US 41A, stay in the bike lane to bear right at mile 3.8. The bike lane ends just as you start across the Cumberland River. At the first street, beside the KFC, turn right onto Cliff Drive at mile 4.3. You will wind through until you reach the intersection with Buena Vista Pike. This becomes West Trinity Lane. Take the right turn onto Buena Vista Pike at mile 4.8, and just as you begin the downhill, get into

Bike Shops

Cumberland Transit: 2807 West End Ave., Nashville; (615) 321-4069; http://cumberlandtransit.com/cycling/
Eastside Cycles: 103 S. 11th St., Nashville; (615) 469-1079; www.eastside-cycles.com
Green Fleet Bicycle Shop: 1579 Edgehill Ave., Nashville; (615) 379-8687; http://greenfleetbikes.com
Halcyon Bike Shop: 1119 Halcyon Ave., Corner of 12th Ave. S. and Halcyon Ave., Nashville; (615) 730-9344; www.halcyonbike.com

Busy cows

the left lane to prepare for a left turn at the traffic light, again onto Buena Vista Pike, at mile 5.3. There is a short downhill, and you will bear left onto Tucker Road at mile 5.5; Buena Vista goes right. This is easy to miss, so pay attention here.

You will shortly notice Hartman Park at mile 5.9. There are restrooms here. At the T intersection at the middle school, turn right onto Kings Lane at mile 6.6. Turn left at the intersection with Buena Vista Pike at mile 6.9. You are going to be on this road for about 7 miles. You will merge with Whites Creek Pike / US 431 at mile 9.2, but continue in the same direction. There is a Shell market there if you need refreshments.

After you pass the Fontanel complex, if you are looking for a shortcut, turn right at mile 10.0 onto Knight Road. You can rejoin the route at mile 28.3 to get in a 20-mile ride. Otherwise, continue on Whites Creek Pike until you pass the blue water tower in Joelton. You will not miss the climb as you approach Joelton. That big curve is called Devil's Elbow. You are welcome to brag a little after making this climb.

As you get into Joelton you will bear right at mile 14.2, continuing on Whites Creek Pike headed toward I-24 and pass the Baptist Church on your right. At mile 14.4, turn right onto Union Hill Road, the street beside the pharmacy. You will be on Union Hill Road for about 7 miles, but be sure to take the left turn that comes quickly at mile 14.7. You will have an appreciation for the Highland Rim as you make this part of the ride. When you intersect Greer Road, turn right at mile 20.3. Shortly after at mile 20.9, you will bear right onto Lickton Pike.

There is a BP market ahead of you if you need a rest stop. At the parking lot of the market you will turn left and start a short climb. Watch for oncoming traffic as you make this left turn onto Union Hill Road. Down the road, you may notice that the Union Hill Baptist Church has an interesting limestone facade. Just past the church, you will turn right onto Brick Church Pike at mile 21.9.

At the next T intersection, turn right onto Shaw Road. Then at the next T intersection, turn left onto Lickton Pike at mile 24.6. Turn right at the T intersection onto Old Hickory Boulevard at mile 27.3 beside the high school. There is not a shoulder until you intersect Whites Creek Pike / US 431 at mile 28.2. As you make the left turn, Richard's Cafe is on your right. You will immediately turn left at mile 28.3 onto Knight Road. This is where the 20-mile loop will continue.

You will stay on this road until you intersect Whites Creek Pike at mile 32.2. There will be a climb on this leg. Get into the left lane to turn at the traffic light at White Creeks Pike. When you reach the intersection at Trinity Lane, you will go straight at this intersection, at mile 33.7. The street becomes Baptist World Center Drive. At this point you will be on the bluffs above the Cumberland across from downtown. The American Baptist College on the right is a liberal arts college that provides training primarily for African-American Baptist ministers.

Turn right on Vashti Street at mile 34.8. This is easy to miss. The street name changes to Cowan Street as you pass by various warehouses adjacent to the river. Turn right at the traffic light at Spring Street and cross over the Cumberland on the Jefferson Street Bridge. Turn right at 3rd Avenue North, the first street. Turn right at the next street, Madison Street, at mile 36.8; it may be a partly gravel surface. You will approach the railroad tracks. The surface may be gravel for a very short distance. Immediately before the tracks, merge left at mile 36.9 onto the Greenway. You will follow the Greenway until mile 38.2 at the Great Circle Trailhead. This is the end of the ride.

MILES AND DIRECTIONS

0.0 Begin the ride at the Metro Center Levee Greenway Great Circle Road Trailhead. Follow the levee westward.

2.8 Exit the Levee Greenway at the Freelands Station Road Trailhead.

3.2 Turn right at the intersection with Mainstream Drive.

3.4 Turn right onto Rosa L. Parks Boulevard. The bike lane begins here.

3.8 Bear right onto Clarksville Pike / US 41A. The bike lane ends before crossing the bridge.

4.3   Turn right onto Cliff Drive at the KFC restaurant.

4.8   Turn right at the T intersection onto Buena Vista Pike. It becomes West Trinity Lane.

5.3   Turn left at the light continuing on Buena Vista Pike.

5.5   Bear left to go onto Tucker Road.

5.9   Hartman Park is on your left.

6.6   Turn right at the T intersection onto Kings Lane.

6.9   Turn left onto Buena Vista at the T intersection.

9.2   Continue straight at the intersection to merge onto Whites Creek Pike / US 431.

10.0 If you want an optional shortcut, turn right onto Knight Road and join the ride cues at mile 28.3.

14.2 Bear right to continue on Whites Creek Pike.

14.4 Turn right at the drugstore onto Union Hill Road.

14.7 Turn left to continue on Union Hill Road.

20.3 Turn right to continue on Union Hill Road at the intersection with Greer Road.

20.9 Bear right at the merge intersection onto Lickton Pike.

21.0 BP station is on the right.

21.1 Turn left to again pick up Union Hill Road. There is a short climb.

21.9 Turn right onto Brick Church Pike just past the Union Hill Baptist Church.

23.8 Turn right at the T intersection onto Shaw Road.

24.6 Turn left at the T intersection onto Lickton Pike.

27.3 Turn right at the T intersection onto Old Hickory Boulevard.

28.2 Turn left at the intersection with Whites Creek Pike / US 431.

28.3 (10.0)   At the first road turn left onto Knight Road. This is the pickup point for the optional 20-mile ride. The short option mileage is noted in parentheses.

32.2 (13.9)   Turn left onto Whites Creek Pike / US 431 at the traffic light. There is a left turn lane.

33.7 (15.4)   At the traffic light, continue straight across W. Trinity Lane. The street becomes Baptist World Center Drive.

34.8 (16.5)   Turn left onto Vashti Street; it becomes Cowan Street.

36.2 (17.9)   Turn right at Spring Street / Jefferson Street to cross the Cumberland on the Jefferson Street Bridge.

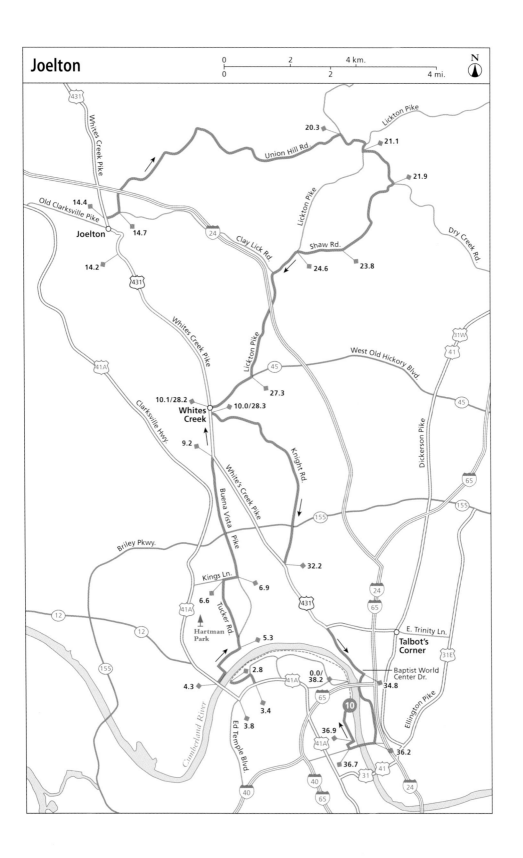

Joelton

36.7 (18.4)   Turn right at the first street, 3rd Avenue North.

36.8 (18.5)   Turn right onto Madison Street, the next street. There may be a short gravel surface here.

36.9 (18.6)   Take a left onto the Greenway before crossing the tracks. Follow the Greenway from here.

38.2 (19.9)   You are back at the Great Circle Road Trailhead of the Metro Center Levee Greenway. This is the end of the ride.

RIDE INFORMATION

Local Events/Attractions

Cedarwood: 3831 Whites Creek Pike, Nashville; (615) 876-9999; http://www.cedarwoodweddings.com/. This historic home was built in 1835 by James Yarbrough. The house is listed on the National Register of Historic Places and offers a beautiful look into the antebellum farmhouse of yesteryear. It is available for weddings and other group events.

A Cowboy Town: 3665 Knight Dr., Whites Creek; (615) 876-1029; www.acowboytown.com. According to their website, this attraction offers "horseback riding, Wild West gunfights, awesome live cowboy music, primitive camping, hiking, picnics, fishing, giant bonfires, hayrides, campfire cookouts, and much more."

Fontanel Mansion: 4225 Whites Creek Pike, Nashville; (615) 724-1600; http://www.fontanelmansion.com. Fontanel Mansion, the former home of country music star Barbara Mandrell and husband and builder, Ken Dudney, was completed in 1987. Today, this 27,000-square-foot mansion—with over twenty rooms, and called the largest log house in the world—is a tourist attraction, and The Woods Amphitheater at Fontanel is a destination for a variety of musical groups. Country music history and memorabilia are included in the tours, available every day from 9 a.m. to 3 p.m.

Local Eateries

BP Market: There is a BP market at mile 21.1 immediately before the turn onto Union Hill Road.

Richard's Cafe: 4420 Whites Creek Pike, Whites Creek; (615) 299-9590; richardscafe.com. Located at mile 10.1 and 28.2 at the intersection of Whites Creek Road and Old Hickory Boulevard, this cafe serves breakfast, lunch, and dinner, and the menu is a Cajun treat!

Restrooms

Mile 5.9: There are restrooms and water at Hartman Park on your left.
Mile 21.1: There are restrooms at the BP Market.

Starbucks to Starbucks

This ride is based on a simple concept of arithmetic: If one is good, then two is better. Hence, the Starbucks to Starbucks ride. This ride follows a bit of the Percy Warner Park ride and then takes off south out of the back end of the park toward Williamson County to Franklin. It is chock-full of local history, dating from roughly the end of the first millennium to the nineteenth-century development of Nashville and Williamson County. It is a great ride, accessible from downtown, and a good workout with a primarily rural feel.

The ride begins in West Nashville at the Belle Meade Starbucks. The turn point is the Franklin Starbucks in the Five Points area of Franklin. There are a couple of climbs if you need some practice!

Start: The ride begins in West Nashville at the Belle Meade Starbucks.

Length: 43 miles, loop ride

Approximate riding time: About 3 hours

Best bike: Any bike

Terrain and trail surface: The terrain is rolling, even hilly in a couple of places. The ride is on paved city/county streets. The section of the ride on Old Natchez Trace is rough in places.

Traffic and hazards: Most of the miles of the ride are on suburban or rural roads. There will be traffic on Harding Road / US 70 South, but it's a short section of the ride. The part of the ride that goes through Percy Warner Park is a narrow road shared by other bikers, walkers, and runners, as well as cars.

Things to see: Meeting of the Waters and Montpier

Maps: DeLorme *Tennessee Atlas & Gazetteer*, page 33, B8

11

THE RIDE

The ride begins in front of the Starbucks store in the Belle Meade Shopping Center. The first one half mile will be the busiest traffic, but there is a wide shoulder and turn lane. If you need bike shop services, Gran Fondo bike shops are less than a mile down Harding Road at the point of the turn at Belle Meade Boulevard.

After you pass through the significant stone entryway into Percy Warner Park, the Percy Warner Golf Course is on the right.

Immediately as you round the turn at mile 3.8, the Warner Woods hiking trail crosses the road. Watch for hikers crossing the road. Also, watch for hikers crossing the road at mile 5.3. There is a portable restroom here.

Continue in this big circle around the park. At mile 8.3, before you start up the hill toward the horse track, turn right. This access road intersects Old

Bike Shops

Cumberland Transit: 2807 West End Ave., Nashville; (615) 321-4069; http://cumberlandtransit.com/cycling/

Gran Fondo: 5133 Harding Rd., Suite A6, Nashville; (615) 354-1090; http://www.granfondocycles.com/

Gran Fondo Trail & Fitness: 5133 Harding Rd., Suite B-1, Nashville; (615) 499-4634; http://www.granfondotrail.com/

Green Fleet Bicycle Shop: 1579 Edgehill Ave., Nashville; (615) 379-8687; http://greenfleetbikes.com

Halcyon Bike Shop: 1119 Halcyon Ave., Corner of 12th Ave. S. and Halcyon Ave., Nashville; (615) 730-9344; www.halcyonbike.com

Mac's Harpeth Bikes: 1100 Hillsboro Rd., Franklin; (615) 472-1002; www.macsharpethbikes.com

MOAB Franklin: 109 Del Rio Pike, Suite 105, Franklin; (615) 807-2035; http://moabbikes.com/

Curious horses

Hickory Boulevard at Vaughn Road. This is where you will exit Percy Warner Park. You will pass a portable restroom on your left. There will be some traffic on Vaughn and especially on Sneed Road. Exercise caution crossing the narrow bridges over the Harpeth River on Vaughn and Sneed.

Just a bit past Temple Road, you will see the historical marker for the Indian mounds, which are believed to date between AD 900 and 1450. Shortly after, you will bear left to continue to follow Old Natchez Trace instead of going up into the subdivision.

After a short climb, you will notice a historical marker for Montpier. This was the home of Nicholas Perkins, the owner of an approximately 12,000-acre farm in the area. The house in the distance dates to 1822.

After you turn left onto Del Rio Pike at mile 15.6 you will shortly pass by Meeting of the Waters on the left side. This was the original plantation of the Perkins family, completed in 1807. It was their son-in-law Nicholas Perkins who developed Montpier, and later inherited and inhabited Meeting of the Waters.

You will enter a residential section when you get to the bike lane at about mile 20. Turn right at the next traffic light at mile 20.6 onto Magnolia Drive. It will become 11th Avenue N. Note the interesting architecture as you proceed down Fair Street. Turn right onto US 431 / Hillsboro Road / TN 106 / 5th Avenue North. Starbucks is on your left; turn in at the parking lot before the intersection at mile 21.7. This is the return point for the ride.

To return, you will go to the intersection at West Main Street and turn right, heading southwest. If you need bike shop services, the MOAB and Mac's Harpeth bike shops are nearest by turning right on Del Rio Pike at mile 22.9.

Proceed on the return through the park. After you go through the traffic light on Harding Road, get into the left lane to prepare for the left turn into the Kroger Store parking lot at mile 42.4. Starbucks is just ahead. This is the end of the ride at mile 42.6.

MILES AND DIRECTIONS

0.0 Begin at the Starbucks Belle Meade; exit the parking lot, turning right onto Harding Road / US 70.

0.5 Turn left onto Belle Meade Boulevard.

3.2 Enter Percy Warner Park at the main park entrance.

3.8 Bear right to continue on the Main Drive.

4.6 Rough road here due to much patching, especially in the curve.

4.9 Bear left to continue on the Main Drive.

5.3 Continue straight here and watch for hikers crossing the road. This is the Deep Well parking lot accessible from Highway 100. There is a portable restroom here.

5.9 A half-mile climb begins here.

Meeting of the Waters

Thomas Hardin Perkins (1757–1838) built Meeting of the Waters, a Federal style house, completing it around 1809. Perkins was a Revolutionary War prisoner of war, and after he was released, he visited his colonial officer, also a POW; later, he married his daughter. He and his wife subsequently migrated to Williamson County, where he became a significant landowner. He amassed a total of 3,300 acres through purchases of land in 1802, 1804, and 1810.

One of his daughters, Mary Hardin Perkins, married her first cousin, Nicholas Perkins (Bigbee). Together they constructed the Montpier estate about 1 mile north, and later they inherited Meeting of the Waters. Through a series of sometimes colorful owners, the family ownership ended in 1989, when the estate was purchased by a local Nashville author and historian. However, the home retains a connection to its origins, as current owners, the Wills family, are also related to the Perkins family.

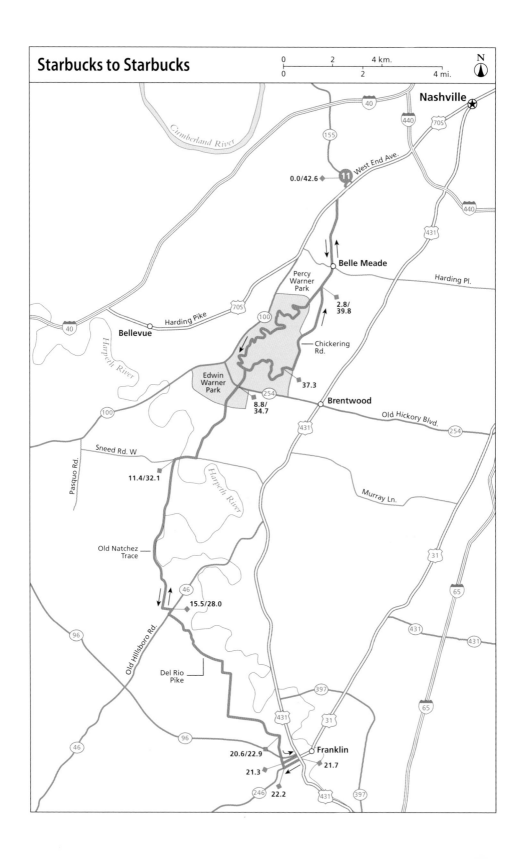

Starbucks to Starbucks

0   2   4 km.
0   2   4 mi.

N

Nashville

Cumberland River

40

440

70S

155

West End Ave.

0.0/42.6 11

431

440

Belle Meade

Percy
Warner
Park

Harding Pl.

2.8/
39.8

70S

Harding Pike

46

Bellevue

40

100

Chickering
Rd.

Harpeth River

Edwin
Warner
Park

37.3

254

Brentwood

8.8/
34.7

431

Old Hickory Blvd.

254

100

Sneed Rd. W

11.4/32.1

Harpeth River

Murray Ln.

Pasquo Rd.

31

Old Natchez
Trace

65

46

15.5/28.0

431

431

96

Old Hillsboro Rd.

Del Rio
Pike

397

65

431   31

96

20.6/22.9   Franklin

46

21.3   21.7

246   22.2   431   397

6.5   Go straight to continue on the Main Drive.

7.4   Bear right to continue on the Main Drive.

8.0   Make a hard left to continue on the Main Drive.

8.3   Turn right onto exit/access road.

8.8   Go across Old Hickory Boulevard at the traffic light onto Vaughn Road.

10.8   Turn right onto Sneed Road W at the T intersection.

11.4   Turn left onto Old Natchez Trace.

15.5   Turn right at the T intersection onto Old Hillsboro / TN 46.

15.6   Turn left onto Del Rio Pike.

17.5   Turn right to continue on Del Rio Pike.

20.6   Turn right onto Magnolia Drive (becomes 11th Avenue North).

21.1   Cross TN 96 and continue on 11th Avenue North / Magnolia Drive.

21.3   Turn left onto Fair Street.

21.7   Turn right onto US 431 / Hillsboro Road / TN 106.

21.7   Turn left into Starbucks; this is the turn point for the ride. To return, from the Five Points intersection in front of Starbucks, turn right onto West Main Street, heading southwest.

22.2   Turn right onto 11th Avenue North / Magnolia Drive.

22.3   Cross TN 96 and continue on 11th Avenue North / Magnolia Drive.

22.9   Turn left onto Del Rio Pike at the traffic light beside the Kroger store.

25.9   Turn left to continue on Del Rio Pike at the stop sign.

27.8   Turn right at the T intersection onto Old Hillsboro / TN 46.

27.9   Turn left onto Old Natchez Trace.

32.1   Turn right onto Sneed Road W at the T intersection.

32.7   Turn left onto Vaughn Road.

34.7   Go across Old Hickory Boulevard at the traffic light.

35.3   Turn right at the intersection with the Main Drive.

37.3   Bear right toward the Chickering Road exit.

37.5   Turn left onto Chickering Road.

38.3   Bear right to remain on Chickering Road.

39.8   Bear right onto Belle Meade Boulevard.

42.0   Bear right on US 70 / Harding Road. Exercise caution at this busy intersection.

42.4 Turn left into the Belle Meade Shopping Center at the Kroger store.

42.6 Starbucks is on your left; this is the end of the ride.

RIDE INFORMATION

Local Events/Attractions

Town of Franklin: This is the best attraction in the area, maintaining a small-town feel even though it's just a 20-minute drive from Nashville. It has active neighborhood involvement and local government support for a variety of events. To get an idea of events and activities, consult the Williamson County Convention and Visitor Bureau at http://www.visitwilliamson.com. For more information about historic Franklin, check out http://www.historicfranklin.com.

Local Eateries

There are various eateries in the Belle Meade Shopping Center and the Hill Center. There are also various shops and restaurants on White Bridge, less than 0.5 mile from the intersection of White Bridge Road and Harding Road.

There are also a number of restaurants in Franklin, including places on West Main Street and side streets. At mile 21.7 you may want to turn left onto West Main Street from Starbucks (the route makes a right turn) and explore some of the local places in the surrounding blocks.

Restrooms

Mile 5.3: Portable restrooms available at the Deep Well Trailhead.

Mile 8.5 and 35.1: Portable restrooms available at the parking area beside the horse track.

Mile 9.4 and 36.0: There are portable restrooms at the dog walk area on the west side of Vaughn Road.

Bicentennial Park to J. Percy Priest Dam

The Music City Bikeway has been improved in recent years to go from the southwest side of Nashville at Percy Warner Park through downtown and around the east side to Percy Priest Dam. The first part was the Deep Well to Bicentennial Park ride. This ride completes the loop, covering part of the Shelby Bottoms Greenway ride.

This ride is an out-and-back ride on the same track. Although it is on the Music City Bikeway, it covers two greenway sections. The first one you encounter is the Shelby Bottoms Greenway (SB). When you cross over the Cumberland River, you are on the Stones River Greenway (SR) for the rest of the outbound leg of the ride. Both of these greenways have signage designating either SB or SR, respectively, along with a mileage number embossed on a large wooden post. The posts appear in either 0.25- or 0.5-mile increments.

Start: The ride begins at the crosswalk on 7th Avenue North at the Bicentennial Capitol Mall State Park. There is a Music City Bikeway sign pointing east toward a bike/pedestrian path.

Length: 32 miles, out-and-back ride

Approximate riding time: 2 to 3 hours

Best bike: Any bike

Terrain and trail surface: Most of this ride is on paved bike paths. Otherwise, it is on paved streets with a bike lane, except for a short section through downtown.

Traffic and hazards: Most of this ride is a bike path. The trail may be crowded with other bikers, runners, walkers, and in-line skaters, especially on weekends. There are wooden bridges that narrow the trail and may be slick if there has been any rain or heavy fog. Parts of the trail have hairpin turns; take it slow, and watch for oncoming trail users. Part of the bike path trail is located in the Stones River floodplain, so the trail is sometimes covered with water after very extended rainy periods. Also, the part of the trail between Lebanon Road and the dam encourages motorized wheelchair users.

The downtown section of the ride crosses several streets. Although there are pedestrian walks and car traffic should stop for you, it is best to be prepared to stop at these streets if necessary. Also, a couple of the turns are very short, so caution rather than speed on this section is best.

Things to see: Cumberland River, Stones River, J. Percy Priest Dam

Maps: DeLorme *Tennessee Atlas & Gazetteer*, page 34, A1

Getting there by car: Bicentennial Capitol Mall State Park, known as Bicentennial Park, is located at 600 James Robertson Parkway in downtown Nashville, at the foot of the State Capitol between James Robertson Parkway and Jefferson Street, 6th and 7th Avenues. Exits from the interstates are marked Bicentennial Mall. Take I-65 to the Rosa Parks / 8th Avenue North exit. Head south toward downtown for 0.7 miles and turn left at Jefferson Street and right onto 7th Avenue North. Parking is on the street. **GPS:** N36 10.12' / W86 47.15'

THE RIDE

The early part of the ride weaves through the downtown Nashville business district, and it may feel a bit like a maze. The key is to follow the Music City Bikeway signage. At the beginning of the ride you are on a downtown section of the Music City Bikeway. If you are coming from Harrison Street on 7th Avenue North, you will see the Music City Bikeway sign that directs you to turn to go east. You will cross six streets in the first 0.7 mile of the ride. Depending on day of week and time of day, these cross streets will be busy, so stop and look both ways before crossing. There will be plenty of open riding once you cross over the Cumberland River at mile 2.2. The crossing

Bike Shops

Eastside Cycles: 103 S. 11th St., Nashville; (615) 469-1079; www.eastside-cycles.com
Green Fleet Bicycle Shop: 1579 Edgehill Ave., Nashville; (615) 379-8687; http://greenfleetbikes.com
Halcyon Bike Shop: 1119 Halcyon Ave., Corner of 12th Ave. S. and Halcyon Ave., Nashville; (615) 730-9344; www.halcyonbike.com
Ride615: 3441 Lebanon Rd. #103, Hermitage; (615) 200-7433; www.ride615.com
Sun & Ski: 501 Opry Mills Dr., Nashville; (615) 886-4854; http://www.sunandski.com

Downtown Nashville

at 1st Avenue North has an interesting dogleg! The barrier construction to enforce that 90 degree turn in the sidewalk/bike lane could also be used for automobile traffic instead of bike and pedestrian traffic.

You will cross 1st Avenue North at 0.7 mile, where it gets even more interesting. The bike path is on a sidewalk from here for the next 0.6 mile. At mile 1.25 the bike path ends and the route goes onto 1st Avenue South. Don't worry; it's a relatively quiet street. As you proceed, the buildings on your right are part of Nashville's downtown entertainment venues on 2nd Avenue. Pictures dating from the 1870s show this area to be the Nashville wharf and warehouse district.

From here you will make a square to access the river bridge. You will cross over the beginning of Broadway, passing the Music City Star train station and Riverfront Park. Turn right onto Demonbreun Street at mile 1.6. Turn right onto 3rd Avenue South at mile 1.7, the second street. You will pass the Schermerhorn Symphony Center on your left as you approach the opening to Shelby Street Pedestrian Bridge at mile 1.8. There is a bit of a climb immediately. Ride in the center of the bridge. The bridge is always busy; caution is advised. You may want to stop at the top of the bridge and take a look at downtown Nashville and the Titans Stadium from this vantage point.

As you get to the bottom of the bridge at mile 2.2, turn right onto 1st Street South, which becomes Davidson Street at the curve. You will enter

Shelby Park at mile 3.7. The VinnyLinks Golf Course will be on your left. As you pass by the picnic areas and ball fields, bear right, following the Music City Bikeway. You will continue to bear right, although it will seem like you're going straight at mile 4.7 as you go under the CSX trestle. Just as you pass under the trestle, the Shelby Bottoms Nature Center will appear on your left at mile 4.8. This is the place for restrooms and water. If the Nature Center is closed, you can take the stairs about 50 feet to your right as you face the building and access the restrooms from the other side of the building. If you have ridden the Shelby Bottoms Greenway ride, this section will be familiar.

As you come out of a wooded area and cross a wooden bridge, you won't be able to miss the Cumberland River Pedestrian Bridge access at mile 7.5. Follow the path up the grade, circle around, and cross over the bridge. From this vantage point over the Cumberland, the Opryland Hotel and Convention Center may be visible on the far left. Gaylord Entertainment Company, owner of the Opryland complex, occupies the large redbrick office building.

You will go under a couple of tunnels as you cross under Briley Parkway / TN 155. When you reach the top of the hill, Two Rivers Park and the Wave Country complex is on your right. There are also restrooms and water here at mile 8.2. You can see the skateboarders from the bike path. You will cross over an interior park road; stop here for car traffic. Just as you ride by the Stones River Greenway Trailhead at mile 9.2, you may be able to see the Two Rivers Mansion on your right at the top of the hill.

The bridge at mile 10.3 is over the Stones River, the second of the Two Rivers. The farmland on your right is part of the Ravenwood Farm. The golf course that begins as you make the sharp turn at mile 11.3 is the Ravenwood Country Club and Golf Course.

The very wide section of trail you encounter at mile 12.7 was the old Lebanon Pike / US 70. Be cautious as you make the hairpin turn, as the trail narrows and you make a blind-curve turn at mile 13.0. The trail will follow the Stones River most of the way from this point until you reach the J. Percy Priest Dam. You should also be aware of persons who may be traveling in wheelchairs from this point on.

At mile 14.8 the trail narrows as you enter an elevated boardwalk section over the Stones River. Be especially aware of other trail users on this section. It is a straight path beside the river most of the rest of the way to the J. Percy Priest Dam Trailhead. Take the left turn at the Y intersection that directs the wheelchairs to go right.

You will reach the parking lot and trailhead at mile 15.8. You can't miss the dam in front of you. There are portable restrooms here, but no water. This is the turnaround point for the ride.

Do you remember those couple of nice downhill sections as you were coming out on the path? There will be a couple of climbs on the inbound leg back to Bicentennial Park. Overall this is a very pleasant ride by the usually peaceful Stones River.

Remember as you cross over the Cumberland River, you will bear right to remain on the Music City Bikeway. At mile 31.6, you are back at Bicentennial Park, the end of the ride.

MILES AND DIRECTIONS

0.0 Begin at the crosswalk on 7th Avenue North beside the farmers' market complex. There is a Music Bikeway sign on the right side of the street as you approach from Harrison Street (south) pointing east toward a bike/pedestrian path. Head east toward downtown.

1.25 Turn left onto 1st Avenue South onto the street.

1.6 Turn right onto Demonbreun Street.

1.7 Turn right onto 3rd Avenue South.

1.8 Turn right onto the Shelby Street pedestrian bridge. Prepare for an immediate climb.

2.2 Turn right onto 1st Street South. This becomes Davidson Street.

3.7 Enter Shelby Park at mile 3.7. The VinnyLinks Golf Course will be on your left. As you pass by the picnic areas and ball fields, bear right, following the Music City Bikeway.

4.7 Proceed through Shelby Bottoms Greenway on the Music City Bikeway.

4.8 Shelby Bottoms Nature Center is on your left.

7.5 Cross the Cumberland River.

8.2 The Two Rivers Park and the Wave Country complex are on your right.

10.3 Cross the Stones River on the pedestrian bridge.

11.3 Ravenwood Golf Course and Country Club is on your left.

12.7 Cross the Stones River on Old Lebanon Pike.

13.0 Caution, there is a blind curve turn here.

14.8 This is a narrow boardwalk section beside the Stones River.

15.8 This is the J. Percy Priest Dam Trailhead and the turnaround point for the ride.

31.6 You are back at Bicentennial Park, and this is the end of the ride.

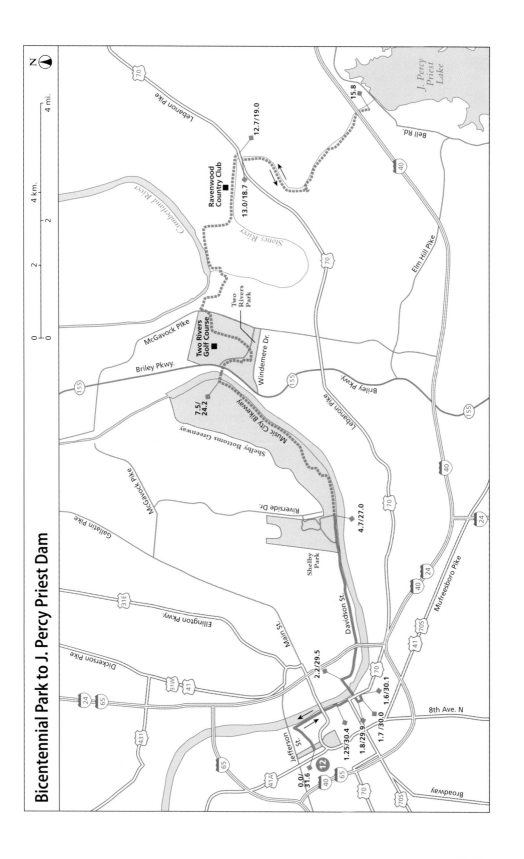

Bicentennial Park to J. Percy Priest Dam

N

4 mi.

4 km.

Lebanon Pike

70

Cumberland River

12.7/19.0

Ravenwood Country Club

13.0/18.7

Stones River

15.8

Bell Rd.

40

J. Percy Priest Lake

McGavock Pike

Two Rivers Golf Course

Two Rivers Park

Windemere Dr.

Briley Pkwy.

155

70

Elm Hill Pike

7.5/24.2

Music City Bikeway

Shelby Bottoms Greenway

155

Lebanon Pike

Briley Pkwy.

155

Riverside Dr.

4.7/27.0

Shelby Park

70

40

24

McGavock Pike

Gallatin Pike

Ellington Pkwy.

31E

Davidson St.

Main St.

2.2/29.5

70

41

705

Murfreesboro Pike

Dickerson Pike

24

65

31W

41

431

1.6/30.1

8th Ave. N

1.25/30.4

1.8/29.9

1.7/30.0

Jefferson St.

12

0.0/31.6

41A

65

40

65

40

70

705

Broadway

RIDE INFORMATION

Local Events/Attractions

The Parthenon: 2500 West End Ave., Nashville; (615) 862-8431; http://www
.nashville.gov/Parks-and-Recreation/Parthenon.aspx. The Parthenon is a rep-
lica of the original Parthenon in Athens. It is the centerpiece of Centennial
Park, which is about 0.5 mile from the Music City Bikeway via the 28th Avenue connector to Charlotte Pike. The website notes that the Parthenon was
originally part of the 1897 Centennial Exposition. It is noteworthy for its recreation of "the 42-foot statue Athena," and also houses a "permanent collection of sixty-three paintings by nineteenth- and twentieth-century American
artists, donated by James M. Cowan."

Schermerhorn Symphony Center: Nashville Symphony, One Symphony
Pl., Nashville; (615) 687-6500 and Box Office (615) 687-6400; http://www
.nashvillesymphony.org/. This attraction is located downtown at the corner
of Demonbreun Street and 3rd Avenue South and 4th Avenue South, across
the street from the entrance to the Shelby Street pedestrian bridge. Although
the Nashville Symphony's origins date back to the end of World War II, the
completion of the Schermerhorn Symphony Center in 2006 has brought even
more attention to Music City for the diversity of music. As noted from their
website, the hall "has attracted global attention for its acoustical excellence
and distinctive neoclassical architecture, and its opening marked the beginning of an exciting new chapter in the history of the Nashville Symphony."

Music director Giancarlo Guerrero has already led the Nashville Symphony's
efforts to capture four Grammy Awards. A variety of musical events are scheduled;
for more information and to schedule a tour, you can check out their website.

Local Eateries

There are eating places in the farmers' market area at the Bicentennial Park at
mile 0.0. When you make the turn onto Demonbreun Street at mile 1.6, you
are near many restaurants. If you want to turn right and ride up 2nd Avenue,
you will find something to eat, mostly nicer restaurants. The Schermerhorn
Symphony Center also offers casual food at the Symphony Café. There is a
convenience market on Davidson Street before you get to Shelby Park.

Restrooms

Mile 0.0: There are restrooms in the farmers' market complex.
Mile 4.8 and **Mile 20.6:** There are restrooms and water at the Shelby Bottoms
Nature Center. Facilities are available even when the center is closed.
Mile 8.2 and **Mile 23.6:** There are restrooms and water at the Two Rivers Park
and Wave Country.

Shelby Bottoms Greenway (SBG)

The Shelby Bottoms Greenway (SBG) is part of the larger Music City Bikeway system and is sometimes included in organized marathons and half marathons from the downtown area. This ride follows a two-way paved trail on the east side of the Cumberland River. You can see some of the downtown area from different points on the trail. The Shelby Bottoms Nature Center is the starting point. There are exhibits and maps describing SBG. The living green roof is an example of the conservation efforts under way at Metro Parks. No bike—no problem. You have two options: B-cycle is now in Nashville. Check out the Visiting Music City section near the end of the book for how to use this service. Your second option is a free bike via the Nashville Green Bikes program; see the write-up about the Nature Center in the Local Events/Attractions section.

Start: The trailhead is at the Shelby Bottoms Nature Center, 1900 Davidson Street, Nashville.

Length: 8 miles total, out and back on the same trail

Approximate riding time: 1 hour or less

Best bike: Any bike

Terrain and trail surface: Flat ride on a paved asphalt bike path

Traffic and hazards: There will be no car traffic, but the trail may be crowded with other bikers, runners, walkers, and in-line skaters, especially on weekends. There are six wooden bridges that narrow the trail and may be slick if there has been any rain or heavy fog. The bridge near the observation deck includes several winding turns; take it slow here, and watch for oncoming trail users.

Maps: DeLorme *Tennessee Atlas & Gazetteer*, page 34, B1. Park map: http://www.nashville.gov/Portals/0/SiteContent/Parks/images/greenways/small-shelby%20bottom.jpg

THE RIDE

The SBG is an 820-acre natural area park located in the Cumberland River floodplain. The area was under agricultural cultivation as recently as the 1950s. Metro Parks of Nashville has chosen to return most of it to a natural area.

The ride route includes a loop on either end; it is 4 miles including both loops, beginning at the Nature Center going to Forrest Green Drive Trailhead.

There are two connectors to local neighborhoods: Fortland Connector and Shadow Lane Connector (not included in the 4 miles). The first loop has an observation tower at mile 0.5; you may want to get a picture!

How did the early settlers ever get across the river to settle the downtown area? John Shelby, a local doctor, obtained 640 acres in the area in 1817, and was the first to build a bridge across the Cumberland River. For his efforts, SBG, Shelby Park, Shelby Street, and the Shelby Street Bridge were named in his honor.

Fortland, one of the early farms in the area, has a connection to World War II aviation. The Fort family owned part of the land now occupied by SBG. Cornelia Fort, a local debutante, became fascinated with flying. She joined the Women's Auxiliary Ferrying Squadron (WAFS) in 1940. WAFS was responsible for flying planes across the United States in preparation for use in the war effort. Cornelia Fort died

Bike Shops

Eastside Cycles: 103 S. 11th St., Nashville; (615) 469-1079; www.eastside-cycles.com
Green Fleet Bicycle Shop: 1579 Edgehill Ave., Nashville; (615) 379-8687; http://greenfleetbikes.com
Halcyon Bike Shop: 1119 Halcyon Ave., Corner of 12th Ave. S. and Halcyon Ave., Nashville; (615) 730-9344; www.halcyonbike.com
Ride615: 3441 Lebanon Rd., #103, Hermitage; (615) 200-7433; www.ride615.com
Sun & Ski: 501 Opry Mills Dr., Nashville; (615) 886-4854; http://www.sunandski.com

View from SBG Observation Deck

in 1943 while en route from California to Dallas; her plane crashed when another pilot clipped her wings in midair. The Cornelia Fort Air Park was named in her honor.

SBG also includes several primitive walking and hiking trails. Trail rules are very specific that bikers must use only paved trails.

The first loop from the Nature Center includes the Observation Deck and a river-overlook platform. In summer, you will ride down level, paved trails curtained with trees and shrubs. The best views of downtown are in the winter months when there are no leaves on the trees.

The trail is marked every 0.25 or 0.5 mile (for example, "SB 2.5" will be carved on a wooden post beside the trail). Turn left onto the main trail at 0.7 mile. On the trail, you will cross a bridge; you may miss the marker (SB 2.5), but you won't miss the overhead bridge. This is a bicycle and pedestrian bridge over the Cumberland River. Do not take this (see the Bicentennial Park to J. Percy Priest Dam ride). Stay on the level path continuing straight at the intersection and follow the loop to the Forrest Green Drive Trailhead.

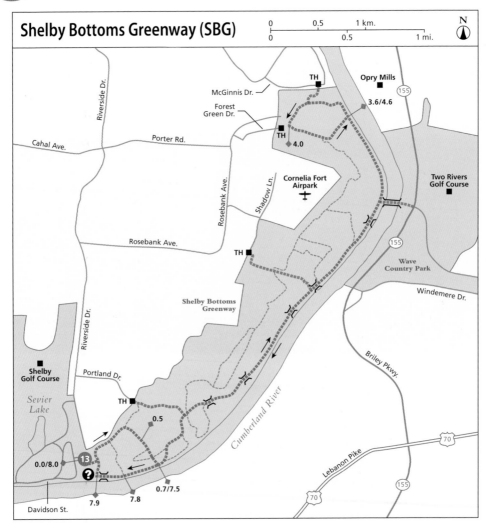

Shelby Bottoms Greenway (SBG)

0   0.5   1 km.
0   0.5   1 mi.

N

Opry Mills

TH

McGinnis Dr.

Forest
Green Dr.

3.6/4.6

155

Riverside Dr.

Porter Rd.

Cahal Ave.

TH

4.0

Rosebank Ave.

Shadow Ln.

Cornelia Fort
Airpark

Two Rivers
Golf Course

Rosebank Ave.

TH

155

Wave
Country Park

Shelby Bottoms
Greenway

Windemere Dr.

Riverside Dr.

Briley Pkwy.

Shelby
Golf Course

Portland Dr.

TH

Cumberland River

Sevier
Lake

0.5

70

0.0/8.0

13

Lebanon Pike

?

0.7/7.5

70

155

7.9   7.8

Davidson St.

At mile 4.0 the trail begins the return loop when you make a left turn. If you
need restroom facilities, turn right to go to the Forrest Green Trailhead; it is
.05 miles to the right. After you pass over a wooden bridge, turn right at the
fork at mile 7.9 to return to the start. Then when you reach the circle, you will
turn left to return to the parking lot at mile 8.0.

MILES AND DIRECTIONS

0.0 Begin at the Shelby Bottoms Nature Center. Take a left turn at the loop after you cross the wooden bridge.

0.5 Observation tower is on the left.

0.7 Turn left onto the main trail.

2.5 Continue straight on the SBG trail.

4.0 This is the turnaround point. Turn left to return to the Nature Center.

7.8 Viewpoint—Cumberland River.

7.9 Turn right to return to the Nature Center.

8.0 Turn left and arrive back at the Shelby Bottoms Nature Center.

RIDE INFORMATION

Local Events/Attractions

Shelby Bottoms Nature Center: 1900 Davidson St., Nashville; 615-862-8400; http://www.nashville.gov/parks/nature/sbnc/index.asp. This nature center offers various learning activities for all ages and is one of the rental points for Nashville GreenBikes, a bike-share program (http://nashvillebikeshare.org/). The website even shows the number of bikes available at each location. Visiting Nashville? You don't have to be a resident to rent one for free if you return it in a timely fashion. You can even get a helmet!

Local Eateries

Five Points at the intersection of Woodland Street and South 11th Street, approximately 2 miles from Shelby Bottoms Nature Center, is a good area for eateries and local crafts. You can catch the Tomato Art Fest in early August.

Restrooms

Mile 0.0: There are restrooms available at the Shelby Bottoms Nature Center.
Mile 4.0: There is a restroom facility at Forrest Green Drive Trailhead.

East Nashville

Nashville was settled on both sides of the Cumberland River beginning in the late 1700s. The east side of the Cumberland has had a varied history since it was first developed, beginning with the exclusive Edgefield residential community. This was followed by Lockeland Springs and other local neighborhoods. A great fire in 1916 and a tornado in 1933 destroyed many of the fine Victorian homes in the area. These two events sparked some out-migration from the area to newer sections of the city. But some areas have been preserved, and the East End has become a rising star in Nashville, even surviving a tornado in 1998. You can see many of the preserved homes on Russell, Woodland, and Fatherland Streets.

This ride is an introduction to the east side of Nashville. It includes some residential, park, and commercial areas. Residential development in this community has included restoration of many early-twentieth-century bungalows and even older Victorian homes. The view on the ride through the area is a bit of a step back in time of residential architecture, combined with trendy shops and restaurants that service the local residents. One of the recent additions in the city has been the Tennessee Titans stadium, known as LP Field. This ride circles the stadium.

Start: The ride begins in the Five Points area.

Length: 9 miles, loop ride

Approximate riding time: 1 hour

Best bike: Any bike

Terrain and trail surface: The terrain is generally flat with some rolling parts. The entire route is on paved city streets. Most of the route has a bike lane.

Traffic and hazards: The traffic depends mainly on time of day. This is not a good ride to attempt during rush hour, but most any other time should be fine. Part of the ride, from the Titans Stadium past the I-24 interchange, about 0.5 mile, is busy.

Things to see: Eastside Cycles Mural

Maps: DeLorme *Tennessee Atlas & Gazetteer*, page 34, A1

Getting there by car: From downtown Nashville, take the James Robertson Parkway, which becomes Main Street when you cross over the Cumberland River. Follow Main Street 1.0 miles until you get to South 10th Street. Turn right on South 10th, then immediately left onto Woodland Street. Five Points, where Woodland, Clearview, and 11th Streets intersect, is the starting point.

From other parts of the city, take I-24 through the downtown loop; take the Shelby Avenue exit, exit 49, and drive east to the traffic light at South 5th Street; turn left (north). Follow South 5th Street, then turn right at the intersection of South 5th and Woodland Street. Then proceed to Five Points, where you will intersect South 11th Street. **GPS:** N36 10.39' / W86 44.58'

THE RIDE

As you begin the ride from the parking lot of Eastside Cycles, turn right onto Woodland Street. Before you do, take a good look at the wall mural on the side of the Eastside Cycles building. You will see immediately that this area is an eclectic mix of residential and light commercial development. You may want to make your own mental notes of places to visit or eat later. The ride follows the bike lane as marked until you reach Shelby Park. At 0.2 mile, turn left at the four-way stop sign at North 14th Street. Be aware of the cross-street stop signs. Turn right at Eastland Avenue at 0.6 mile. You will ride by condos, restaurants, a coffee shop, and other commercial businesses.

Bike Shops

Eastside Cycles: 103 S. 11th St., Nashville; (615) 469-1079; www.eastside-cycles.com
Ride615: 3441 Lebanon Rd., #103, Hermitage; (615) 200-7433; www.ride615.com
Sun & Ski: 501 Opry Mills Dr., Nashville; (615) 886-4854; http://www.sunandski.com

At the stop sign, mile 1.3, bear left onto Porter Road. You will follow the street as it bears right just before mile 2.3. Turn right onto Riverside Drive at mile 2.3 at the stop sign. You will see a mix of established houses and renovations, demonstrating the popularity of this area.

Shelby Park entrance

At mile 4.0, get into the right turn lane; turn right here onto Huntleigh Drive. You will now enter Shelby Park. The sign indicates the Greenway is to the left. Turn left in less than 0.1 mile.

You will ride by Sevier Lake and the ball fields inside the park. Shelby Park was opened on July 4, 1912. The mockingbird statue is part of the park's centennial celebration.

Turn right at the T intersection onto Davidson Street at mile 4.8. This segment is on the Music City Bikeway. This is near the starting point for the Shelby Bottoms Greenway ride. There is a bike lane on this segment until you reach the stadium.

At the noticeable turn in the street, approximately mile 6.8, Davidson becomes South 1st Street. You will ride under the Korean Veterans Boulevard as the Titans Stadium comes into view. Turn left onto Victory Avenue at mile 7.0. Then take the first right onto Titans Way at mile 7.1.

Turn right at mile 7.4 onto Titans Way / Russell Street. At mile 7.6, turn left at South 2nd Street for one block. Be cautious at the right turn onto Woodland Street. This is the busy traffic corridor until you get past the I-24 interchange, about 0.5 mile. Continue on Woodland Street until you reach the light at Five Points, at mile 9.0. This is the end of the ride.

MILES AND DIRECTIONS

0.0 Beginning at the corner of the parking lot of Eastside Cycles, turn right on Woodland Street.

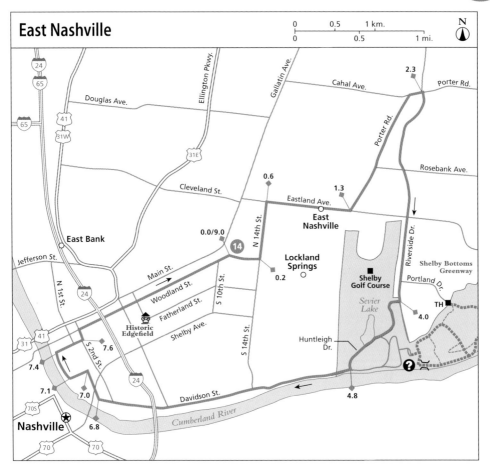

East Nashville

0.2   Turn left at North 14th Street.

0.6   Turn right at Eastland Avenue.

1.3   Bear left at the stop sign onto Porter Road.

2.3   Turn right at Riverside Drive.

4.0   Turn right at Huntleigh Drive. Make the first left after entering Shelby Park.

4.8   Turn right at the T intersection with Davidson Street.

6.8   Continue on 1st Street toward LP Field.

7.0   Turn left at Victory Avenue.

7.1   Turn right at Titans Way.

14

7.4 Turn right at Titans Way / Russell Street.

7.6 Turn left at South 2nd Street.

7.6 Turn right at Woodland Street.

9.0 This is the end of the ride at Five Points.

RIDE INFORMATION

Local Events/Attractions

There are a variety of events that go on all year long in east Nashville, including the Tomato Art Fest, an annual event in August. An exciting addition is the Faux Paw Fashion Show ("paw" is the key here). During Christmastime, there is a historic home tour. For more information, visit http://www.lockelandsprings .org/ and http://www.east-nashville.com/.

Local Eateries

This ride is specially designed to introduce you to many places to eat; the first part of the ride is best. Here are the best spots on the ride to explore local eateries: Five Points; the intersection of North 14th Street and Woodland; the intersection of Eastland Avenue and Chapel Avenue for a few blocks; and a few places on Porter. For more information, visit http://www.east-nashville .com/destinations/restaurants.

Restrooms

Mile 4.4: There are seasonal restrooms behind the mockingbird statue.
Alternatives: Sometimes there are portable toilets around Shelby Park. However, at mile 4.8, you can turn left (the route turns right) and watch for signs for the Shelby Bottoms Nature Center, 0.6 mile one-way. These restrooms are open when the park is open.

Top O'Woodland Historic Inn

Top O'Woodland is representative of the renaissance of East Nashville. This Queen Anne Victorian home was completed by a Dr. and Mrs. J. B. Hyde in 1904. It served as Dr. Hyde's second office, in addition to his main office in Nashville. Dr. Hyde was the great-grandson of one of Nashville's early pioneers. The present owner purchased the property in 2000. The home has been substantially restored to its original grandeur and is now a B&B and wedding venue.

East Nashville Cumberland River

The Cumberland River starts in Kentucky, flows through Tennessee, including Nashville, and then back into Kentucky, where it merges into the Ohio River. This entire ride is encompassed by one of the bends in the Cumberland River. From the west side, downtown Nashville is the prominent vista, and on the east side, the Opryland Hotel complex and the Two Rivers business district are bounded by the flow of the Cumberland. This ride combines a bit of Cumberland River sightseeing, the Opryland complex, Shelby Bottoms Greenway, and the Music City Bikeway. It is very accessible and a good workout ride near downtown.

East Nashville is generally considered the area bounded by the Cumberland River, I-65, I-24, and Briley Parkway. But inside the larger expanse are several smaller communities, which have separate names and, in some cases, formerly separate governance structures—that is, until the Metropolitan Government of Nashville was formed in 1963. These communities include Historic Edgefield, East End, Lockeland Springs, Shelby Hills, Boscobel Hills, Rolling Acres, Eastwood Maxwell, Inglewood, and Greenwood. This ride goes through East End, Edgefield, Lockeland Springs, and Inglewood. As you ride through, you will see architectural styles spanning a range of 150 years.

Start: The ride begins in the Historic Edgefield area at the East Park Community Center.

Length: 18 miles, loop ride

Approximate riding time: Less than 2 hours

Best bike: Any bike

Terrain and trail surface: The terrain is rolling. There is one steep but short climb; most of the ride is generally flat to rolling. The surface is all paved streets or paved bikeways.

Traffic and hazards: Approximately 3 miles of the ride is on the Shelby Bottoms Greenway, a paved bike and pedestrian trail. Be aware of other bikers, and especially pedestrians and runners. You should announce as you pass people on the trail. Most of the rest of the ride is on city streets with a bike lane. The first 0.5 mile of McGavock Pike is busy. The other streets where there is not a bike lane are quiet residential streets.

Things to see: View of Opryland Complex

Maps: DeLorme *Tennessee Atlas & Gazetteer*, page 34, A1

Getting there by car: From downtown Nashville, you can cross the Cumberland River on Union Street, which becomes Woodland Street on the east side of the river. It is about 0.2 mile to South 7th Street from I-24. Turn left onto South 7th Street at the East Park Community Center. There is parking behind the center, which is accessible on the left as you make the turn at South 7th Street. If you approach from I-24, take the Shelby Avenue exit, exit 49; follow Shelby Avenue east to the traffic light. Turn left at South 5th Street and follow it to Woodland Street; turn right. **GPS:** N36 10.19' / W86 45.42'

THE RIDE

As you exit the parking lot, turn right. At the intersection, turn right when you reach Woodland Street and head east. You will ride through the Five Points area. The wall mural on the side of the Eastside Cycles building gives a hint of the eclectic mix of residential and light commercial development in the area. You may want to make your own mental notes of places to visit or eat later. Turn left at the four-way stop sign on South 14th Street at mile 1.1. Be aware of the cross-street stop signs. Turn right at Eastland Avenue at 1.5 miles. You will ride by condos, restaurants, coffee shops, and other commercial businesses. At the stop sign, mile 2.2, bear left onto Porter Road. You will follow the street as it bears right at mile 3.2. Turn left onto Riverside Drive at mile 3.3 at the stop sign.

Turn right at the traffic light at McGavock Pike at mile 4.0. Proceed when you encounter the stop sign and the caution sign that announces McGavock Pike ends in 1,000 feet. Before McGavock Pike ends, turn right at mile 5.3 onto Moss Rose Drive. The houses on the left side are built on the bluffs of the Cumberland River. As you are able to get a peek between the houses,

Bike Shops

Eastside Cycles: 103 S. 11th St., Nashville; (615) 469-1079; www.eastside-cycles.com
Ride615: 3441 Lebanon Rd. #103, Hermitage; (615) 200-7433; www.ride615.com
Sun & Ski: 501 Opry Mills Dr., Nashville; (615) 886-4854; http://www.sunandski.com

Cumberland River pedestrian bridge

you will see the Opryland Complex and the business district around the Two Rivers area. As you reach the top of the hill, you will experience a Nashville dogleg. Turn right onto Claypool Street at mile 5.5, then quickly turn left onto Moss Rose Drive.

At the Shelby Bottoms Greenway sign you will proceed straight into the greenway at mile 6.7, when Moss Rose Drive makes a right turn. The access may seem a bit long here; turn right onto the Greenway at mile 6.8. Turn left at the intersection at mile 7.0 to remain on Shelby Bottoms Greenway. You can turn right here for restrooms and water at the Forrest Green Drive Trailhead.

At the next intersection turn right and proceed down the Shelby Bottoms Greenway heading toward the Shelby Bottoms Nature Center. Remain on the Greenway as you pass under the bike/pedestrian bridge over the Cumberland River. Turn right at the Fortland Drive connector at mile 10.0. There will be one of the Shelby Bottoms Greenway signposts here. You will exit the Greenway onto Fortland Drive and then make a right onto Barclay Drive at mile 10.4. You will make a 90-degree turn and then ask yourself if you are on the right road. Yes, you do have to make this short, but admittedly steep, climb to continue on Barclay Drive.

Turn right onto Riverside Drive at mile 10.8. Follow the route and turn right at Rosebank Avenue at mile 12.0. You will stay on Rosebank as it loops around and start a descent; you may miss the left turn at Porter at mile 13.6.

Two Rivers Mansion

If the old ferry still existed where McGavock Pike ends at the Cumberland River, you could ferry across, then ride a short distance to Two Rivers Mansion, located at 3130 McGavock Pike, between Two Rivers Middle School and McGavock High School.

Two Rivers, one of the earliest and best preserved of the early Italianate houses in middle Tennessee, was part of an 1,100-acre plantation located on fertile, rolling land between the Stones and Cumberland Rivers. The junction of the two rivers suggested the name given to the place by an early owner, William Harding. (See the Percy Warner Park loop and Edwin Warner Park ride for information about William Harding's brother, John Harding.)

The McGavock family inhabited the mansion, built by David McGavock in 1859, for three generations, until 1965. The Metropolitan Government of Nashville and Davidson County purchased the property in 1966. The 14-acre tract, which includes the mansion and a small brick house built in 1802, is listed in the National Register of Historic Places.

Today, the mansion is a popular venue for weddings and receptions. There are currently no public operating hours for the mansion, but the main house, gazebo, and surrounding grounds can be rented for private functions. Reservations and availability inquiries can be made by telephone (615-885-1112). Prospective renters may view the interior of the mansion by appointment.

Just past the traffic light at Riverside Drive, bear left at mile 14.5 to remain on Porter Road. At mile 15.5 you will bear right as you merge into Eastland Avenue. After you pass the commercial development, turn left onto North 16th Street at mile 15.9. Turn right at mile 16.6 onto Fatherland Street. You will see quite an eclectic mix of architectural styles that highlights the East End as you proceed down this street. Turn right at South 7th Street at mile 17.7. Turn into the parking lot of the community center at mile 17.9. This is the end of the ride.

MILES AND DIRECTIONS

0.0 Begin at the parking lot at the East Park Community Center. Turn right onto South 7th Street; then turn right onto Woodland Street heading east.

1.1 Turn left at North 14th Street.

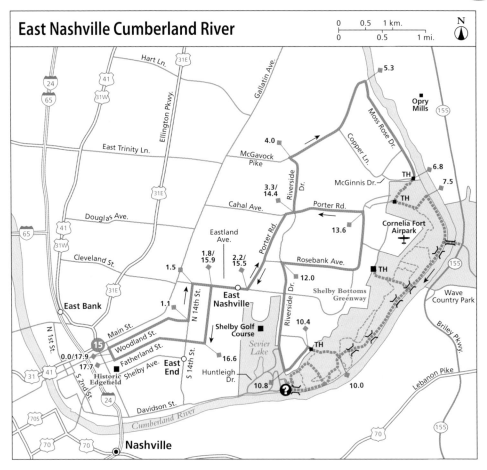

East Nashville Cumberland River

1.5 Turn right at Eastland Avenue.

2.2 Turn left onto Porter Road at the stop sign.

3.2 Continue on Porter Road as it bears right.

3.3 Turn left onto Riverside Drive.

4.0 Turn right at McGavock Pike.

5.3 Turn right onto Moss Rose Drive.

5.5 Turn right onto Claypool Street, then turn left onto Moss Rose Drive.

6.7 Proceed straight into the Shelby Bottoms Greenway.

6.8 Turn right as you approach the trail on Shelby Bottoms Greenway.

7.0 Turn left to remain on the Shelby Bottoms Greenway.

7.5 Turn right to follow the main Shelby Bottoms Greenway.

10.0 Turn right at the Fortland Drive connector.

10.4 Turn left onto Barclay Drive.

10.8 Turn right onto Riverside Drive.

12.0 Turn right onto Rosebank Avenue.

13.6 Turn left onto Porter Road.

14.5 Bear left to remain on Porter Road.

15.5 Turn right onto Eastland Avenue.

15.9 Turn left at North 16th Street.

16.6 Turn right at Fatherland Street.

17.7 Turn right onto South 7th Street.

17.9 Turn right into the East Park Community Center.

RIDE INFORMATION

Local Events/Attractions

There are a variety of events that go on all year long in east Nashville. For example, the second Saturday each month, from May through December, is the East Nashville Art Crawl. There is a different activity each month, like the Tomato Art Fest in August. An exciting addition is the Faux Paw Fashion Show ("paw" is the key here). During Christmastime, there is a historic home tour. For more information, visit http://www.lockelandsprings.org/ and http://www.east-nashville.com/.

Local Eateries

There are places to eat everywhere on this ride. Here are the best spots on the ride to explore local eateries: Five Points; the intersection of North 14th Street and Woodland; the intersection of Eastland Avenue and Chapel Avenue for a few blocks; and a few places on Porter. For more information, visit http://www.east-nashville.com/destinations/restaurants.

Restrooms

Mile 0.0: There are restrooms inside the East Park Community Center.
Mile 7.0: There are portable toilets and a water fountain at the Forrest Green Drive Trailhead in about 50 yards if you turn right (instead of the left turn on the route).

Bells Bend

Bells Bend was the center of a recent controversy that played out in the Nashville media when a local developer wanted to buy property and turn this agrarian area into a retail and residential complex. The May Town proposal failed, but local residents fear it may come back again. When you see Bells Bend you will understand why there was such uproar.

The last ferry service in Nashville/Davidson County was Cleeces Ferry, which ended in 1990. It docked at the end of Old Hickory Boulevard at Bells Bend. Once you get to Bells Bend and look across the Cumberland River, you will wonder how you can be this close to Nashville and experience this.

This is a great ride with both short and long options. The description and cues will note both as needed to get you there. The long option will be a good workout on some rural roads in Davidson and Cheatham Counties. You will pass some scenic areas, including Beaman Park. If you are riding the long option, make sure you have two full water bottles and snacks at the start. There are no stores after you turn onto Eatons Creek Road until you reach Ashland City Highway.

Start: The ride begins in West Nashville at the Belle Meade Starbucks.

Length: 52 miles (short option, 35 miles), loop ride

Approximate riding time: 4 to 5 hours; about 3 hours or less for the short option

Best bike: Road bike or hybrid bike

Terrain and trail surface: The terrain is rolling. There is one noteworthy climb and a few honorable mentions on the long option. The short option is a bit flatter, without any big climbs. All the roads, mainly rural, are paved.

Traffic and hazards: There are two places where there will be some traffic. The only bridge over the Cumberland River is via Briley Parkway. There will be traffic, but there is a wide shoulder, and the total distance on this street is about 1 mile each way. The other traffic spot is Ashland

City Highway / TN 12 / Hydes Ferry Pike. There is a very wide shoulder for most of this part of the ride. However, watch for trash, especially on the shoulder of these two roads.

Things to see: A rural part of Davidson County

Maps: DeLorme *Tennessee Atlas & Gazetteer*, page 33, B8

Getting there by car: From Nashville, proceed west. Follow US 70 South / Broadway / West End Avenue / Harding Road to the Belle Meade area. Turn right into the Belle Meade Shopping Center just as you pass the intersection with White Bridge Road at the traffic light. Alternatively, from downtown, take I-440 to I-40 West; take the White Bridge Road exit and turn left. Follow White Bridge Road to the intersection with Harding Road / US 70 South. **GPS:** N36 07.30' / W86 50.55'

THE RIDE

The first 7 miles of the ride will be in and out of some high-traffic areas. But there will be adequate shoulder for biking. The section around 51st Avenue and Centennial Boulevard is commercial/industrial without a shoulder, but the streets are wide. In this segment, watch for trash you should not run over on your bike. At mile 4.8, use the shoulder and turn right onto the Briley Parkway access ramp. Stay on the shoulder and cross the Cumberland River. At the end of the County Hospital Road exit, get into the right turn lane. You will make somewhat of a diagonal across County Hospital Road at mile 5.9; this is Stewarts Lane. The first street that turns right from Ashland City Highway is Eatons Creek Road. If you are taking the long option, turn right here at mile 7.7.

If you are taking the short option, here it is. Bells Bend begins about 4 miles ahead. Continue straight on Ashland City Highway and go over Briley Parkway at mile 8.2. From this point Ashland City Highway is a four-lane divided highway. The shoulder is considered a bike lane and is adequate. Turn left at mile 9.8 onto Old Hydes Ferry Pike; watch for oncoming

Bike Shops

Cumberland Transit: 2807 West End Ave., Nashville; (615) 321-4069; http://cumberlandtransit.com/cycling/
Gran Fondo: 5133 Harding Rd., Suite A6, Nashville; (615) 354-1090; http://www.granfondocycles.com/
Gran Fondo Trail & Fitness: 5133 Harding Rd., Suite B-1, Nashville; (615) 499-4634; http://www.granfondotrail.com/

Bells Bend Park entrance

traffic as you make the left turn. At the stop sign where Old Hickory Boulevard intersects Old Hydes Ferry Pike, turn left onto Old Hickory Boulevard, at mile 11.1. The Bells Bend Outdoor Center is 4 miles ahead of you, and the rest of the ride for the short option begins at mile cue 31.9.

When you make the turn onto Eaton's Creek Road, this is the long option; you have about 18 miles of rural roads ahead. Follow Eatons Creek Road; after you cross under Briley Parkway at mile 8.7 you can prepare for a climb. It will get steeper at the end. At mile 11.9, go across Old Hickory Boulevard, but don't enjoy the downhill too much, because there is a left turn onto Little Marrowbone Road at mile 12.8. Follow Little Marrowbone Road through the hills and valley. You will begin to see the escarpment bluffs above the Cumberland River. Although Ashland City Highway is a busy thoroughfare, the shoulder is wide and you can ride outside the rumble strips. As Ashland City Highway begins to bear left, turn right onto River Trace at mile 23.9. Then turn left at mile 24.1 to continue on River Trace. This is a neat section along the banks of the Cumberland River. Much of this was flooded in the 2010 middle Tennessee flood. There is a short climb up the bluff before you will turn right onto Old Hydes Ferry Pike at mile 26.7 and immediately cross the railroad tracks.

You will join with the short option at mile 27.6 at the stop sign (11.1 for the short option); here you will turn right onto Old Hickory Boulevard. This community was serviced via ferry across the Cumberland River until the 1960s, when the Briley Parkway Bridge over the Cumberland River was completed. The Bells Bend Outdoor Center is at the second Bells Bend park sign at mile 31.9. You will want to stop here.

Exit the Outdoor Center and turn right to go all the way down to the river. Stop and turn around at the Cumberland River at mile 34.1 (short option 17.6) and retrace the route back to the intersection of Old Hickory Boulevard and Old Hydes Ferry Pike, where you will turn right onto Old Hydes Ferry Pike at mile 40.2 (short option 23.7) before the railroad tracks.

It is about an 11-mile roll back to Starbucks. Once you make the turn on County Hospital Road at mile 45.4 (short option 28.9), get onto the shoulder to make the right turn onto the Briley Parkway access ramp. Continue on Briley Parkway, using the shoulder, and cross the Cumberland River. Take the first exit for Centennial Boulevard. At the end of the ramp, get into the middle lane to make the left turn onto Centennial Boulevard. The traffic may be quite busy here, but it will be brief. The streets in this area are named after states. You will pass New York and California (Avenues), proceeding on Centennial Boulevard. Depending on your state of mind, by this time you may need ice cream. If so, turn right at Charlotte Pike; the ride route goes straight. Bobby's Drive-In is about 0.25 mile down Charlotte Pike, on the left.

Regardless of your ice cream inclination, follow 51st Avenue until you intersect Wyoming Avenue at mile 49.8 (short option 33.3) and turn right. You may have noticed the Music City Bikeway sign pointing in the same direction. Turn right to get on the Richland Creek Greenway toward White Bridge Road at mile 49.9 (short option 33.4). You will cross over Richland Creek twice, then turn right to access the White Bridge Road Trailhead at mile 51.2 (short option 34.7). This is the end of the ride at Starbucks at mile 51.9 (or 35.4, if you took the short option). In either case, you got to experience Bells Bend!

MILES AND DIRECTIONS

0.0 Begin the ride at the Starbucks in Belle Meade. Ride toward Publix from Starbucks under the overpass and turn left to cross over the tracks on the White Bridge Road pedestrian bridge beside Publix.

0.3 Turn right onto the Richland Creek Greenway.

0.7 Turn left to access the main Richland Creek Greenway, following the direction of the Music City Bikeway.

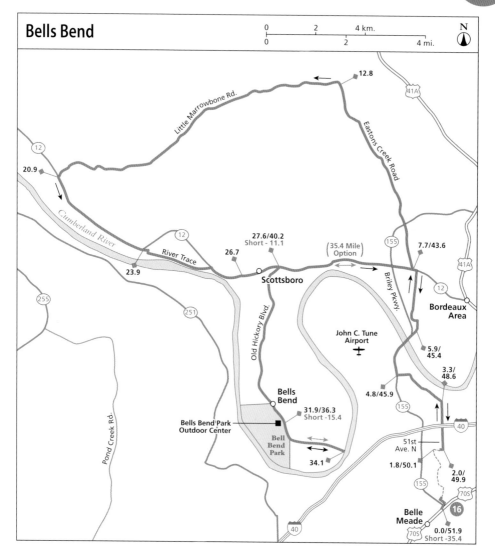

Bells Bend

0 2 4 km.
0 2 4 mi.
N

12.8

41A

Little Marrowbone Rd.

Eastons Creek Road

12

20.9

Cumberland River

River Trace

12

27.6/40.2
Short - 11.1

26.7

(35.4 Mile)
Option

155

7.7/43.6

41A

23.9

Scottsboro

12

Bordeaux
Area

255

251

Old Hickory Blvd.

Briley Pkwy.

John C. Tune
Airport

5.9/
45.4

3.3/
48.6

Bells
Bend

4.8/45.9

Pond Creek Rd.

Bells Bend Park
Outdoor Center

31.9/36.3
Short -15.4

155

Bell
Bend
Park

34.1

51st
Ave. N

40

1.8/50.1

155

2.0/
49.9

70S

Belle
Meade

16

40

70S

0.0/51.9
Short -35.4

1.8 Exit the Greenway at the Wyoming Avenue Trailhead and turn right onto Wyoming Avenue; go one block, then turn left onto 51st Avenue.

3.3 Turn left onto Centennial Boulevard.

4.5 The now-closed Tennessee State Prison is on your right.

4.8 Turn right onto the Briley Parkway ramp (use the shoulder). Cross the Cumberland River (on the shoulder).

5.7   Exit at County Hospital Road.

5.9   Follow the right turn lane, then go across County Hospital Road onto Stewarts Lane.

7.6   At the T intersection, turn left on Ashland City Highway / TN 12 / Hydes Ferry Pike.

7.7   Turn right onto Eatons Creek Road. The short option continues straight at this point.

The go-short option continues on Ashland City Highway / TN 12, and is as follows:

8.2   Cross over Briley Parkway and continue on Ashland City Highway.

9.8   Turn left onto Old Hydes Ferry Pike. Watch for oncoming traffic.

11.1   Turn left at the stop sign, at the intersection with Old Hickory Boulevard.

Follow the ride cues for the long option beginning at mile 31.9. The short option cues are noted in parentheses.

8.7   Cross under Briley Parkway and prepare for a long climb; it's steeper at the end.

11.9   Cross Old Hickory Boulevard.

12.8   Turn left onto Little Marrowbone Road.

20.9   Turn left onto Ashland City Highway.

23.9   Turn right onto River Trace.

24.1   Turn left to continue on River Trace.

25.7   Turn right at the T intersection onto Ashland City Highway.

26.7   Turn right on Old Hydes Ferry Pike and cross the railroad tracks.

27.6   Turn right onto Old Hickory Boulevard at the stop sign.

31.9 (15.4)   Turn right at the second Bells Bend Park sign into the outdoor Center, then continue in the same direction on Old Hickory Boulevard to the river.

34.1 (17.6)   Stop, turn around at the Cumberland River and return following Old Hickory Boulevard.

40.2 (23.7)   Turn right onto Old Hydes Ferry Pike before the railroad tracks.

41.6 (25.1)   Turn right onto Ashland City Highway.

43.0 (26.5)   Cross over Briley Parkway.

43.7 (27.2)   Turn right onto Stewarts Lane.

45.4 (28.9)	Turn right onto County Hospital Road, cross over Briley Parkway (45.6), and bear right onto the access ramp for Briley Parkway. Use the shoulder.
45.9 (29.4)	Continue on Briley Parkway (use the shoulder) and cross the Cumberland River on the shoulder.
47.0 (30.5)	Turn right at the Centennial Boulevard exit.
47.2 (30.7)	Turn left onto Centennial Boulevard at the bottom of the ramp.
48.6 (32.1)	Turn right onto 51st Avenue.
49.3 (32.8)	Cross Charlotte Pike.
49.9 (33.3)	Turn right onto Wyoming Avenue following the Music City Bikeway.
50.1 (33.5)	Turn left then right to access the Richland Creek Greenway toward White Bridge Road.
51.2 (34.7)	Turn right at the White Bridge Road Trailhead at the old railroad overpass.
51.7 (35.2)	Turn left to go over the railroad tracks on the White Bridge Road pedestrian bridge.
51.8 (35.3)	Turn right to go to Starbucks.
51.9 (35.4)	This is the end of the ride at Starbucks at mile 51.9 (short option, at mile 35.4).

The Tennessee State Prison

The Tennessee State Prison is a former correctional facility located at mile 4.5 on the ride. State-owned buildings and land are available to filmmakers free of charge. According to the Tennessee Film, Entertainment and Music Commission, the former prison is a popular setting for filmmakers: "The former Tennessee State Penitentiary in Nashville has been used without a location fee for numerous projects, including Walk the Line, The Last Castle, The Green Mile, Last Dance, and HBO's Against the Wall." The facility was built with inmate labor in 1898, and opened with 800 cells. It was replaced with a newer facility in 1992.

RIDE INFORMATION

Local Events/Attractions

The Bells Bend Outdoor Center: 4187 Old Hickory Blvd., Nashville; (615) 862-4187; http://www.nashville.gov/Parks-and-Recreation/Nature-Centers -and-Natural-Areas/Bells-Bend-Outdoor-Center.aspx. This environmental education and outdoor recreation facility is managed by the Nashville Metropolitan Board of Parks and Recreation. The center serves as a jumping-off point for exploring the 808 acres of Northwest Davidson County's Bells Bend Park. It offers a wide range of environmental education programs, school field trips, educator training workshops, outdoor recreation programs, and other special activities for people of all ages.

The entire campus includes the Bells Bend Outdoor Center, which houses various natural and cultural history displays and programming space; a library with a collection of natural and cultural history titles and local history folders; the historic 1842 Buchanan House; a demonstration garden by the Friends of Bells Bend; and the main trailhead for 6 miles of hiking trails.

Local Eateries

There are various restaurants at the start/end of the ride. The Belle Meade Shopping Center and the Hill Center both have several options, including Starbucks. About 0.25 mile past the turn to the Richland Creek Greenway, there are various shops and restaurants on White Bridge Road at the intersection of Post Road (the first street) and White Bridge Road.

The route crosses Charlotte Pike. There are several places situated within a few blocks of the intersection with the route. There are also eateries on 51st Avenue. There are stores at the intersection of Hydes Ferry and Old Hickory Boulevard. This is less than 0.5 mile north of the route at mile 27.6/40.2, or 11.1 for the short option.

Restrooms

Mile 0.3: There is a portable restroom at the entrance to the Richland Creek Greenway.
Mile 31.9 (short option, 15.4): Bells Bend Outdoor Center has restrooms and water. They are open during all park hours, even when the Outdoor Center is closed.

Adjoining Counties

Covered bridge

There are six counties that surround Davidson County (Nashville). There are a couple of counties in the mid-state, one county away, that are represented in this group of rides. Each county has rides that vary depending on the terrain, local surroundings, and, in some cases, the unique impact of historical events. But in every case, there are both rural and suburban rides that are easily accessed from Nashville.

Beginning in Dickson County, Montgomery Bell State Park west of Nashville has one of the premier single-track rides. If you proceed clockwise outside Nashville to Cheatham County, you can experience one of the few rails-to-trails rides in the area. Next, in Sumner County, the Old Hickory Lake and surrounding Lock 4 and neighboring lake community, Hendersonville, is adjacent to the Long Hollow ride. The Watertown ride in Wilson County will give you a feel for rural rides and interesting small towns.

The Civil War was fought all around Tennessee, and Murfreesboro was the site of one particularly bloody battle; you will experience this firsthand on the Stones River National Battlefield ride. In nearby Bedford County, a Civil War veteran founded a school in Bell Buckle, the namesake for that ride.

Traveling south of Nashville is Williamson County, a longtime favorite of bikers, likely due to the Natchez Trace Parkway. The historic movement of goods that created the development of The Trace is a common thread for many of the rides in Williamson County. Some rides are actually on The Trace, while others are in the area due to its influence on local development and commerce since the early nineteenth century.

A mix of rural scenery and commercial development into the twenty-first century is a common theme of the Iris City, Arrington, and Factory rides. Technically, there are two rides that begin about 0.5 mile north of Williamson County, in Davidson County, but they are otherwise similar to the rural feel of Williamson County roads: Moran Road and Model Airplane Field to Puckett's.

Conservation is the key theme of the single-track ride at Bowie Nature Park in Fairview. Be sure to take in all of the park's other activities as well.

To complete the circle, go a bit farther west to catch the most unique ride: a gravel-grinder in neighboring Hickman County.

You can get to most of these rides in less than an hour from Nashville, and in most cases, in about 30 minutes. If you live in Franklin, Gallatin, Hendersonville, Murfreesboro, or Fairview, there are rides in your own neighborhoods to check out. Hopefully, these rides will give you enough knowledge of the area to spur you on to further explore other local rides. You can also check out the Bike Clubs section in the Appendix for possible networking opportunities with other cyclists.

Hickman Creek Crossing

If you are looking for something a bit different, this may be it. Although this is a country-roads ride, it doesn't fit in either the single-track or road category. It is primarily on unpaved country roads in rural eastern Hickman County.

There are several reasons to consider this ride. If you enjoy creek crossings and rural surroundings, this is the ride for you. This may be an important ride for you if you want to shame those friends of yours who keep their mountain bikes really clean. You will see several creeks at the real water level!

Hickman County is southwest of Nashville. Centerville is the county seat and the largest town in the county.

Start: The ride begins at the East Hickman High School on TN 7 / New Highway 7 in Lyles.

Length: 28 miles

Approximate riding time: About 3 to 4 hours

Best bike: Hybrid or mountain bike (mountain bike recommended)

Terrain and trail surface: The terrain is rolling; there are a few climbs. The majority of the ride is on unpaved rural roads that are maintained by road grader. There are approximately eight creek crossings (without bridges).

Traffic and hazards: There will be little to no traffic, but the roads are narrow. Depending on the weather, the creek crossings may be slick. The crossings on Tom Patton Road may not be passable except by walking. In this rural area, most people have dogs. They may or may not be penned or tied. If you miss a turn, TN 7 / New Highway 7 bisects the route, and most roads end up there.

Things to see: Rural country

Maps: DeLorme *Tennessee Atlas & Gazetteer*, page 32, E4

Getting there by car: From Nashville, take I-40 West. From the I-440 West intersection with I-40, proceed west 33 miles and take exit 172, TN 46 Centerville/Dickson. Turn left onto TN 46 and proceed south about 6.5 miles. You will intersect TN 100. Follow TN 100 west and turn left at the intersection with TN 7 / New Highway 7. It is about 1 mile to the high school on the right. The address is East Hickman High School at 7700 Highway 7, Lyles. Alternatively, if you want to avoid I-40, follow US 70 / Broadway / West End Avenue / Harding Road through the Belle Meade area. At the Y intersection of US 70 and TN 100, get in the left lane and follow TN 100 for 28.7 miles to the TN 46 intersection. **GPS:** N35 55.485683' / W87 17.13955'

THE RIDE

The ride counter begins at the intersection of the high school drive and TN 7 / New Highway 7. Turn right onto TN 7 / New Highway 7 and proceed south. Make an acute left turn onto North Lick Creek Road at mile 0.6. Follow North Lick Creek Road and turn right at mile 1.1 onto Barren Fork Lane. Turn right at mile 2.0 onto Barren Fork Bridge Road (Barren Fork Lane goes left). You will make a couple of creek crossings on this leg. At mile 4.1, at the T intersection,

Bike Shops

Cumberland Transit: 2807 West End Ave., Nashville; (615) 321-4069; http://cumberlandtransit.com/cycling/
Gran Fondo: 5133 Harding Rd., Suite A6, Nashville; (615) 354-1090; http://www.granfondocycles.com/
Gran Fondo Trail & Fitness: 5133 Harding Rd., Suite B-1, Nashville; (615) 499-4634; http://www.granfondotrail.com/
Mac's Harpeth Bikes: 1100 Hillsboro Rd., Franklin; (615) 472-1002; www.macsharpethbikes.com
MOAB Franklin: 109 Del Rio Pike, Suite 105, Franklin; (615) 807-2035; http://moabbikes.com/
R.B.'s Cyclery: 3078 Maddux Way, #300, Franklin; (615) 567-6633; www.rbscyclery.com
REI: 261 Franklin Rd., Brentwood; (615) 376-4248; www.rei.com
Sun & Ski: 545 Cool Springs Blvd., Franklin; (615) 628-0289; http://www.sunandski.com
Trace Bikes: 8080B TN 100, Nashville; (615) 646-2485; http://tracebikes.com/

Farm on Beech Valley Road

turn left onto Old Locust Creek Road. You will enjoy this paved road for a change! At mile 4.8, bear left to continue on Old Locust Creek Road.

If you have enjoyed the ride thus far, you will really like Bud Qurriel Road. At mile 5.2, turn right onto Bud Qurriel Road. You will ride across a valley on this leg. There is a significant curve to the left on the downhill section. At mile 6.9, you will turn right onto McFarlin Road. You will make a right turn to continue at mile 8.5. This is Davis Branch Road. Just past this turn, at mile 8.8, bear left onto Old Hadley School Road. A little past the Church of Christ at Parham's Chapel, turn left onto Warf Road at mile 10.2.

At the next intersection, you will go straight. Just past a 90-degree turn in the road, turn left to continue on Warf Road at mile 11.4. At mile 13.0, turn right onto South Lick Creek Road. You will get to enjoy a bit of paved road. At mile 14.5, the route intersects TN 7 / New Highway 7. If you feel the need to bail out, turn right onto TN 7 / New Highway 7 and proceed north about 8 miles to return back to the high school. There is a wide shoulder on TN 7.

Continue the route by going across TN 7 / New Highway 7 and slightly left. At mile 15.9, bear right to continue onto Beech Valley Road. It is a gravel surface. At the T intersection with the paved road, mile 17.2, turn right onto Primm Springs Road. You will turn right at mile 17.6 onto the gravel surfaced Tom Patton Road. There will be three creek crossings on this leg. The first creek crossing is at mile 18.9. These are different because there is not a concrete bottom; the bottom is just creek gravel. It will be sticky when wet. You may not notice the intersection of South Tatum Creek Road and Tom Patton Road at mile 19.7. You will turn left to continue on Tom Patton Road. At mile 19.9, you will bear left, although it may feel like you are going straight to access Willow Springs Road. There is a small sign at mile 20.6; bear right here.

Proceed on Willow Springs Road to the T intersection at mile 23.3 with Brown Hollow Road (paved), and turn right. It is an easy return from here. At mile 26.0, turn left onto TN 7 / New Highway 7. Turn left at mile 27.9 into the high school drive. This is the end of the ride.

MILES AND DIRECTIONS

0.0 Begin at the TN 7 / New Highway 7 intersection and school drive entrance; turn right onto TN 7 / New Highway 7.

0.6 Turn (hard) left onto North Lick Creek.

1.1 Turn right onto Barren Fork Lane.

2.0 Turn right onto Barren Fork Bridge Road. Barren Fork Lane goes left.

4.1 Turn left onto Old Locust Creek / County Highway 1841 at the T intersection.

4.8 Bear left to continue on Old Locust Creek / County Highway 1841.

5.2 Turn right onto Bud Qurriel Road.

Silver Leaf Country Inn

The Silver Leaf Country Inn (615-670-3048) is west of the ride start on TN 100. This log structure was built in 1815 and sits behind a large modern house on Norma Crow's 500-acre farm. Since 1980 it has been serving southern specialties like country ham, fried chicken, fresh vegetables, and homemade breads and desserts at the dining room. They are open Friday and Saturday night and Sunday for brunch. There are ten guest rooms furnished with antiques, and a guest cottage. At Christmastime there are live trees in every room. Once each month from late spring through early fall, there is entertainment in the outdoor amphitheater.

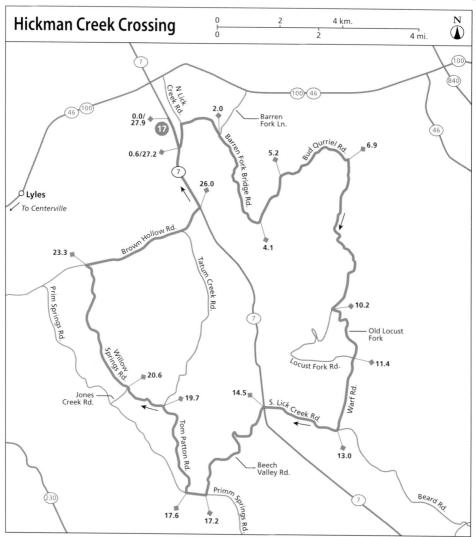

Hickman Creek Crossing

0   2   4 km.

0   2   4 mi.

N

6.9   Turn right onto McFarlin Road.

8.5   Turn right to continue on Davis Branch Road.

8.8   Bear left onto Old Hadley School Road.

10.2   Turn left onto Warf Road.

11.4   Turn left to continue on Warf Road just past a 90-degree turn.

13.0   Turn right onto South Lick Creek Road.

14.5 Cross TN 7 / New Highway 7; the road name is now Beech Valley Road.

15.9 Bear right to continue onto Beech Valley Road.

17.2 Turn right onto Primm Springs Road / County Highway 963.

17.6 Turn right onto Tom Patton Road.

18.9 This is the first of three creek crossings on this leg.

19.7 At the intersection of South Tatum Creek Road and Tom Patton Road, turn left onto Tom Patton Road.

19.9 Bear left (feels like straight) onto Willow Springs Road.

20.6 Bear right at the sign for Willow Springs Road.

23.3 Turn right onto Brown Hollow Road / County Highway 1850 at the T intersection.

26.0 Turn left onto TN 7 / New Highway 7.

27.9 Turn left into the high school drive. This is the end of the ride.

RIDE INFORMATION

Local Events/Attractions

Hickman County's hometown celebrity is Grand Ole Opry's Minnie Pearl. Local lore states she is from Grinder's Switch. Join the Grinder's Switch Music and Arts Festival held annually in September on the square in Centerville. For more information, check out the Hickman Chamber of Commerce website at www.hickmanco.org.

Local Eateries

You may want to drive west on TN 100 about 17 miles to Centerville. You can check out the local eateries there. Breece's Cafe on the square is one option. Another option for a weekend dinner or a Sunday brunch is the Silver Leaf Country Inn. Alternatively, there are restaurants in Fairview and Bellevue if you travel on TN 100.

Restrooms

There are no public restrooms on the ride.

Watertown

Where else can you ride your bike around two town squares and have a nice rural ride in between? Yes, it is the Watertown ride. These squares are paved; no cobblestones here. This is a great, relatively flat ride in Wilson County. Watertown and Alexandria have preserved the village feel while accommodating twenty-first-century residents.

This ride offers the best of rural riding, and is an easy trip east of Nashville. The local Veloteers Bicycle Club sponsors an annual ride in June. You may want to check it out, at www.bighillchallenge.com. You will see some farm country on this ride.

Start: The ride begins in Watertown on the southwest corner of the square, where Depot and Main Streets intersect.

Length: 32 miles, loop ride

Approximate riding time: 2 to 3 hours

Best bike: Any bike

Terrain and trail surface: The terrain is flat to barely rolling. There is one tiny climb on the ride, which features mostly rural paved roads.

Traffic and hazards: There is very little traffic on these roads except for the short sections on TN 26 / US 70 / Sparta Pike. But the shoulder is adequate and marked as a bike route. Watch for gravel on the shoulders of these roads.

Things to see: Two country towns, lots of rural country

Maps: DeLorme *Tennessee Atlas & Gazetteer*, page 35, B7

Getting there by car: From Nashville, take I-40 East toward Knoxville. From the I-440 East intersection with I-24/I-40, drive 27 miles and take exit 239A, Lebanon/Watertown. Turn right onto TN 26 / US 70 / Sparta Pike and drive about 10 miles. Turn left onto Depot Street. The Watertown square is just ahead. **GPS:** N36 6.016433' / W86 7.9864166'

Alexandria Square

THE RIDE

Begin the ride at the southwest corner of Watertown Square. Head east from the square to start the ride. You will not cross over the railroad tracks the first two times you encounter them. Turn left beside the tracks at mile 0.5; the street name is now Church Avenue. Just down the road at mile 0.7, the street name changes to Holmes Gap Road. You are quickly in the country on this ride, with mostly farms along the route.

Again, as you approach the tracks, turn left to continue on Holmes Gap Road at mile 1.7. Turn right at the intersection onto Haley Road at mile 3.5. There will be a few places on this section of the ride where the route uses some of the old and new roads. There will be some traffic on these sections. The new road, TN 26 / US 70 / Sparta Pike is marked as a bike route; the shoulder is wide enough to ride outside the rumble strips. At mile 5.5, turn left onto Old Alexandria Road at the T intersection. At mile 6.4, turn left onto TN 26 / US 70 / Sparta Pike. At mile 7.0, turn left onto Old Alexandria Road. The street name changes at mile 7.2 to West Main Street.

You will not miss the village of Alexandria. At the stop sign at the end of the square, turn right onto High Street at mile 8.7. The next turn is easy to miss at mile 9.3; turn left onto Hall Road. When you cross TN 53 at mile 9.5, the street name changes to Lower Helton Road. You will stay on this road nearly 8 miles until you get to the T intersection. As you round a curve at mile 15.6, you will bear left around the church to continue on Lower Helton Road. When you reach the T intersection at mile 17.7, turn left onto TN 264 North / Hickman Road. This begins the looping segment of the return. You will be on this road about 2 miles. There is not a street marker, but turn left at mile 19.3 onto New Hope Road. At mile 24.8, continue on this street; along the way, the street name changes to Main Street. You will cross TN 53 again at mile 25.1 and continue west toward Alexandria. There is a market to your left on TN 53 at the intersection if you need refreshment.

> ## Bike Shops
>
> **Biker's Choice:** 11493 Lebanon Rd., Mt. Juliet; (615) 758-8620; www.thebikers choice.com
>
> **Ride615:** 3441 Lebanon Rd., #10, Hermitage; (615) 200-7433; www.ride615.com
>
> **Sun & Ski:** 501 Opry Mills Dr., Nashville; (615) 886-4854; http://www.sunandski.com

You will ride through Alexandria with a slight dogleg and continue on Main Street until you intersect TN 26 / US 70 / Sparta Pike at mile 27.4. Turn right here. Turn right again onto Old Alexandria Road at mile 28.1, beside the cemetery. At mile 29.3, turn right onto TN 26 / US 70 / Sparta Pike. This will be the most traffic you will see on the route, but the shoulder is adequate to ride outside the rumble strip. Watch for debris, especially gravel along this section. Turn right onto Depot Street at mile 32.2. This is the end of the ride, when you reach Watertown Square at mile 32.3.

MILES AND DIRECTIONS

0.0 Begin at the southwest corner of the square. Turn right (east) onto East Main Street.

0.5 Turn left onto Church Avenue. (Do not cross the railroad tracks.)

0.7 Street name changes to Holmes Gap Road. Continue on Holmes Gap Road.

1.7 Turn left to continue on Holmes Gap Road. (Do not cross the railroad tracks.)

3.5 Turn right at the intersection onto Haley Road.

5.5 Turn left at the T intersection onto Old Alexandria Road.

6.4 Turn left onto TN 26 / US 70 / Sparta Pike.

7.0 Turn left onto Old Alexandria Road.

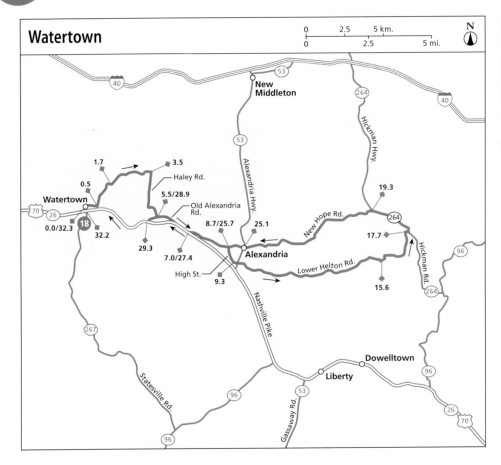

Watertown

0 2.5 5 km.
0 2.5 5 mi.

N

7.2 Street name changes to West Main Street.

8.7 Turn right at the stop sign onto High Street.

9.3 Turn left onto Hall Road.

9.5 The street name changes at the intersection to Lower Helton Road. Continue on Lower Helton Road.

15.6 Bear left here to continue on Lower Helton Road.

17.7 Turn left at the T intersection onto TN 264 North / Hickman Road.

19.3 Turn left onto New Hope Road. There is no marker.

24.8 Continue on this street. The street name becomes Main Street.

25.1 Continue on West Main Street at the stop sign at the intersection of TN 53.

Watertown Square

27.4 Turn right onto TN 26 / US 70 / Sparta Pike.

28.1 Turn right onto Old Alexandria Road.

29.3 Turn right onto TN 26 / US 70 / Sparta Pike.

32.2 Turn right onto Depot Street.

32.3 This is the end of the ride at the Watertown Square.

RIDE INFORMATION

Local Events/Attractions

You will want to look around in Watertown and see why Watertown has its own song: "1997," by Tom T. Hall. Or, you may wish to schedule a day trip from Nashville to Watertown on the Tennessee Central Railroad. Check out the schedule at http://www.tcry.org/pass_ops.htm. Also, check out the annual Watertown Arts and Music Festival at http://watertownmusicandarts.com.

Local Eateries

There are several local eateries on or near the square in Watertown. There are also several restaurants on TN 26 / US 70 / Sparta Pike.

Restrooms

There are no public restrooms on the route.

Cumberland River Bicentennial Trail

The Cumberland River Bicentennial Trail is a 9-mile, one-way trail in Ashland City. There are two sections of the trail: The Eagle Pass section is gravel and not recommended for road bikes; the rest of the trail is paved. Otherwise, it is family-friendly biking, with a comfort station available and plenty of eating opportunities in nearby Ashland City.

The Cumberland River Bicentennial Trail has several things to recommend it. First, it's one of the rails-to-trails bike paths. If you are looking for a flat ride, this is it. It is also in the woods—great for summer heat. It goes beside the lake and is a scenic ride. It is a relatively short 18-mile round-trip, but if you want shorter, it is an out-and-back ride, so you can return anytime. The trail is very well maintained, including brush removal. It does not seem to be busy, so you can expect a quiet ride. It has good creature comfort support along the trail and is easy to access from Nashville. Overall, it makes for a nice outing.

The Central Tennessee Railroad started this trail when it built a railroad from Nashville to Clarksville to transport lumber, ore, and other products in the early twentieth century. The rest of the story picks up in the 1990s, when municipalities and individuals began to try to preserve the abandoned rails as a trail. The work has continued, with excellent results. Running between the bluffs and the lake and Cumberland River, it is a scenic, woodsy ride. The first mile of the trail has arboretum markers identifying local plants along the way. You may want to walk this first section to study the vegetation more carefully.

Start: The ride begins at the trailhead pavilion adjacent to the parking lot.

Length: 18 miles, out-and-back trail

Approximate riding time: 1 to 2 hours

Best bike: Hybrid or mountain bike

Terrain and trail surface: The first 4 miles of the trail are paved bike path. The next 2.5 miles are gravel. There is a 2.0-mile paved section at the end. Except for trail access and a creek crossing, the trail is very flat.

Traffic and hazards: The ride is entirely on closed bike paths. There will be no car traffic, but the trail may be crowded with other bikers, runners, and walkers. Bicycles are the largest and fastest thing on the trail; it is best to announce when you approach walkers and runners. The first mile of the trail is especially attractive to walkers.

Things to see: Woodsy bike path

Maps: DeLorme *Tennessee Atlas & Gazetteer*, page 12, F2

Getting there by car: From Nashville, take I-40 West, then take exit 204A / Briley Parkway / TN 155 North. Proceed on Briley Parkway about 4.5 miles, then take exit 24 onto TN 12 North to Ashland City. Turn left on TN 12 at the ramp. Follow TN 12 for 14.6 miles through Ashland City. Just past the Deerfield Inn, turn left on Chapmansboro Road. The parking lot is on the right in less than 0.2 mile. There is a prominent sign. **GPS:** N36 17.1199833' / W87 4.7500166'

THE RIDE

The ride begins at the Mark's Creek Trailhead. You may want to stop at the Turkey Junction comfort station at mile 1.1 and review the displays about the environmentally friendly restroom.

The crossing at the old trestle is a great viewpoint. The locals have taken advantage of the environment in their lakeside homes and docks. At mile 4.0 the paved trail ends at the Sycamore Creek Trailhead. You will pass beside a road barrier, go down a slight grade, and cross Chapmansboro Road, then bear left as depicted on the sign to the Eagle Pass Trailhead. The railroad trestle over the creek has been removed. After this slight grade, the trail is flat.

At mile 6.7, the Eagle Pass trail ends. This is the beginning of the Cheatham Lock and Dam recreational area and campgrounds. You will bear right slightly past the lock office area and follow the street as it parallels the lake. When you reach the boat launch ramp directly in front, at mile 9.1, this is the turnaround point for the ride.

Bike Shops

Cumberland Transit: 2807 West End Ave., Nashville; (615) 321-4069; http://cumberlandtransit.com/cycling/
Gran Fondo: 5133 Harding Rd., Suite A6, Nashville; (615) 354-1090; http://www.granfondocycles.com/
Gran Fondo Trail & Fitness: 5133 Harding Rd., Suite B-1, Nashville; (615) 499-4634; http://www.granfondotrail.com/

Cumberland River Trail entrance

You will retrace the route back to the pavilion. Remember just past the entry point of Cheatham Lock and Dam recreational area, you will bear left slightly; the trail may be a bit hard to notice here. Be aware of possible oncoming traffic when you cross Chapmansboro Road when the Eagle Pass trail ends. Follow the bike path back to the pavilion, at mile 18.2; this is the end of the ride.

MILES AND DIRECTIONS

0.0 Begin at the pavilion adjacent to the parking lot.

1.1 There is a restroom on the left.

3.2 The crossing at the old railroad trestle is a nice viewing point.

4.0 The paved trail ends. Cross Chapmansboro Road and bear slightly left. The Eagle Pass gravel trail begins.

6.7 The Eagle Pass trail ends at the Cheatham Lock and Dam recreational area.

9.1 This is the turnaround point on the ride at the boat launch ramp on the Cheatham Lock and Dam.

18.2 This is the end of the ride, at the pavilion.

Cumberland River Bicentennial Trail

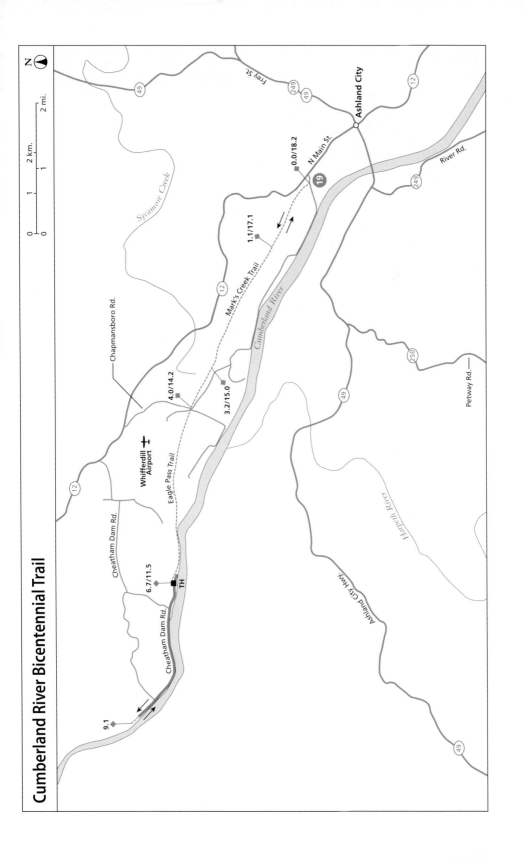

Environmentally friendly comfort station

RIDE INFORMATION

Local Events/Attractions

The Cheatham Lock and Dam: 1798 Cheatham Dam Rd., Ashland City; (615) 792-5697; http://corpslakes.usace.army.mil/visitors/projects.cfm?Id=H303040. Maintained by the US Army Corps of Engineers, this camping, boating, and swimming area offers many activities for campers at the recreational area.

Friends of the Cumberland River Bicentennial Trail: This active group is planning trail additions; for more information, visit http://www.cumberland rivertrail.org/friends.htm.

Local Eateries

There are various local eateries as you drive through Ashland City.

Restrooms

Mile 0.0: There is a portable toilet at the trailhead near the pavilion.

Mile 1.1: There is an interesting environmental display at this comfort station, which includes restrooms.

Mile 4.0: There is a portable toilet here.

Mile 6.7: There is a restroom at the end of the Eagle Pass trail as you enter the campgrounds.

Mile 9.0: There is a restroom on the right just before the boat launch ramp.

Montgomery Bell

Montgomery Bell State Park in Dickson County is known for its mountain bike trail. This trail goes back to an initial 6-mile trail, which opened in the winter of 1996. The goal was to build a sustainable mountain biking trail that upset nature as little as possible. Today, the trail consists of five separate trails, for a total of 20.6 miles; we will be covering two of the trails in this chapter, the Red and Blue Trails. There is something for every skill level in the park. It is an easy drive from Nashville, and you can take advantage of other activities and services available at Montgomery Bell State Park.

The trails are well signed, and access to the trails and parking is very adequate. The website states that the trails are designated for mountain bikes only. You may want to check out the Tennessee Mountain Bike website for more information (http://tennesseemountainbike.com/board/montgomery-bell-bike-trail.php).

Start: The mountain bike trail begins on Jones Creek Road. It is signed.

Length: The Red Trail is 3.3-mile loop ride; the Blue Trail is 5.7-mile loop ride.

Approximate riding time: Red Trail, about 1 hour; Blue Trail, about 2 hours

Best bike: Mountain bike

Terrain and trail surface: This is a single-track ride. The Red, Blue, and White Trails are in the woods. The area is rolling. Some of the trail is through heavy pine growth, and most is through hardwoods growth. There are several relatively narrow creek crossings.

Traffic and hazards: To get to the trails from the parking lot and trailhead, you will cross Jones Mill Road. Be sure to check for traffic from both directions before you cross, especially coming from the parking lot, because you are on a slight downhill. Otherwise, there will be no traffic on these trails. However, the trails run beside US 70, which means you may suddenly hear some truck or traffic noise. In addition to trees, these trails seem to have abundant poison oak and poison ivy; in fact, the pavilion map has some recommendations for trail users, including using insect repellent in the summer months.

Things to see: Lots of woods and wildlife

Maps: DeLorme *Tennessee Atlas & Gazetteer*, page 32, B4. Nashville Mountain Bike Map: http://www.nashvillemountainbike.com/maps2009/l4map_2005.jpg

Getting there by car: From Nashville, take I-40 West. From the I-440 West intersection with I-40, proceed west 13 miles to exit 192, McCrory Lane / Pegram. Turn right onto McCrory Lane and proceed 1.2 miles to the T intersection past the railroad tracks. Turn left onto US 70 West and proceed about 13 miles before the next turn. There is a sign for Montgomery Bell State Park. You will go through the communities of Pegram and White Bluff. As you leave the White Bluff community, from the TN 47 turnoff to Charlotte, proceed 1.3 miles and turn right onto Jones Creek Road. There is a sign for the Montgomery Bell mountain bike trail, along with a sign for the Ebbtide boat company.

Go nearly 1 mile on Jones Creek Road, just past the mountain bike trail sign; turn right onto Bill Duke Road. The parking lot and trailhead are an immediate right.

If you miss Jones Creek Road on US 70 and you get to the main entrance to Montgomery Bell State Park, you are close, but don't turn into the park. Continue on and prepare to turn right at the next road, 0.1 mile past the park entrance, onto Laurel Furnace Road. In 0.5 mile, at the T intersection, turn right onto Jones Creek Road and proceed 0.8 mile, then turn left onto Bill Duke Road. **GPS:** N36 6.75' / W87 16.009966'

THE RIDE

Red Trail

Montgomery Bell mountain bike trail consists of five separate trails, designated Red, White, Blue, Green, and Yellow. (The latter two are for advanced riders only, so will not be covered here. The White trail is described on the map as an intermediate trail that is "easy grade but rooty," and is not covered here.) The network of trails is designed so that you can ride one and then return to the parking lot for a break. The parking lot has water, a portable restroom, and a picnic table near a large shade tree. You may want to bring a picnic lunch so you can stay for a few hours and ride more than one trail.

Trail lengths according to the map are: Red—3.1 miles, White—3.7 miles, Blue—4.3 miles, Green—3.6 miles, and Yellow—6.0 miles. This ride will cover the Red and Blue Trails. These trails will help you explore the range of the park from east to west. A pavilion at the trailhead offers a good map of all the trails. There are also maps available at the Montgomery Bell State Park office as you enter the park on US 70. There are other trail names on the park map. For example, the Expressway Trail is a length of the Red and Blue trails that overlap, mostly. There are also places where a numerical marker has been placed on a tree beside the trail. Although they were likely placed for an event, they help to tell you approximately where your are. They are noted on the rides.

According to the summary of the trails from the website and map, the Red Trail is a beginner-level route with moderate grades, smooth turns, and smooth tread; the Blue Trail is at an intermediate level, with more hills, wider turns, and variable tread smoothness. There are blazes on trees beside the trail denoting each one, along with numerical markers for reference.

Bike Shops

Cumberland Transit: 2807 West End Ave., Nashville; (615) 321-4069; http://cumberlandtransit.com/cycling/
Gran Fondo: 5133 Harding Rd., Suite A6, Nashville; (615) 354-1090; http://www.granfondocycles.com/
Gran Fondo Trail & Fitness: 5133 Harding Rd., Suite B-1, Nashville; (615) 499-4634; http://www.granfondotrail.com/
Trace Bikes: 8080B TN 100, Nashville; (615) 646-2485; http://tracebikes.com/

Although the Red Trail is for beginners, there is plenty to keep you engaged. It begins from the trailhead. After crossing Jones Creek Road, you will see the first trail sign. Take the Red Trail left. This is "Perimeter Red," as shown on the trail sign. The Red Trail makes a few serpentine curves, then begins a loop, heading first east, then south. At mile 1.5 there is an intersection of the Blue, Red, and Green Trails. The trail sign has "Downhill, Blue and Red." Continue on the Red Trail, following the sign to the right. Both the Red and Blue Trails will follow this part of the path, except when the Blue Trail cuts off for short loops.

At mile 2.1, the Red Trail branches at the number 15 marker. The route goes left here for a short out-and-back loop. At mile 2.5, the Red Trail ends; the sign is less than clear, but this is the starting point for the Yellow Trail. Turn around here and follow the trail back to the branch point.

At mile 2.9, you are back to the branch point, number 15. Here, the Red Trail goes left. You can follow Red Trail and trailhead signs from here. At mile

Montgomery Bell Trailhead pavilion

3.3, you are back to Jones Creek Road. The route goes back across the road to the trailhead pavilion. This is the end of the Red Trail ride, at mile 3.3. The Red Trail has 309 feet of ascent. (The Red Trail is not shown on the map.)

Blue Trail

The Blue Trail is longer and has more climbs that the Red. It is a well-designed trail because it has signs for the loops, so you can omit them and continue on the main trail. Compared to the Red Trail, the Blue has many more spiderwebs, and more bugs!

The Blue Trail route is a combination of the Blue Trail, with the Red Trail for connectors. It begins at the map pavilion and crosses Jones Creek Road. The trail sign points to the right (west) for the Blue Trail. The Blue heads south, then meanders on the "Lonesome Blue" Trail, and then intersects the Expressway Trail at mile 0.9. You can turn right here and ride the "Cat Track" loop. At mile 1.5, the number 17 marker, turn right and double back to numbered marker 15.

From that marker, at mile 1.7, the Blue Trail heads east with several short loops. Then at mile 3.2, the four-points junction, it loops west. This part is called "Back Blue." At the number 18 marker, at mile 4.8, the Blue merges with

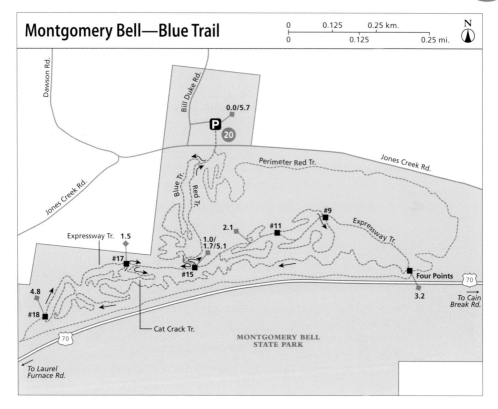

Montgomery Bell—Blue Trail

the Expressway Trail; continue on this trail. When you get back to number 15 at mile 5.1, turn left and follow the Main Street Trail and signs to the trailhead to return. You will cross Jones Creek Road and reach the pavilion at mile 5.7. This is the end of the Blue Trail ride. The mileage differs a bit from the Blue Trail as shown on the trail map at the pavilion.

MILES AND DIRECTIONS

Red Trail

0.0 Begin at the trailhead pavilion and follow the gravel path down and across Jones Creek Road. Watch for oncoming traffic from both directions. Take the Red Trail left.

1.5 The Green Trail begins here.

1.9 Information—trail marker here is "peanut."

2.1 The Red Trail branches at number 15 marker. Proceed left here for a short loop.

2.2 Information—trail marker here is 17.

2.5 This is the turnaround point for the Red Trail.

2.8 Information—trail marker here is 17.

2.9 Turn left at number 15 and follow the Red Trail and trailhead signs to return to the pavilion.

3.3 This is the end of the Red Trail ride at the pavilion.

Blue Trail

0.0 Begin at the trailhead pavilion and follow the gravel path down and across Jones Creek Road. Watch for oncoming traffic from both directions. Follow the trail sign pointing to the right (west) for the Blue Trail.

0.9 This is number 15 marker; turn right and head west.

1.5 This is number 17 marker; double back and head east toward the number 15 marker.

1.7 Head east from the number 15 marker.

2.1 Information—trail marker here is "peanut."

3.2 This is the four-points junction. Follow the Blue Trail signs to continue on the "Back Blue" trail.

4.8 This is number 18 marker; continue on the Expressway Trail.

5.1 This is the last turn to pass the number 15 marker. Turn left onto Main Street Trail.

5.7 This is the end of the Blue (combo) Trail ride.

RIDE INFORMATION

Local Events/Attractions

Montgomery Bell State Park: 1020 Jackson Hill Rd., Burns; park office (615) 797-9052, Park Inn (615) 797-3101; http://www.tn.gov/environment/parks/MontgomeryBell. This is one of the state parks in Tennessee that offers a more extensive array of services, including meeting facilities, a conference center, a golf course, an inn, plus hiking trails and camping facilities.

Local Eateries

There is a restaurant at the Montgomery Bell State Park Inn. There are also various local eateries in White Bluff and Pegram.

Restrooms

Mile 0.0: There is a portable restroom at the trailhead. There are other facilities at the Montgomery Bell State Park on US 70.

Garrison Creek

The Natchez Trace Parkway, about 20 miles from downtown Nashville, is a unique treasure in the area. It was the "road" from Natchez, Mississippi, to Nashville during the period of 1790 through 1812. General Andrew Jackson and his army used this route as they fought the Battle of New Orleans. During its heyday, people of all kinds who had crops and goods to sell from the frontier points of Kentucky and Ohio would raft their goods and produce down the Mississippi River to the Port of Natchez, where the merchandise could be sold or shipped to New Orleans. Even the wooden barges were disassembled for lumber. The return trip was only possible overland; hence, the Natchez Trace Parkway, or The Trace.

Its use was overshadowed by the modern steamboat technology of the day. In 1812 the steamboat New Orleans arrived in Natchez on its voyage upriver from New Orleans, and the new age of travel began. But The Trace's short life contributed much to the history of the fledgling United States. Much of this history is depicted in nature trails, signs, and observation points all along the route.

Today's modern Trace began during the Great Depression. Although it was mostly completed in the twentieth century, the entire 444-mile, two-lane parkway opened on May 21, 2005. It is a unit of the National Park Service. It posts a 50-mph speed limit, which helps to calm the traffic, and is closed to commercial traffic, which greatly reduces the traffic—both contributing to its popularity as a great place to ride a bike. On weekends and holidays, you will always meet bikers, but during off-peak times, like weekdays in summer, it can be an eerily quiet place, especially given its proximity to Nashville.

Start: This ride starts at the parking lot at milepost 440 on The Trace.

Length: 26 miles, out-and-back ride

Approximate riding time: 2 hours

Best bike: Any bike

Terrain and trail surface: Two-lane paved parkway with good surface, but no paved shoulder. The terrain is rolling; there is a 0.5-mile climb on the return, and several shorter climbs both directions.

Traffic and hazards: The Trace is bike friendly, but you should still watch for cars and observe the single-file rule. The shoulder is grassy, and you can pull onto it almost anywhere. Traffic can get a little crazy on the bridge at Birdsong Hollow; it's best not to stop your bike on the bridge.

Things to see: Natchez Trace Parkway

Maps: DeLorme *Tennessee Atlas & Gazetteer*, page 33, D7

Getting there by car: From Nashville, proceed west. Follow US 70 / Broadway / West End Avenue / Harding Road through the Belle Meade area. At the Y intersection of US 70 and TN 100, get in the left lane and follow TN 100 for 7.8 miles. Take the ramp onto the Natchez Trace Parkway. Proceed about 2 miles to the parking lot on the right at milepost 440. **GPS:** N36 00.28' / W86 58.42'

THE RIDE

Begin the ride by making a right turn out of the parking lot. The Trace runs generally north-south. Because this is the rolling part, you should enjoy some of the easy descents. You will want to stop at Birdsong Hollow at mile 1.9.

Birdsong Hollow parking lot is at milepost 438.2. There is a descriptive sign and a short walk out to the overlook. The overlook is the best place to view the bridge without exiting The Trace. This is one of the more incredible observation points on the ride. This bridge is only one of two post-tensioned, segmental concrete arch bridges in the world. There is a photo posted by the Federal Highway Administration at http://www.fhwa.dot.gov/eihd/images/natchez.jpg. You are looking at TN 96 below. At the highest point, it is 155 feet high. This bridge won the Presidential Award for Design Excellence in 1995. There is plenty of room to walk out onto the bridge to snap a few pictures. Turn right from the parking lot to continue the ride south to Garrison Creek.

After you go over the bridge, the exit for TN 96 is at mile 2.6. This is the best route to Franklin. You may wish to ride down the ramp to get a better view of the bridge structure from TN 96; however, it will be a climb back onto The Trace.

A bit farther south, you will ride over a bridge over a hollow below that substantially levels out the road elevation. This is another great example of the design of The Trace. The road and area below that you see are intact, with minimal disruption to the view of the area.

Garrison Creek

As you proceed a bit farther, you will know you are going down Backbone Ridge. You will enjoy this descent. The road sweeps gently to the left as you descend and makes another left sweep as you get to the bottom of this ridge. This is one of the climbs as you proceed north and another design example of The Trace. Although you have a nice vista as you make this climb, you are looking at private land; the average width of The Trace is only 800 feet for the entire 444 miles!

As you descend across this large open area, you will see Hillsboro Middle School on your left. You will cross over Pinewood Road. The exit to Leiper's Fork is just ahead, at mile 11.1. Leiper's Fork is about 3 miles from The Trace; the signs will direct you.

As you pass this exit and make another short climb, you will start to descend what seems to be an open field. You will pass over Garrison Creek Road—the stream beside it is Garrison Creek—and then you will see The Trace's Garrison Creek rest area on your left, at mile 12.8. This rest stop is a great place to meet other cyclists, particularly on summer weekends. There is a hiking trail that departs behind the building. This is the southern end of the ride.

As you leave Garrison Creek, turn right, heading north, to return to the parking lot at milepost 440.

Retrace the route. At mile 25.6, turn left into the parking lot; this is the end of the ride.

Bike Shops

Cumberland Transit: 2807 West End Ave., Nashville; (615) 321-4069; http://cumberlandtransit.com/cycling/

Gran Fondo: 5133 Harding Rd., Suite A6, Nashville; (615) 354-1090; http://www.granfondocycles.com/

Gran Fondo Trail & Fitness: 5133 Harding Rd., Suite B-1, Nashville; (615) 499-4634; http://www.granfondotrail.com/

Mac's Harpeth Bikes: 1100 Hillsboro Rd., Franklin; (615) 472-1002; www.macsharpethbikes.com

MOAB Franklin: 109 Del Rio Pike, Suite 105, Franklin; (615) 807-2035; http://moabbikes.com/

R.B.'s Cyclery: 3078 Maddux Way, #300, Franklin; (615) 567-6633; www.rbscyclery.com

REI: 261 Franklin Rd., Brentwood; (615) 376-4248; www.rei.com

Sun & Ski: 545 Cool Springs Blvd., Franklin; (615) 628-0289; http://www.sunandski.com

Trace Bikes: 8080B TN 100, Nashville; (615) 646-2485; http://tracebikes.com/

You will enjoy many great vistas as you travel north that may not have been in your line of sight on the southbound route. Also, the things you notice depend on the season of the year. Do this ride in March to see the redbuds in bloom; in April, to see the blooming dogwoods; and in October, to enjoy the incredible beauty of autumn in Tennessee. This ride never seems to become routine. If you want to add a few miles, you can always ride a bit farther south before you turn around to make the return trip to the parking lot.

MILES AND DIRECTIONS

0.0 Turn right onto The Trace to begin the ride.

1.9 Stop at Birdsong Hollow parking lot.

2.6 This is the TN 96 exit ramp.

11.1 This is the Pinewood Road / TN 46 / Leiper's Fork Road exit ramp.

12.8 Turn left into the Garrison Creek area. This is the turnaround point for the ride.

25.6 Turn left into the parking lot. This is the end of the ride.

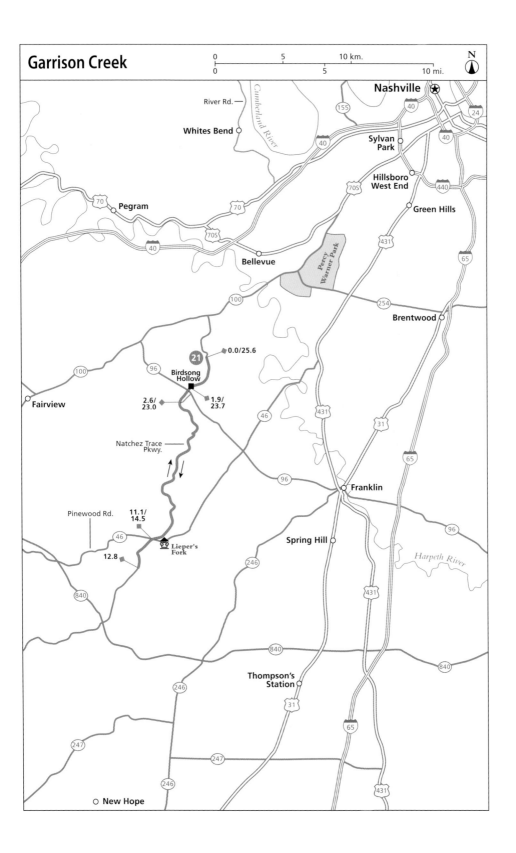

Garrison Creek

RIDE INFORMATION

Local Events/Attractions

Adventure Cycling Association: http://www.adventurecycling.org. Many bikers cycle the entire Trace, or longer sections of it. The Adventure Cycling Association shows the Natchez Trace Route on their Great Rivers South route. You can also check out http://www.natcheztracetravel.com/.

Leiper's Fork Village: http://www.visitleipersfork.com/events. This community has been a fixture in the area since 1801 and has become a magnet for locals and tourists alike.

National Park Service: http://www.nps.gov/natr. There are many things to enjoy on The Trace, including biking, hiking, horseback riding, and camping.

Local Eateries

The most storied eatery near The Trace is Loveless Cafe (www.lovelesscafe .com). They feature southern cooking with an emphasis on country ham and biscuits. There are numerous restaurants of all kinds in Franklin. From the TN 96 exit off The Trace, follow TN 96 east approximately 8 miles to Franklin.

Leiper's Fork is the home of Puckett's Grocery, at 4142 Old Hillsboro Road, Franklin; http://www.leipersfork.net/html/events_html. They have a restaurant that doubles as a music venue on weekend nights.

The community of Bellevue is near the end of The Trace. There are several restaurants and shopping available on TN 100, about 2 miles east of The Trace.

Restrooms

Mile 12.8: Garrison Creek rest area

Leiper's Creek

This ride explores Leiper's Fork, providing a good introduction to the general area. It's a great workout ride, as it includes some climbing, and starts from the southern end at Thompson's Station. Geographically, Nashville is in a basin. As such, an escarpment surrounds it on all sides. This is known as the Highland Rim, which you will experience firsthand. There are three stores in the first 15 miles of the ride if you need a break.

Start: The ride begins at Thompson's Station Park.

Length: 40 miles, loop ride

Approximate riding time: 3 to 4 hours

Best bike: Road or hybrid bike

Terrain and trail surface: The terrain is rolling, and there will be climbs. Although a couple of them are steep, they are short. The climb on Sycamore Road is a 170-foot ascent in about 0.5 mile. There is a climb of note on Wilkins Branch Road. There is a very short but steep climb on McMillan Road. But there will be plenty of rolling terrain to get in some climbing practice. The rural roads are all paved. As always, watch for limbs or debris that may have fallen into the road and that you should not run over.

Traffic and hazards: There will be some traffic on Thompson's Station Road and Carters Creek Pike. For most of the ride, there will be very little traffic. This route is well known among locals, so you may see some other cyclists.

Maps: DeLorme *Tennessee Atlas & Gazetteer*, page 54, A4

Getting there by car: From Nashville, at the intersection of I-440 and I-65 South, take I-65 South 21 miles and exit on I-840 exit 59B, toward Memphis and Dickson. You will go about 3 miles, then take exit 28, the second exit off I-840 toward Columbia/Franklin. You will be going toward Thompson's Station and Spring Hill. Turn left onto Franklin Road / US 31 South and go about 2 miles. Just past the church on your left, turn right onto Thompson's Station Road beside the BP station. Thompson's Station Park is 0.2 mile ahead, on the left. **GPS:** N35 47.869866' / W86 54.493966 '

THE RIDE

To begin the ride, set your odometer just as you make the left turn out of Thompson's Station Park onto Thompson's Station Road. This bit of the route winds through the Thompson's Station community, past the train station and some residential and business districts. As with many communities in the area, the railroad was a key element to growth in the early twentieth century. The train station was torn down in 1952 after truck traffic and better roads caused the obsolescence of the railroad. The present station was rebuilt in 1996 and houses the Town Hall.

You will quickly find yourself in open farm country. Turn left onto Evergreen Road at mile 1.8. Welcome to the rolling terrain of Williamson County. Things have changed, as evidenced by the vacant school building on your right, now in private ownership. Turn right at the T intersection onto Popes Chapel Road at mile 5.1.

The country store at Burwood at mile 6.3 is a good place for a break. Most so-called country stores sell fast food and drinks but this store has true charm, judging by its Case knives sales. From here, turn right onto Carters Creek Pike / TN 246. This was a toll road between 1850 and 1917, and also figured in the Battle of Franklin, November 1864, when Confederate general John Bell Hood tried to frustrate Union general William Tecumseh Sherman's march to

Bike Shops

None of the bike shops are near the ride route. In the case of an emergency, you will need to get back to your car.
Mac's Harpeth Bikes: 1100 Hillsboro Rd., Franklin; (615) 472-1002; www.macsharpethbikes.com
MOAB Franklin: 109 Del Rio Pike, Suite 105, Franklin; (615) 807-2035; http://moabbikes.com/
R.B.'s Cyclery: 3078 Maddux Way, #300, Franklin; (615) 567-6633; www.rbscyclery.com
REI: 261 Franklin Rd., Brentwood; (615) 376-4248; www.rei.com
Sun & Ski: 545 Cool Springs Blvd., Franklin; (615) 628-0289; http://www.sunandski.com

A bed-and-breakfast in Boston

the Deep South. Now I-840 looms; turn left just after you pass it, onto Johnson Hollow Road at mile 6.7.

This is country riding at its best. Turn right onto Sycamore Road at mile 7.8. You will have a climb ahead of you; then it flattens out a bit, followed by another short ascent. Overall, you will climb about 170 feet from the last turn. This is the beginning of the big loop. You will be at the other end of some of these roads in a few miles.

You will get to a Y intersection at Bear Creek Road. At mile 10.1, bear left; watch for traffic coming over the hill from your left as you enter Bear Creek. You will have a nice descent into the Boston community.

At the T intersection with Robinson Road, turn right at mile 11.0. The Boston Church of Christ on your right as you turn was founded in 1854. Davis Store at Boston will be another place for a rest stop on your left as you approach Leiper's Creek Road. Turn right onto Leiper's Creek Road at mile 11.2. This is a pleasant, relatively flat section where you will enjoy the well-manicured farms along the way. This road used to be the railroad bed of the Middle Tennessee Railroad, from 1910 to 1927.

Leiper's Fork Market and Shell Station will be your next signal for a turn, at mile 14.9. Turn left onto Wilkins Branch Road. This entire area is an interesting mix of longer-term residences and newer farms that have populated the area. This segment is another climbing opportunity. Before you reach Hargrove Road, you will ascend about 250 feet. In the next approximate 0.5 mile, you will have three turns: Turn right onto Hargrove Road at mile 17.6. At the T intersection with Old State Highway 96, turn right at mile 18.1. Immediately, turn left onto Parker Branch Road at mile 18.2.

After all the climbing, you will cross over The Natchez Trace Parkway. Enjoy this downhill stretch most of the way to the next turn onto Old Hillsboro Road / TN 46. At the T intersection with Old Hillsboro Road / TN 46, turn left at mile 21.6. You will enter the Bingham community as you approach the next turn. Turn right onto Boyd Mill Pike at mile 22.2. You will make another quick right turn after you cross over the bridge onto Blazer Road at mile 22.4. After the sharp left turn, turn right onto Boxley Valley Road at mile 22.7. Turn right onto McMillan Road at mile 24.1. Prepare for a climb. You will ascend about 80 feet in the next 0.25 mile.

At the T intersection you will turn right onto Southall Road at mile 24.7. Continue the big loop at mile 25.6, where you will turn left onto Carl Road. At the T intersection with Carters Creek Pike / TN 246, turn right at mile 28.6. There is usually traffic on Carters Creek Pike / TN 246, but there is a usable shoulder. You will enjoy this bit of rolling countryside.

This is a bit of a side tour through the countryside. Turn right onto Bear Creek Road at mile 29.3. Shortly after you make this turn, there is a historical society sign for the Mayberry-Bailey Plantation. Turn left onto Gray Lane, the first road at mile 29.9. At the T intersection, turn left onto Perkins Road at mile 31.2. At the next T intersection, turn left onto Carters Creek Pike / TN 246 at mile 31.6. You may notice another historical sign for Colonel Hardy Murfree.

Mayberry-Bailey Plantation

Just after the turn onto Bear Creek Road at mile 29.3, you may notice the historical marker for this large antebellum house, set back from the road. Built in 1856, the house was named Beechwood Hall. The two-story brick and stucco structure features, per the roadside marker, are "Greek Revival and Italianate influences, [and is] famous for the freestanding spiral walnut staircase in the 40-by-60-foot central hall." The house remained in the family until 1949, and was owned briefly in the early 1950s by country music star Hank Williams Sr.

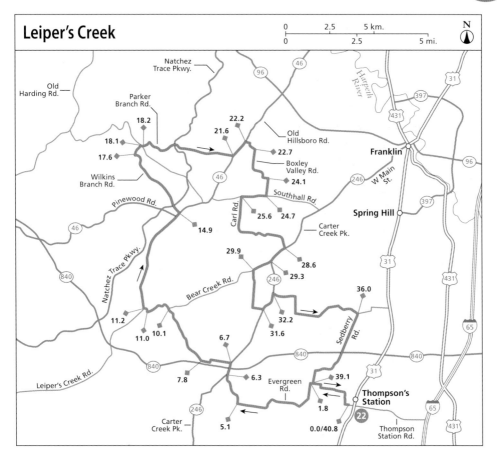

Leiper's Creek

This was the original land grant for the Mayberry-Bailey Plantation. Turn right onto West Harpeth Road at mile 32.2.

Farm country continues on this leg of the route. Turn right onto Sedberry Road at mile 36.0. Turn left onto Thompson's Station Road at mile 39.1, at the T intersection. You will retrace the route from here, and turn right into Thompson's Station Park at mile 40.8. This is the end of the ride.

MILES AND DIRECTIONS

0.0 Start/end Thompson's Station Park. Turn left onto Thomson Station Road.

1.8 Turn left onto Evergreen Road.

5.1 Turn right at the T intersection onto Popes Chapel Road.

6.3 Bear right onto Carters Creek Pike / TN 246. The Burwood Country Store is at this intersection.

6.7 Turn left onto Johnson Hollow Road.

7.8 Turn right onto Sycamore Road.

10.1 Bear left at the intersection onto Bear Creek Road.

11.0 Turn right at the T intersection onto Robinson Road.

11.2 Turn right onto Leiper's Creek Road.

14.9 Leiper's Fork Market and Shell Station is on your left. Turn left onto Wilkins Branch Road.

17.6 Turn right onto Hargrove Road.

18.1 Turn right onto Old State Highway 96.

18.2 Turn left onto Parker Branch Road.

21.6 Turn left onto Old Hillsboro Road / TN 46.

22.2 Turn right onto Boyd Mill Pike.

22.4 Turn right onto Blazer Road.

22.7 Turn right onto Boxley Valley Road.

24.1 Turn right onto McMillan Road.

24.7 Turn right at the T intersection onto Southall Road.

25.6 Turn left onto Carl Road.

Thompson's Station

Although Thompson's Station was incorporated on August 15, 1990, its roots date back to the 1780s, when the first white settlers began to inhabit Native American land in the area. After being known by other names, and suffering many trials and tribulations, in 1856, Dr. Elijah Thompson donated land for the village, and Thompson's Station was begun in earnest. The 1866 census counted 200 residents. The 2010 census counted 2,194 residents.

Thompson's Station figured in the Civil War as a battlefront. The local hero of the battle was Nathan Bedford Forrest. During the battle, his horse Roderick was killed. A monument to this historic steed was dedicated on March 5, 2008.

Thompson's Station continues to recognize its traditions even as it looks to the future, recently adding two national company headquarters to its community of businesses.

28.6 Turn right onto Carters Creek Pike / TN 246.

29.3 Turn right onto Bear Creek Road.

29.9 Turn left onto Gray Lane (first road).

31.2 Turn left onto Perkins Road.

31.6 Turn left onto Carters Creek Pike / TN 246.

32.2 Turn right onto West Harpeth Road.

36.0 Turn right onto Sedberry Road.

39.1 Turn left onto Thompson's Station Road.

40.8 Turn right into Thompson's Station Park.

RIDE INFORMATION

Local Events/Attractions

Thompson's Station Park is the site during September for the Thompson's Station Fall Festival / Craft Fair. It is a fund-raising event for the Town of Thompson's Station Community Association.

Local Eateries

There are three country stores along the route. Burwood Country Store at mile 6.3 will make sandwiches to order at the counter. Davis Market in Boston at mile 11.2 has the usual offerings and will also make sandwiches. They also grill burgers around the lunch hour. Leiper's Fork Market is located at mile 14.9. Instead of retracing the drive back on I-840, you can follow US 31 / Franklin Road / Columbia Pike north into Franklin. There are a variety of eateries in Franklin in the downtown area.

Restrooms

Mile 0.0 and **40.8:** There are public restrooms at Thompson's Station Park.
Mile 14.9: Leiper's Fork Market has restrooms.

Country Church Tour

Many small communities thrived during earlier times when roads were not as good as they are today. This route travels through College Grove, Arno, Peytonsville, and Rudderville, and explores the southern and eastern parts of Williamson County—"east of 65," as the locals call it. See The Factory ride in this book for another route in this area.

Although many small communities no longer support the commerce of local stores, they continue to have a community church. They have accumulated the history of these communities in interesting ways, through maintaining adjoining cemeteries. This route goes by three community churches: Epworth United Methodist Church, Westwood Community Baptist Church, and Cool Springs Primitive Baptist Church. At mile 28.4 (or 9.3, where the short option turns around), you can turn left onto Peytonsville Road and go about 0.25 mile to view the two front entrances of Peytonsville Methodist Church.

The ride start point is easily accessible from I-65 South, and quickly gets into some nice rural roads. There is a short option (19 miles) if you are pressed for time or just beginning your adventures in biking. This route is structured to start at the edge of the busy traffic rather than riding the first few miles on busy roads. To accomplish this, the ride counter begins at the intersection of Carothers Parkway and TN 96 / Murfreesboro Road. There is a strip mall, Williamson Medical Center, and other places in this vicinity to park.

Start: The ride begins at the intersection of Carothers Parkway and TN 96 / Murfreesboro Road.

Length: 38 miles (short option, 19 miles), loop ride

Approximate riding time: 2 to 3 hours

Best bike: Road or hybrid bike

Terrain and trail surface: The ride is part of the local rolling terrain, but there are not any difficult climbs. Most of the route is made up of well-maintained, rural roads.

Traffic and hazards: There will be traffic at the beginning on Carothers Parkway. As always in urban riding, ride on the right side of the road, be aware of traffic, and ride in a predictable manner. The traffic will thin after the first mile. There are short sections on roads that accommodate local traffic, with speed limits of 50 mph or more—Arno Road and Horton Highway / US 41A.

Maps: DeLorme *Tennessee Atlas & Gazetteer*, page 33, E8. NPS map: http://www.nps.gov/natr/planyourvisit/upload/NATRmap1_2011 _ForWeb_340_444.pdf

Getting there by car: From Nashville, take I-65 South. From the I-65 South intersection with I-440 West, drive 14.9 miles south toward Huntsville. Take the TN 96 / Murfreesboro exit, exit 65. Turn left onto Murfreesboro Road / TN 96 and go over the interstate. Turn left onto Carothers Parkway at the second traffic light. There are a variety of places to park in the area. **GPS:** N35 54.47' / W86 49.10'

THE RIDE

The ride counter begins at the intersection of Carothers Parkway and TN 96 / Murfreesboro Road. Proceed south on Carothers Parkway. The busy traffic should diminish quickly within the first mile or so. Enjoy the ride! Turn right at the T intersection with Arno Road at mile 4.0. The first country church, Epworth United Methodist, is on your right. Turn right at mile 5.3 onto Gosey Hill Road. This route will omit the hill part of this road, but it's a beautiful jaunt if you are interested. At mile 6.6, turn left onto Crowder Road. At mile 7.4, continue on the same road, which becomes Meeks Road.

You encounter the second country church, Westwood Community Baptist, at the intersection of Crowder Road and Peytonsville Trinity Road. It will be on your left. This is the split point for the short option. The short

Bike Shops

Mac's Harpeth Bikes: 1100 Hillsboro Rd., Franklin; (615) 472-1002; www.macsharpethbikes.com
MOAB Franklin: 109 Del Rio Pike, Suite 105, Franklin; (615) 807-2035; http://moabbikes.com/
R.B.'s Cyclery: 3078 Maddux Way, #300, Franklin; (615) 567-6633; www .rbscyclery.com
REI: 261 Franklin Rd., Brentwood; (615) 376-4248; www.rei.com
Sun & Ski: 545 Cool Springs Blvd., Franklin; (615) 628-0289; http:// www.sunandski.com

Epworth United Methodist Church

option is easy, as follows: Turn right onto Peytonsville-Trinity Road at mile 7.4. Proceed for 1.9 miles. The Peytonsville Market is at mile 9.3, at the intersection of Peytonsville Trinity Road and Peytonsville Road just before the I-840 overpass. Turn around and retrace the route back to the intersection of Crowder Road and Peytonsville Trinity Road. Pick up the long-option route at mile 30.3.

The long option continues on Crowder Road at mile 6.6, and follows an irregular loop to College Grove. The street name changes to Meeks Road at this intersection. At mile 9.3, cross over Arno Road. The street name changes to McDaniel Road. Turn right at the T intersection onto Cox Road at mile 12.1. Turn right onto Horton Highway / US 41A at the T intersection at mile 14.7. This is a main highway, so expect some traffic and rumble strips!

US 41 Alt splits off toward Shelbyville at mile 15.4, but you will continue to bear right on Horton Highway / US 41A. You enter College Grove and turn right onto Arno-College Grove Road at mile 16.9. If you need a break, instead of making this turn, continue for about 0.1 of a mile to the College Grove Grocery. From there you can go out Depot Street, or retrace the route; either way, get on Arno-College Grove Road heading west.

Turn right onto Eudaley-Covington Road at mile 17.8. This leg of the route is a mix of rural roads and new residential developments; the closer you get to I-840, the more residential it becomes. Turn left onto Arno Road at mile 22.2. At the intersection of Arno-Peytonsville Road at mile 23.9, you will continue on this road; the street name becomes Arno Allisona Road. At mile 24.7, turn right onto Bethesda-Arno Road. At mile 26.0, turn right onto Cool Springs Road.

The third country church is on your right, on Cool Springs Road: Cool Springs Primitive Baptist Church. Two early-twentieth-century Grand Ole Opry stars, Sam and Kirk McGee, are recognized on a historic sign near the church. Continue on the same road at the intersection of Cool Springs Road and Peytonsville Trinity Road, at mile 27.8. The street name becomes Peytonsville Trinity Road. Go under I-840 just ahead, at mile 28.1.

At mile 28.4, the short option merges into the route. The Peytonsville Market is on the left at this intersection. From the market, turn left to continue on Peytonsville Trinity Road north. Turn left onto Crowder Road at mile 30.3 at the Westwood Community Baptist Church. From this point, the remainder of the route retraces the outbound route.

Turn right onto Gosey Hill Road at the T intersection at mile 31.1. Turn left onto Arno Road at the T intersection at mile 32.5. Just past the Epworth United Methodist church, turn left onto Carothers Parkway at mile 33.7. At mile 37.7, this is the end of the ride at the intersection of TN 96 / Murfreesboro Road and Carothers Parkway.

Churches in Arno and Peytonsville

According to one source, at one time there were forty-four separate communities in Williamson County. Most of them have long since disappeared, as roads to Franklin have improved and lifestyles have changed. But on a bicycle, one can imagine how each community must have thrived and been an integral part of the lives of many citizens.

Churches are the main survivors of these communities. Arno and Peytonsville currently are home to six churches, two in Arno and four in Peytonsville. One of the earliest churches in the area was the Cool Springs Primitive Baptist Church. Located on Arno-Peytonsville Road, it was built by "the big cool springs." Records date from 1818. In 1839, the church was moved, log by log, to its present site. It is located on the long route on Cool Springs Road, before you get to I-840.

Another interesting church building phenomenon occurred in 1856 with the Peytonsville Methodist Church, whose meetinghouse design included the dual entrances that were popular at the time—one for men and one for women. This church is about 0.25 mile off the route on Peytonsville Road, past the Peytonsville Market at mile 28.4 (9.3, short route).

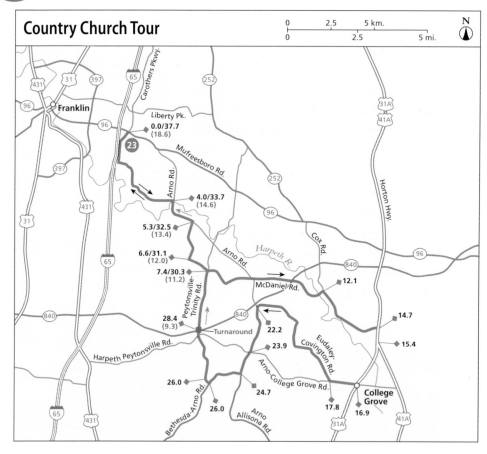

Country Church Tour

MILES AND DIRECTIONS

0.0 Begin at the intersection of Carothers Parkway and TN 96 / Murfreesboro Road. Proceed south on Carothers Parkway.

4.0 Turn right onto Arno Road at the T intersection.

5.3 Turn right onto Gosey Hill Road.

6.6 Turn left onto Crowder Road.

7.4 Continue on the same road; the street name becomes Meeks Road.

The short option splits here, and is as follows:

7.4 Turn right onto Peytonsville-Trinity Road

9.3 The short route turns around here and merges with long route return directions. The Peytonsville market is at this intersection. Check for oncoming traffic, and continue on the same road. The street name becomes McDaniel Road at the intersection with Arno Road.

12.1 Turn right onto Cox Road at the T intersection.

14.7 Turn right onto Horton Highway / US 41A at the T intersection.

15.4 Bear right to continue on Horton Highway / US 41A.

16.9 Turn right onto Arno-College Grove Road.

17.8 Turn right onto Eudaley-Covington Road.

22.2 Turn left onto Arno Road.

23.9 Continue on the same road. The street name becomes Arno Allisona Road at the intersection with Arno-Peytonsville Road.

24.7 Turn right onto Bethesda-Arno Road.

26.0 Turn right onto Cool Springs Road.

27.8 Continue on the same road. The street name becomes Peytonsville-Trinity Road at the intersection with Harpeth Peytonsville Road.

28.1 Continue under I-840.

28.4 Continue north on Peytonsville-Trinity Road at the intersection with Peytonsville Road.

28.4 (9.3) The short route turns around here and continues with the long route; Peytonsville market is at this intersection. The short option mileages are shown in parentheses.

30.3 (11.2) Turn left onto Crowder Road.

31.1 (12.0) Turn right onto Gosey Hill Road at the T intersection.

32.5 (13.4) Turn left onto Arno Road at the T intersection.

33.7 (14.6) Turn left onto South Carothers Parkway.

37.7 (18.6) This is the end of the ride at the intersection of TN 96 / Murfreesboro Road and Carothers Parkway.

Local Events/Attractions

The Tennessee Renaissance Festival: 2124 New Castle Rd., Arrington; http://www.tnrenfest.com/index.htm. This festival site is only a few miles northeast from the turn onto Horton Highway / US 41A, at mile 14.7, near Franklin, in Arrington. The festival is held on weekends in May and offers a series of events for the whole family, celebrating sixteenth-century England. The Village of Covington Glen comes alive with the bustle of a Renaissance marketplace, with more than sixty vendors displaying the wares of skilled artisans.

Cool Springs Primitive Baptist Church

Weekends are given to various themes: Celtic Weekend, Pirate Invasion Weekend, and Royal Jousting Tournament Weekend. Yes, there are period costumes, including full body armor. The tour of Castle Gwynn includes displays of needlework and tapestry collections.

Local Eateries
At mile 16.9, the College Grove Grocery is 0.1 mile ahead. (Do not make the right turn, per the route.) At mile 28.4 (mile 9.3, short option), the Peytonsville market is on the left.

Restrooms
Mile 16.9: There are restrooms at the College Grove Grocery.
Mile 28.4: The Peytonsville Market has portable restrooms.

Country Store Tour

Williamson County once had forty-four separate communities, according to the chamber of commerce. Not much remains of the store, church, post office, and other businesses that were built as the center of these communities, but this ride is an introduction to three country stores in Williamson and Maury Counties: Fly's, Hilltop, and Davis Markets. The ride incorporates part of the Natchez Trace Parkway, and it's a very convenient drive to the ride start from Nashville.

The convenience of the interstate and much improved road systems have reduced the need for the neighborhood market. Nonetheless, these markets provide a great place to take a quick rest stop on a bike ride.

Start: The ride begins at the Garrison Creek rest stop on the Natchez Trace Parkway. The official Natchez Trace Parkway mile marker is 427.6.

Length: 37 miles

Approximate riding time: About 3 hours

Best bike: Road or hybrid bike

Terrain and trail surface: The terrain is definitely rolling. There is one climb of note on Woolard Road. The roads are generally rural, paved, and well-maintained.

Traffic and hazards: There will be little traffic on these roads. You may encounter some traffic on Natchez Trace Parkway. Some of the roads are narrow, country roads with a lot of trees. It is always advisable to watch for new potholes or debris in the road, such as fallen branches or gravel that sometimes accumulates.

Things to see: Bona fide country stores

Maps: DeLorme *Tennessee Atlas & Gazetteer*, page 33, F6

THE RIDE

The mileage counter begins immediately in front of the shelter at the Garrison Creek rest stop on the Natchez Trace Parkway. Turn left to head south when you get to The Trace. You will begin near mile marker 427. At mile 11.8, turn right at the TN 7 exit toward Columbia/Dickson, near Trace mile marker 416. At mile 12.0, turn left on TN 7 (toward Columbia), at the T intersection (bottom of ramp). Turn left at Fly's Market (the first store on the route), at the bottom of the hill, at mile 13.7. You will want to look around in the antiques area beside the store if it is open. Fly's will make sandwiches if you are hungry.

Continue in the same direction by turning left as you exit Fly's at mile 13.7. Turn left at Hay Hollow Road at mile 14.2. You have about 10 miles of country roads ahead. Turn right onto Woolard Road at mile 15.3. There is sometimes a pile of gravel just at the turn. There is a story that buffalo migrating through the area first created early roads. You may think they have continued on the next few turns. The climb of note happens just ahead. There are two switchbacks. At the Y intersection, take the left fork at mile 17.2 onto Chestnut Ridge Road. Don't go down the hill.

Bike Shops

Cumberland Transit: 2807 West End Ave., Nashville; (615) 321-4069; http://cumberlandtransit.com/cycling/
Gran Fondo: 5133 Harding Rd., Suite A6, Nashville; (615) 354-1090; http://www.granfondocycles.com/
Gran Fondo Trail & Fitness: 5133 Harding Rd., Suite B-1, Nashville; (615) 499-4634; http://www.granfondotrail.com/
Mac's Harpeth Bikes: 1100 Hillsboro Rd., Franklin; (615) 472-1002; www.macsharpethbikes.com
MOAB Franklin: 109 Del Rio Pike, Suite 105, Franklin; (615) 807-2035; http://moabbikes.com/
R.B.'s Cyclery: 3078 Maddux Way, #300, Franklin; (615) 567-6633; www.rbscyclery.com
REI: 261 Franklin Rd., Brentwood; (615) 376-4248; www.rei.com
Sun & Ski: 545 Cool Springs Blvd., Franklin; (615) 628-0289; http://www.sunandski.com
Trace Bikes: 8080B TN 100, Nashville; (615) 646-2485; http://tracebikes.com/

Davis General Merchandise

At the three-way intersection at mile 17.8, bear left to continue on Chestnut Ridge Road. Another example of road naming is just ahead at mile 18.4; you will go straight to continue on Chestnut Ridge Road, even though the roads are Gaskill and Raleigh Beard. But it's not over yet; at mile 20.0, turn left at the T intersection with Godwin. Immediately you will turn right at mile 20.1, to continue on Chestnut Ridge Road. It is not all downhill from here, but at least the roads will make more sense.

At the intersection with TN 247 / Les Robinson Road, turn left at mile 23.7. Hilltop Market is just ahead on the left at mile 24.3. This serves as the local farmers' market in summer, with fresh vegetables on display. When you exit Hilltop Market, you will turn right at mile 24.3, retracing the route to the next road and turning right at mile 24.4 onto Sulphur Springs Road. You should enjoy this downhill section. Turn right at the T intersection onto Leiper's Creek Road at mile 27.2. You will get to the Boston community at mile 30.5; Davis Market is on the right. They make sandwiches at lunchtime; one summer, they even grilled hamburgers at lunch! (This may have been due to the traffic caused by the I-840 construction project, which is now completed.)

Turn right as you exit Davis Market and continue heading north on Leiper's Creek Road. You will probably see the new firehouse on your left as

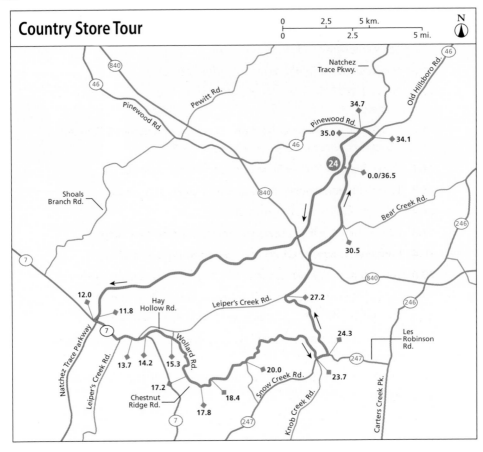

Country Store Tour

you approach TN 46 / Pinewood Road at mile 34.1; turn left. As you pass Hillsboro Middle School, you will go under The Trace; get into the left turn lane and turn left onto the Natchez Trace Parkway access ramp, at mile 34.7. Turn right onto The Trace at the T intersection at mile 35.0 and head south toward Tupelo to return to Garrison Creek. Turn left into the Garrison Creek rest area at mile 36.4. This is the end of the ride as you get to the rest stop shelter at mile 36.5.

But this is not the end of the country stores. Hint: Nett's is farther south of Boston on Leiper's Creek Road, and don't miss the one at Burwood! Go up Garrison Creek to the intersection with Bending Chestnut and see what you can find!

MILES AND DIRECTIONS

0.0 Begin at Garrison Creek rest stop and turn left onto the Natchez Trace Parkway.

11.8 Turn right at TN 7 exit toward Columbia/Dickson.

12.0 Turn left on TN 7 (toward Columbia) at the T intersection (bottom of ramp).

13.7 Turn left at Fly's General Store (the first store on the route). Turn left out of Fly's General Store to continue on TN 7.

14.2 Turn left at Hay Hollow Road (the second road to the left).

15.3 Turn right onto Woolard Road (possibly gravel at the turn).

17.2 Turn left at Chestnut Ridge Road.

17.8 Bear left at Gaskill and Lewis to continue on Chestnut Ridge.

18.4 Continue straight at Gaskill and Raleigh Beard (not marked).

20.0 Turn left at the T intersection at Chestnut Ridge and Godwin (right).

20.1 Turn right immediately, continuing on Chestnut Ridge Road.

23.7 Turn left on TN 247 / Les Robinson Road at the T intersection.

24.3 Turn left at the Hilltop Market (second store). Turn right out of Hilltop Market.

24.4 Immediately turn right at Sulphur Springs Branch Road.

27.2 Turn right at the T intersection on Leiper's Creek Road.

30.5 Turn right at the Davis Store (third store).

34.1 Turn left at TN 46 / Pinewood Road.

34.7 Turn left onto the Natchez Trace Parkway access ramp.

35.0 Turn right onto The Trace, heading south toward Tupelo.

36.4 Turn left into the Garrison Creek rest area.

36.5 This is the end of the ride, at the Garrison Creek rest area shelter.

RIDE INFORMATION

Local Events/Attractions

Town of Franklin: Williamson County Visitor Center, 209 E. Main St., Franklin; (866) 253-9207; http://www.visitwilliamson.com/. The town of Franklin has managed to preserve their history even as they have accommodated twenty-first-century growth. There is a lot to see; according to their website, there are twenty-five walking and driving tours of Franklin and the surrounding area.

Fly's General Store

There is a self-guided walking tour of downtown Franklin's historic district that includes homes, churches, and local history landmarks.

Local Eateries

Any culinary needs you may have can be filled at the three aforementioned stores. Here are the particulars:

Davis General Merchandise is at mile 30.5 on the ride; 5600 Leiper's Creek Rd., Franklin; (615) 794-1066.

Fly's General Store is at mile 13.7 on the ride; 5661 Leiper's Creek Rd., Santa Fe; (931) 682-2356.

Hilltop Market is at mile 24.3 on the ride; 2278 Les Robinson Rd., Columbia; (931) 381-4025.

Restrooms

Mile 0.0 and **36.5:** The Garrison Creek rest area on the Natchez Trace Parkway has restroom facilities. During warm months the outdoor water fountain is operational, but the water inside is also potable.

Factory

The Factory ride is a good introduction to the southern areas of Williamson County. The terrain is relatively flat, there are country stores dispersed along the route if you need a snack, and there is a 27-mile short option. The Factory is a storied site and a favorite destination in Franklin. Formerly a center of manufacturing, it's been converted into a shopping area. On Saturday mornings in the summer, you'll usually find both a flea market and a farmers' market set up in the back parking area.

The town of Franklin has preserved a certain small-town atmosphere while meeting the twenty-first-century needs of its residents. The ride begins at The Factory, but also explores some of the rural areas of Williamson County. Set your odometer at the intersection as you turn onto Liberty Pike from the parking lot.

Length: 39 miles, loop ride (27 miles, short option)

Approximate riding time: About 3 hours, long option (about 2 hours, short option)

Best bike: Road or hybrid bike

Terrain and trail surface: The terrain is rolling, but for Williamson County, it is relatively flat. There are plenty of "rollers," but there are not any difficult climbs. The roads are either urban or well-maintained rural roads. Harpeth Peytonsville Road is a bit rough in places.

Traffic and hazards: There will be traffic in the urban areas. You may expect traffic on Liberty Pike. The route crosses two major thoroughfares, TN 96 and Arno Road, where a complete stop is necessary to check for oncoming traffic from both directions. Although there will be traffic on Carters Creek Pike / TN 246, the shoulder is very adequate.

Things to see: Various local artisans at The Factory

Maps: DeLorme *Tennessee Atlas & Gazetteer*, page 33, E8

Getting there by car: The Factory is about 1 mile east of the Square in Franklin on Franklin Road / US 31. From Nashville, you can take either US 431 / Hillsboro Road / TN 106, or Franklin Road / US 31 South. Or you can take I-65 South from Nashville. From the intersection of I-65 South and I-440, proceed about 12 miles and take the 68B exit off I-65 South. Proceed right on Cool Springs Boulevard about 2 miles to the T intersection with Mack Hatcher Boulevard. Turn right on Mack Hatcher and follow it to the traffic light at the intersection of Franklin Road / US 31 South. Turn left onto Franklin Road / US 31 and proceed 1 mile to the traffic light at Liberty Pike. The Factory water tower will be visible. Turn left onto Liberty Pike and then turn left into The Factory parking lot. This intersection will be the beginning of the ride. **GPS:** N35 55.52' / W86 51.31'

THE RIDE

The ride begins at the entrance to the Factory from the parking lot farthest away from Franklin Road at Liberty Pike. You will stay on this street for nearly 5 miles. After crossing under I-65, you will start through a development, passing a few streets. The next turn is easy to miss. At mile 4.7, turn right onto Market Street. This is a little dogleg to begin the big circle around the south of Franklin.

During the past four decades, this area has transitioned from farms to residential. Many of the properties have enough acreage to graze a few horses or cattle, which makes for interesting scenery along the way. As you get a few miles from Franklin, the area transitions to more traditional farm country. Turn right onto Trinity Road at mile 7.5. This turn will be easy to miss; it is best to look for the only place where you can cross the railroad tracks. You cross the tracks immediately after turning onto Trinity Road. You will be on Trinity Road for about 7 miles, but there are two important intersections. Be

Bike Shops

Mac's Harpeth Bikes: 1100 Hillsboro Rd., Franklin; (615) 472-1002; www.macsharpethbikes.com
MOAB Franklin: 109 Del Rio Pike, Suite 105, Franklin; (615) 807-2035; http://moabbikes.com/
R.B.'s Cyclery: 3078 Maddux Way, #300, Franklin; (615) 567-6633; www.rbscyclery.com
REI: 261 Franklin Rd., Brentwood; (615) 376-4248; www.rei.com
Sun & Ski: 545 Cool Springs Blvd., Franklin; (615) 628-0289; http://www.sunandski.com
Trace Bikes: 8080B TN 100, Nashville; (615) 646-2485; http://tracebikes.com/

The Factory at Franklin

sure to stop completely and look for traffic from both directions that may be traveling fast.

The short-option ride splits off at the Peytonsville Market as follows: Turn right onto Peytonsville Road at mile 14.2. This section will be a bit rolling, but it's a very scenic ride along some very manicured farms and interesting developments. At mile 19.4, the traffic will be busy briefly as you cross over I-65 South near the Williamson County Fairgrounds. Turn right onto Old Peytonsvillle Road at mile 19.5, just past the interstate overpass. This will skirt around some heavy traffic. Turn right onto Lewisburg Pike / US 431 North at mile 20.8. You are now headed back toward Franklin. When you get downtown, turn right onto Church Street at mile 25.3. You can follow Church Street and pick up the long route at mile 37.7.

The long route continues to make a big circle from the Peytonsville Market. At mile 14.3, go under I-840; turn right at the stop sign onto Harpeth Peytonsville Road at mile 14.6. Watch for some rough road surface on Harpeth Peytonsville Road. There will be another market ahead at the intersection with Lewisburg Pike / US 431 South at mile 18.8. This is another short dogleg south to Thompson's Station Road West. It will not be obvious, but turn right onto Thompson's Station Road West at mile 19.6. This leg will fill out the bottom part of the circle.

At mile 23.2, cross busy Columbia Pike / US 31 South. There is a BP station and market on the right. There are restrooms at Thompson's Station Park on your left as you leave the market. There is a roadside marker on Carters Creek Pike for Colonel Hardy Murfree, a Revolutionary War hero, and the recipient of several land grants in this area. He is the namesake of nearby Murfreesboro, Tennessee, and his father was the namesake of Murfreesboro, North Carolina!

There will be some traffic on Carters Creek Pike / TN 246, but the shoulder is adequate. Just as you get to downtown, you will follow the traffic pattern and bear right at the T intersection with 7th Street. Follow this through the traffic light; it becomes Church Street. You will continue to circle around Franklin, then turn left at the T intersection with 1st Avenue at mile 38.0. Take some time to stroll around the shops at The Factory.

MILES AND DIRECTIONS

0.0 Begin the ride from the back of The Factory parking lot and turn left onto Liberty Pike.

1.0 Cross Mack Hatcher Memorial Parkway / TN 397.

2.0 Cross under I-65 South; the street becomes McCay's Mill.

4.7 Turn right onto Market Street.

5.0 Turn left at the T intersection onto Clovercroft Road.

5.7 Turn right at the T intersection onto Wilson Pike.

7.5 Turn right onto Trinity Road and immediately go over the railroad tracks.

9.2 Cross TN 96 / Murfreesboro Road; make a complete stop and watch for traffic from both directions.

11.3 Cross Arno Road; make a complete stop and watch for traffic from both directions. The road becomes Peytonsville Trinity Road.

14.2 The Peytonsville market is on the right.

This is the split for the short option, as follows:

14.2 Turn right onto Peytonsville Road.

19.4 Cross over I-65 South. Watch for traffic.

19.5 Immediately turn right onto Old Peytonsville Road.

20.8 Turn right onto Lewisburg Pike / US 431 North.

25.3 Turn right onto Church Street.

Merge with long route at mile 37.7. Short option mileages are noted in parentheses.

14.3 Go under I-840.

14.6 Turn right at the stop sign onto Harpeth Peytonsville Road.

18.8 Turn left onto Lewisburg Pike / US 431 South.

19.6 Turn right onto Thompson's Station Road.

Factory

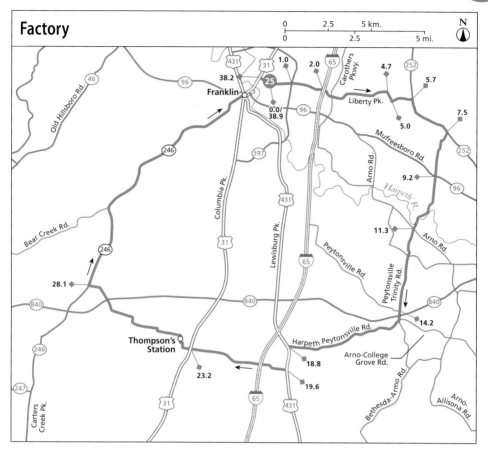

23.2 Cross Columbia Pike / US 31 South. There is a BP station/market on the right.

28.1 Turn right onto Carters Creek Pike / TN 246.

36.0 Carters Creek Pike / TN 246 becomes Main Street.

37.5 Turn right onto 7th Street at the T intersection.

37.7 Continue through the light; the street becomes Church Street.

37.7 (25.3) The short option merges in here.

38.0 (25.6) Turn left at the T intersection onto 1st Avenue.

38.2 (25.8) Turn right onto Main Street / Franklin Road / US 31 North.

38.6 (26.2) Turn right onto Liberty Pike at the second traffic light.

38.9 (26.5) Turn left into The Factory parking lot. This is the end of the ride.

The Factory

Built in 1929, The Factory occupies the complex of ten buildings that once housed the Allen Manufacturing Co, a stove manufacturer. It failed during the Great Depression. Subsequently, Dortch Stove Works occupied the property from 1932 to 1955, followed by Magic Chef (1955–59). Later the Jamison Bedding Company occupied the property (1962–91). "A member of the National Register of Historic Places, The Factory is rich with history, and a very careful renovation has preserved many of The Factory's original features and architectural details. Calvin Lehew bought the sprawling complex [. . .], and after an environmental cleanup, began renovating the facility in sections. Today, The Factory at Franklin has 83 tenants" (per the website).

RIDE INFORMATION

Local Events/Attractions

The Factory: http://www.factoryatfranklin.com. The Factory offers a combination of arts and crafts, craft fair, local shops, and flea market. You can do anything from get a meal or a cup of coffee, watch an artist work, or browse in shops of all kinds. Its proximity to downtown Franklin makes it a destination for all kinds of events as well. It is worth a bit of your time just to check it out.

Local Eateries

There are all kinds of eatery options at The Factory. If you want other options, downtown Franklin has many places to eat and shop, and is less than a mile from The Factory. If you need a snack along the route, there are some markets: the Peytonsville Road Market at mile 14.2; a gas station/market at mile 18.8, at the intersection of Peytonsville Trinity Road and Columbia Pike / US 431; and a BP station/market at mile 23.2.

Restrooms

Mile 0.0: The Factory identifies areas by building number. There are restrooms in all the buildings. Building 8 is relatively accessible from the back parking lot.
Mile 23.2: There are restrooms at Thompson's Station Park. It will be on your left just past the BP station/market.

Kingston Springs Pegram Tour

This ride originates on the Natchez Trace Parkway and proceeds west in a loop to Kingston Springs and Pegram in Cheatham County. The Harpeth River runs 125 miles through middle Tennessee and empties into the Cumberland River. In earlier days it was the source of energy for commerce. Some of this history is depicted a few miles north of this ride route, at Harpeth River State Park. A special attraction at this park is Newsome's Mill, one of the oldest gristmills in Davidson County.

This ride features quite a bit of climbing—seven climbs, in fact. You will see some beautiful vistas, agricultural areas, and two small towns on this ride that make up the Harpeth River Valley in Cheatham County.

Start: The ride begins at the 440-mile marker parking lot on the Natchez Trace Parkway.

Length: 35 miles, loop ride

Approximate riding time: About 3 hours

Best bike: Hybrid or road bike

Terrain and trail surface: The terrain is rolling, and there are seven climbs on this route. The roads are paved and generally rural.

Traffic and hazards: For most of the ride, there will be very little traffic. The part of the ride on US 70 will have traffic, along with the section that crosses over I-40 at Kingston Springs, although with the latter, the shoulder is wide. The turn at South Harpeth Road requires special caution to negotiate the angle of the turn on a bit of a downhill slope.

Maps: DeLorme *Tennessee Atlas & Gazetteer*, page 33, D7

Getting there by car: From Nashville, proceed west. Follow US 70 / Broadway / West End Avenue / Harding Road through the Belle Meade area. At the Y intersection of US 70 and TN 100, get in the left lane and follow TN 100 for 7.8 miles. Take the ramp onto the Natchez Trace Parkway. Proceed about 2 miles to the parking lot on the right at milepost 440. **GPS:** N36 00.28' / W86 58.42'

THE RIDE

Turn left, heading north on the Natchez Trace Parkway to begin the ride. Enjoy this long downhill; you will see it from the other direction on the return! As The Trace ends, follow it straight, then bear left on the ramp to go straight (west) onto TN 100 at mile 2.7, toward Fairview. Turn right at the first road onto Old Harding Pike, at mile 2.9. The first climb will begin as soon as you make the right turn at the next road, at mile 3.1, onto Lewis Road. Just as you get to the top of the hill, it is easy to miss the left turn onto Griffith Road, at mile 3.7. When you get to the T intersection on Poplar Creek Road at mile 5.1, turn left.

The next turn is so acute, you will have to stop and then turn or weave into the oncoming lane to make the right turn onto South Harpeth Road at

Bike Shops

Cumberland Transit: 2807 West End Ave., Nashville; (615) 321-4069; http://cumberlandtransit.com/cycling/

Gran Fondo: 5133 Harding Rd., Suite A6, Nashville; (615) 354-1090; http://www.granfondocycles.com/

Gran Fondo Trail & Fitness: 5133 Harding Rd., Suite B-1, Nashville; (615) 499-4634; http://www.granfondotrail.com/

Mac's Harpeth Bikes: 1100 Hillsboro Rd., Franklin; (615) 472-1002; www.macsharpethbikes.com

MOAB Franklin: 109 Del Rio Pike, Suite 105, Franklin; (615) 807-2035; http://moabbikes.com/

R.B.'s Cyclery: 3078 Maddux Way, #300, Franklin; (615) 567-6633; www.rbscyclery.com

REI: 261 Franklin Rd., Brentwood; (615) 376-4248; www.rei.com

Sun & Ski: 545 Cool Springs Blvd., Franklin; (615) 628-0289; http://www.sunandski.com

Trace Bikes: 8080B TN 100, Nashville; (615) 646-2485; http://tracebikes.com/

Cornfield on South Harpeth Road

mile 7.2 Be cautious of traffic from both directions. Turn right onto Luyben Hills Road (unmarked) at mile 12.3. There is another climbing opportunity on this leg. You will cross over I-40 at mile 12.9. If you want to take a break, there are various options until you reach the next turn.

As you approach the T intersection, get into the left turn lane. There will be some traffic as you make the left turn at the traffic light onto West Kingston Springs Road at mile 13.3. There will be a bit more traffic here, and there is not much shoulder, but this leg is only about a mile. As you get into the community of Kingston Springs, turn right at the T intersection beside the Church of Christ onto Main Street, at mile 14.6. At mile 14.8, continue straight through the stop sign and cross the railroad tracks, and then turn right onto Park Street / Pinnacle Hill Road.

There will be a significant climb to the top of Pinnacle Hill. You will enjoy the downhill as you proceed to the T intersection at US 70; at mile 17.3, turn right here onto US 70. There is limited shoulder on this section and there are rumble strips, but it will only be about 1.5 miles. As you approach the Tanglewood subdivision, turn left onto Tanglewood Drive at mile 18.9. There will be a short climb, and the route will feel like you are going straight when you turn left onto Lone Oak Road at mile 19.5.

At mile 20.1, turn left at the intersection onto Sams Creek Road / TN 249. Just ahead at mile 20.4, turn right onto Marshall Woodard Road. You get some downhill on this leg. On one of those descents, Marshall Woodard Road actually merges into Hannah Ford Road. You will turn left here onto Hannah Ford Road at mile 21.7. Just ahead at mile 22.0, you will cross US 70 at the traffic light. The street becomes Thompson Road. If you need refreshment, turn right onto US 70 and ride to a market about 0.3 mile west.

You will cross over the railroad tracks just as you cross US 70 on Thompson Road. The Pegram train station will be on your left. The road bears right past the caboose and train station. Just past the Pegram City Park, turn left onto Riverview Drive at mile 22.3. When you go under I-40 at mile 23.6, the road name changes to Anderson Road. You will have another climb ahead.

At the T-intersection, turn left onto South Harpeth Road (unmarked) at mile 25.8. The road is not marked. This begins the retrace of the outbound route. At mile 27.8, you will negotiate a left turn onto Poplar Creek Road. Be

Harpeth River State Park

The State of Tennessee Park system has been innovative in preserving some key natural areas in the state. Harpeth River State Park, located along the Harpeth River and US 70, mainly in Cheatham County, is one example. This linear park offers various cultural and scenic views of the Harpeth River Valley and is noted for canoeing, kayaking, and hiking. It comprises ten sites that are all connected by the river. The major ones are Newson's Mill, Hidden Lake, the Gossett Tract, Mace Bluff, Mound Bottom, and the Narrows of the Harpeth.

Highlights include:

- The Bluff Trail, one of the hiking trails at the Narrows of the Harpeth, leads to a promontory point above the valley where you will see Table Top Rock.
- The Pattison Forge—part of the early iron-making business in the area, powered by the Harpeth River—leads to the back side of the Narrows opening, "where water that drove the mill cascades back from the tunnel into the river via a waterfall" (per the roadside marker).
- Mace Bluff provides views of the Mound Bottom, a large Mississippian Period Indian Mound complex, and is also the site of a petroglyph of a mace. Archaeologists believe the site was important in Native American functions dating from AD 900 to 1300.
- Park rangers offer guided tours on a regular schedule to these sites, October through March. Some of the sites are sensitive.

Contact: (615) 952-2099; www.tnstateparks.com

Kayaking on the Harpeth River

cautious here; you may have to go straight and then do a U-turn to follow the return route on Poplar Creek Road.

Turn right onto Griffith Road at mile 30.0. There will be a significant climb ahead. Turn right at the intersection onto Lewis Road at mile 31.3. At the bottom of this descent, turn left onto Old Harding Pike at mile 32.0. Just ahead, come to a full stop and check for oncoming traffic from both directions at the intersection with TN 100. Turn left onto TN 100 East at mile 32.2. The entrance ramp to the Natchez Trace Parkway is just ahead at mile 32.4. You will have another climb up to the parking lot. Turn right into the parking lot at the 440-mile marker, at mile 34.8; this is the end of the ride.

MILES AND DIRECTIONS

- **0.0** Begin at the 440-mile marker parking lot on the Natchez Trace Parkway; turn left.
- **2.7** Continue (straight) onto TN 100 West toward Fairview.
- **2.9** Turn right onto Old Harding Pike.
- **3.1** Turn right onto Lewis Road.
- **3.7** Turn left onto Griffith Road at the top of the hill.
- **5.1** Turn left onto Poplar Creek Road at the T intersection.
- **7.2** Turn right onto South Harpeth Road at the Y intersection.

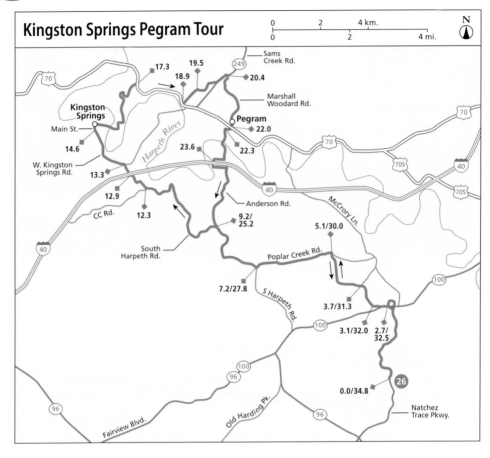

Kingston Springs Pegram Tour

12.3 Turn right onto Luyben Hills Road (unmarked).

12.9 Continue over I-40.

13.3 Turn left onto West Kingston Springs Road.

14.6 Turn right at the Church of Christ onto Main Street.

14.8 Continue straight across the railroad tracks and turn right onto Park Street / Pinnacle Hill Road.

17.3 Turn right onto US 70 (rumble strips) at the T intersection.

18.9 Turn left onto Tanglewood Drive at the Tanglewood subdivision entrance.

19.5 Turn left onto Lone Oak Drive.

20.1 Turn left at the stop sign onto Sams Creek Road / TN 249.

20.4 Turn right onto Marshall Woodard Road.

21.7 Turn left onto Hannah Ford Road.

22.0 Continue across US 70 onto Thompson Road and bear right past the railroad tracks.

22.3 Turn left onto Riverview Drive.

23.6 Continue under I-40; the street name changes to Anderson Road.

25.8 Turn left onto South Harpeth Road (unmarked).

27.8 Turn left onto Poplar Creek Road.

30.0 Turn right onto Griffith Road.

31.3 Turn right onto Lewis Road.

32.0 Turn left onto Old Harding Pike.

32.2 Turn left onto TN 100 East.

32.4 Turn right onto the Natchez Trace Parkway.

34.8 Turn right into the parking lot at mile 440.

RIDE INFORMATION

Local Events/Attractions

Harpeth River State Park: (615) 797-6096; www.tnstateparks.com. This linear park along the Harpeth River is located on Cedar Hill Road. Annual events include a spring wildflower walk in April and the Mound Bottom / Paint Rock Tour in October.

Local Eateries

There are various eating places at the intersection of the route and I-40 at mile 12.9. You may want to check out eating options in Kingston Springs, beginning at mile 14.6. There is a market 0.3 mile west of the route at mile 22.0 on US 70, at the intersection of US 70 and Hannah Ford Road.

The Loveless Cafe (www.lovelesscafe.com) is at the end of the Natchez Trace Parkway. They feature southern cooking with an emphasis on country ham and biscuits. The community of Bellevue is just east of the Natchez Trace Parkway. There are several restaurants and shopping available on TN 100 about 1 mile east of The Trace.

Restrooms

Mile 22.2: There are restrooms at the Pegram City Park.

If you need an adjective to describe it, then bucolic is the one to go with for this ride. It is a bit longer, but experiencing some of the Williamson County country-side will make you forget the distance and just take in the scenery. Williamson County once had forty-four separate communities according to the chamber of commerce. You will ride through three of those communities: Hillsboro, Southall, and Kingfield. For most of them, the only thing remaining of the store, church, post office, and other businesses that used to form the heart of the community is the church.

The ride begins at the Williamson County municipal park across from the Edwin Warner Park office. There are several ball fields there, but the notable activity that has given the park its nickname is flying model airplanes. The Model Airplane Field is at the intersection of Old Hickory Boulevard and Vaughn Road, on the east side, across from the park office.

Start: The ride begins at the entrance at Vaughn Road.

Length: 50 miles, loop ride

Approximate riding time: 3 to 4 hours

Best bike: Road or hybrid bike

Terrain and trail surface: The terrain is rolling. There are a few climbs along the way, but they are usually short. The roads are mainly suburban or rural, and, for the most part, they are well-maintained paved surfaces.

Traffic and hazards: There is not much traffic on the ride. Most of the traffic will be on the short sections of Vaughn Road and TN 100.

Things to see: Bucolic countryside

Maps: DeLorme *Tennessee Atlas & Gazetteer*, page 33, C8

Getting there by car: From Nashville, proceed west. Follow US 70 South / Broadway / West End Avenue / Harding Road through the Belle Meade area. At the Y intersection of US 70 South and TN 100, get in the left lane and follow TN 100 about 3 miles to the major intersection at Old Hickory Boulevard. Turn left at the traffic light and proceed 0.6 mile on Old Hickory Boulevard east, until you get to the first traffic light at Vaughn Road and turn right. Go about 100 yards and turn left into the park entrance. There are several parking lots left and ahead of you to the right. **GPS:** N36 03.151' / W86 53.996'

THE RIDE

The ride route begins at Vaughn Road at the parking lot entrance. Be aware of busy traffic on this section before you go left onto Vaughn Road. But it thins out quickly after you pass the residential developments.

Make a right at the T-intersection onto Sneed Road West at mile 2.0. Just after you cross the Harpeth River, turn left onto Old Natchez Trace at mile 2.5. Just a bit past Temple Road at mile 4.1, you will see the historical marker for the Indian mounds that are believed to date back to AD 900 to 1450. Shortly after, you will bear left at mile 5.6 to continue to follow Old Natchez Trace instead of going up into the subdivision.

After a short climb, you will notice a historical marker for Montpier. This was the home of Nicholas Perkins, who was the owner of a 12,000-acre farm in the area. The house in the distance dates to 1822.

Turn right at the T intersection onto Old Hillsboro Road / TN 46 at mile 6.6. Immediately, turn left onto Del Rio Pike at mile 6.8. You will shortly pass by Meeting of the Waters on the left side. This was the original plantation of the Perkins family. It was their son-in-law Nicholas Perkins who developed Montpier and later inherited and inhabited Meeting of the Waters. Meeting of the Waters was completed in 1807. At mile 8.6, turn right when you encounter the three-way stop to continue on Del Rio Pike.

At the three-way stop at mile 10.2, go straight onto Carlisle Lane. After the sharp curve and short hill, bear left at mile 10.4 to continue on Carlisle Lane. You will cross busy TN 96 at mile 10.8. At this point, the street name is now Old Boyd Mill Pike. Follow it and turn right at mile 11.5, onto Horton Lane. At the T intersection with West Main Street, mile 12.6, turn right. It becomes Carters Creek Pike / TN 246. You will be on this road for about 4 miles. At mile 14.3, you will go through the Southall community; continue straight at the intersection.

Continue on Carters Creek Pike. As you begin a slight climb, turn right onto Carl Road at mile 16.1. You now have about 3 miles of country roads with a couple of short climbs. Turn left at the T intersection with Southall Road at mile 19.2. You may encounter a little more traffic on this section. Turn right at the T intersection with Leiper's Creek Road at mile 20.2. Puckett's Grocery is on your right at mile 20.6, and will have anything you need. There are portable restrooms out back.

Exit Puckett's going in the same direction, then turn right at Old State Highway 96, the first road, at mile 20.7. There will be one climb of note on this section, but the downhill will give it back. Be aware that the downhill section has a couple of curves.

When you intersect TN 96 at mile 34.0, turn right. The view of the bridge on the Natchez Trace Parkway will be your signal that your next turn is coming up. Turn right at the Natchez Trace Parkway access road at mile 36.6. Sorry, but you have to climb up this hill! At the top, turn right onto the Natchez Trace Parkway at mile 37.2. You will now see the ride from the top when you cross the bridge over TN 96. Take the exit at the end of The Trace at mile 42.1 and follow TN 100 toward Nashville. This is a short but busy section. If you need bicycle services, Trace Bikes is nearby. Turn right onto Pasquo Road at mile 42.5. At the 90-degree curve, the road becomes Union Bridge; bear left. Turn

Bike Shops

Cumberland Transit: 2807 West End Ave., Nashville; (615) 321-4069; http://cumberlandtransit.com/cycling/

Gran Fondo: 5133 Harding Rd., Suite A6, Nashville; (615) 354-1090; http://www.granfondocycles.com/

Gran Fondo Trail & Fitness: 5133 Harding Rd., Suite B-1, Nashville; (615) 499-4634; http://www.granfondotrail.com/. (Note: You will drive by both Gran Fondos on the way to the ride.)

Mac's Harpeth Bikes: 1100 Hillsboro Rd., Franklin; (615) 472-1002; www.macsharpethbikes.com

MOAB Franklin: 109 Del Rio Pike, Suite 105, Franklin; (615) 807-2035; http://moabbikes.com/

R.B.'s Cyclery: 3078 Maddux Way, #300, Franklin; (615) 567-6633; www.rbscyclery.com

REI: 261 Franklin Rd., Brentwood; (615) 376-4248; www.rei.com

Sun & Ski: 545 Cool Springs Blvd., Franklin; (615) 628-0289; http://www.sunandski.com

Trace Bikes: 8080B TN 100, Nashville; (615) 646-2485; http://tracebikes.com/

Countryside near Leiper's Fork

right on Temple Road at the traffic light at mile 43.7. This adds a little distance, but eliminates a climb on busy Sneed Road.

When you get to the T intersection, turn left onto Old Natchez Trace at mile 46.1. You are back to the original route. At the T intersection, turn right onto Sneed Road East at mile 47.8. In 0.5 mile, turn left onto Vaughn Road at mile 48.3. At mile 50.4, turn right into the Model Airplane Field parking lot. This is the end of the ride.

MILES AND DIRECTIONS

0.0 Begin at the parking lot entrance of the Model Airplane Field on Vaughn Road; turn left onto Vaughn Road.

2.0 Turn right at the T intersection on Sneed Road West.

2.5 Turn left on Old Natchez Trace.

4.1 Temple Road is on the left.

5.6 Bear left to continue on Old Natchez Trace.

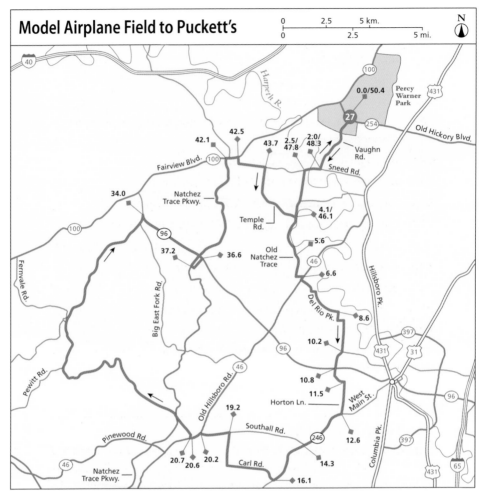

Model Airplane Field to Puckett's

0   2.5   5 km.
0   2.5   5 mi.

N

6.6 Turn right at the T intersection on Old Hillsboro Road / TN 46.

6.8 Turn left at the next road onto Del Rio Pike.

8.6 Turn right at stop sign to continue on Del Rio Pike.

10.2 Continue straight on Carlisle Lane at the three-way intersection.

10.4 Bear left at the sharp curve to continue on Carlisle Lane.

10.8 Cross TN 96; the street name becomes Old Boyd Mill Pike.

11.5 Turn right on Horton Lane.

12.6 Turn right at the T intersection on West Main Street (becomes Carters Creek Pike).

14.3 Continue straight on Carters Creek at the intersection with Southall.

16.1 Turn right on Carl Road.

19.2 Turn left at the T intersection onto Southall Road.

20.2 Turn left at the T intersection onto Old Hillsboro Road / TN 46 / Leiper's Creek Road and follow it into Leiper's Fork.

20.6 Puckett's Grocery is on the right.

20.7 Turn right on Old State Highway 96 (Backbone Ridge) to Fernvale (becomes Old Harding Road).

34.0 Turn right at the T intersection on TN 96.

36.6 Turn right on Natchez Trace Parkway access road.

37.2 Turn right on Natchez Trace Parkway toward Nashville.

42.1 Exit Natchez Trace Parkway onto TN 100 toward Nashville.

42.5 Turn right on Pasquo Road; becomes Union Bridge at the sharp turn.

43.7 Turn right on Temple Road at the traffic light.

46.1 Turn left at the T intersection onto Old Natchez Trace.

47.8 Turn right at the T intersection onto Sneed Road.

48.3 Turn left onto Vaughn Road.

50.4 Turn right into the Model Airplane Field parking lot. This is the end of the ride.

RIDE INFORMATION

Local Events/Attractions

Puckett's Grocery: 4142 Old Hillsboro Road, Franklin; (615) 794-1308; http://www.leipersfork.net/html/events_.html. Puckett's has become a locally well-known establishment for food and entertainment. They have a restaurant that doubles as a music venue on weekend nights.

Natchez Trace Parkway: There are many things to enjoy on The Trace, including biking, hiking, horseback riding, and camping. The National Park Service website is http://www.nps.gov/natr.

Local Eateries

Many country stores in the area have survived since the early days. Most of these are on the route or nearby, and include Puckett's Grocery and Restaurant, Leiper's Fork Market at the Shell station, Country Boy Restaurant, Halfway Market in the Southall community, and Nett's Country Store. More information is available at http://www.visitleipersfork.com/eating.

As you exit The Trace, there are several shops and restaurants. The most famous one is Loveless café (www.lovelesscafe.com).

Restrooms
Mile 0.0: Seasonal and portable restrooms are available in the park near the ball fields.
Mile 20.6: Portable restrooms are located behind Puckett's Grocery.

Three Historic Communities

The Kingfield Community
The noticeable remnant of the Kingfield Community is the Kingfield Seventh Day Adventist Church on Old State Highway 96. David King, who recorded fifty acres in 1846, named the area. His father was a Revolutionary War soldier. A nearby roadside marker noted that the abundant freestone water was available for "the making of whiskey and growing ginseng."

Southall
Southall Community in former times included a country store, a blacksmith shop, Southall School, White's Chapel, and Berea Church of Christ. Berea Church was founded in 1876, and still stands today, along with the Halfway Market, across from the church on Southall Road. Halfway Market is the only surviving store currently in operation in this community. The area is named after James Southall, a fallen hero of the Battle of New Orleans.

Hillsboro and Leiper's Fork
Jesse Benton purchased this community's original land. His widow moved her family to Williamson County in 1801. The name was originally Bentontown, but was renamed to Hillsboro. In 1818 a post office was granted, in part to service traffic on the Natchez Trace Parkway but due to another existing Hillsboro, Tennessee, the post office was named Leiper's Fork from the creek passing through the village. The community had a bank, Bank of Leiper's Fork, organized in 1911. The local blacksmith shop is now the site of Puckett's Market and Restaurant. In 1998 the village was placed on the National Register of Historic Places.

The Arrington community was formerly known as Petersburg. However, when the post office was established in the early nineteenth century, it was determined that Petersburg already existed in neighboring Bedford County. Thus, the Arrington community came to be at its current location. Its central site was always near the intersection of Wilson Pike / TN 252 and TN 96 / Murfreesboro Road. This is at mile 5.7 on the ride. The building at this intersection was the site of the Arrington post office, beginning in 1939 when it was housed in one corner of Paschall's Store. This building is now an antiques shop.

Edwin Paschall was an early settler in the Arrington community in the 1830s. His son, Dr. D. H. Paschall, one of the county's early physicians, served his practice on horseback from Nolensville to College Grove and Franklin. He was also the community's first postmaster. The post office was housed in one corner of his office. Ultimately three successive generations of the Paschall family would serve as postmaster, until Hill Paschall retired in 1971. The Arrington post office is now located on TN 96 / Murfreesboro Road, just before the turn onto Cox Road.

More recently, Arrington has become known as the home of Arrington Vineyards at mile 8.0 on the ride. Due to availability of parking, the ride begins at Trinity Park, also known as Cecil Lewis Park, at 3680 North Chapel Road in Franklin.

Start: The ride begins at the entrance to Trinity Park at North Chapel Road.

Length: 44 miles, loop ride

Approximate riding time: 3 to 4 hours

Best bike: Hybrid or road bike

Terrain and trail surface: The terrain is relatively flat for Williamson County. There are no significant climbs on the ride. The roads are all paved; some are urban thoroughfares, but most are rural roads.

Traffic and hazards: Generally, most roads on this ride are quiet. During rush hour there will be traffic on TN 96 / Murfreesboro Road and North Chapel Road, the first and last 6 miles of the ride. Although the ride on TN 96 / Murfreesboro Road is only 0.1 mile, use great caution when entering this busy road; there is very little shoulder, and the traffic is usually traveling fast compared to bicycle speeds.

This ride has the distinction of going through Williamson County's only one-way railroad underpass at mile 2.1 and 42.3. Be cautious here; slow to a near stop and make sure there is no traffic already in the underpass from the opposite direction.

One other point of caution is Horton Highway / US 31A / US 41A at mile 32.7. First, this road will be busy, as it is a through road in the College Grove community. This is an inverted Y intersection, but only two legs of the traffic stop. Northbound traffic merges from Horton Highway and Shelbyville Road; both stop to allow southbound traffic to access Shelbyville Road. When you stop, make sure to wait for oncoming traffic turning left in front of you; they have the right-of-way, and do not stop.

Things to see: Arrington Vineyards

Maps: DeLorme *Tennessee Atlas & Gazetteer*, page 34, E1

Getting there by car: From Nashville, take I-65 South. From the I-65 South intersection with I-440 West, drive 14.9 miles south toward Huntsville. Take the TN 96 / Murfreesboro exit, exit 65. Turn left on TN 96 / Murfreesboro Road and proceed 3.1 miles to North Chapel Road. Turn left onto North Chapel and go 0.7 mile to Trinity / Cecil Lewis Park. **GPS:** N35 54.06' / W86 46.19'

THE RIDE

The ride begins at the intersection of the Trinity Park entrance and North Chapel Road. Turn right onto North Chapel Road. Turn right at the T intersection at mile 1.2 onto Wilson Pike. As the road parallels ever closer to the adjacent railroad bed, it will seem to disappear at mile 2.1. There is just enough room for a car to turn out to the right to allow oncoming traffic from the other side of the one-way railroad underpass to go through. Caution is advised!

There is a sign that you are entering the Arrington community shortly before the next intersection at mile 5.7. There is a left turn lane onto TN 96 / Murfreesboro Road. This is a dogleg; turn right onto Cox Road in about 0.1

mile, at mile 5.8. You will pass the current Arrington post office on your right before the turn. Proceed on Cox Road; you will go under I-840 at mile 7.4. Turn left onto Patton Road at mile 7.8. Just ahead, on your right, the entrance to Arrington Vineyards is at mile 8.0. You cannot miss those huge casks! If you go up to the vineyards, proceed with caution. The road that you climb is paved, with some loose gravel.

Exiting from Arrington Vineyards, turn right to continue on Patton Road. At mile 9.9, there is another dogleg. Turn right at the T intersection onto Horton Highway / US 31A / US 41A, and then, in 0.1 mile, turn left onto Patterson Road at mile 10.0. At mile 13.5, turn right beside the Patterson Baptist Church to continue on Patterson Road. At mile 17.3, turn right onto Windrow Road. Just ahead, at mile 17.5, at the inverted Y intersection, go straight to access Snail Shell Cave Road. Turn right at mile 20.0 onto Old Jackson Ridge Road North.

Go through the next intersection where you'll see Bo Jacks Country Market on the right, at mile 21.4. At mile 21.5, turn right to continue on Old Jackson Ridge Road North. At mile 22.3, turn left onto Taylor Road. Watch for traffic from both directions before turning onto Taylor Road. Another dogleg is at mile 24.4; turn left onto North Lane, and then turn right onto Swamp Road, at mile 24.5. The next T intersection is difficult to see, but turn right onto

Bike Shops

Franklin
Mac's Harpeth Bikes: 1100 Hillsboro Rd., Franklin; (615) 472-1002; www.macsharpethbikes.com
MOAB Franklin: 109 Del Rio Pike, Suite 105, Franklin; (615) 807-2035; http://moabbikes.com/
R.B.'s Cyclery: 3078 Maddux Way, #300, Franklin; (615) 567-6633; www.rbscyclery.com
REI: 261 Franklin Rd., Brentwood; (615) 376-4248; www.rei.com
Sun & Ski: 545 Cool Springs Blvd., Franklin; (615) 628-0289; http://www.sunandski.com
Trace Bikes: 8080B TN 100, Nashville; (615) 646-2485; http://tracebikes.com/

Murfreesboro
Murfreesboro Outdoor and Bicycle (MOAB Murfreesboro): 310 North Maple St.; (615) 893-7725; http://moabbikes.com/
Smoopy's Vintage Bicycles: 2042 Lascassas Pike; (615) 410-3928; http://www.smoopysbicycles.com/

Arrington Vineyards entrance

Shoemaker Road at mile 26.4 when you reach the intersection. At the next intersection, turn left onto Rocky Glade Road at mile 27.9.

Turn right onto US 41 Alt at the T intersection at mile 29.1. Turn left onto College Grove Road at mile 29.8. The street name changes to Bellenfant Road. At the T intersection with Horton Highway / US 31A / US 41A, turn right beside the Methodist Church at mile 31.2.

Stop at the intersection at mile 32.7. Watch for oncoming traffic turning left in front of you; they have the right-of-way, and do not stop. There is a market here if you need refreshment.

At mile 33.4, near the bottom of the descent, turn left onto Cox Road. At mile 36.6, you will pass the intersection with Patton Road on the right; the remainder of the route is a retrace. Turn left onto TN 96 / Murfreesboro Road at mile 38.6. Caution is advised; this is a busy intersection. Turn right onto Wilson Pike / TN 252 immediately at mile 38.7. You will encounter the one-way railroad underpass at mile 42.3. Turn left onto North Chapel Road at mile 43.2. Turn left into Trinity / Cecil Lewis Park at mile 44.4. This is the end of the ride.

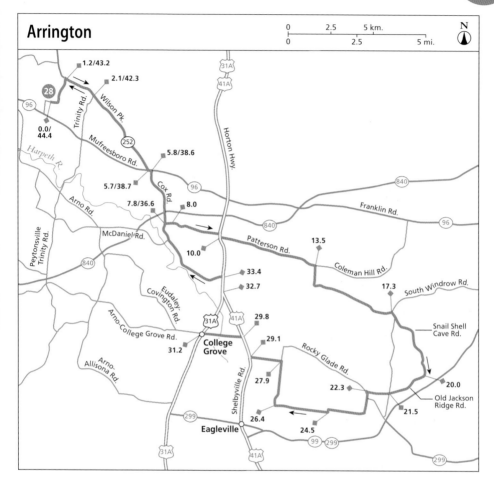

Arrington

0   2.5   5 km.
0   2.5   5 mi.

N

MILES AND DIRECTIONS

0.0 Begin at Trinity Park at the intersection of the park entrance and North Chapel Road. Turn right onto North Chapel Road.

1.2 Turn right onto Wilson Pike / TN 252 at the intersection of North Chapel Road and Wilson Pike.

2.1 Caution is advised at the one-way railroad underpass.

5.7 Turn left onto TN 96 / Murfreesboro Road.

5.8 Turn right onto Cox Road.

7.4 Cross under I-840.

7.8 Turn left onto Patton Road.

8.0   Arrington Vineyards is on the right. Look for the wine casks!

9.9   Turn right onto Horton Highway / US 31A / US 41A. (This is a dogleg.)

10.0   Turn left onto Patterson Road.

13.5   Turn right to continue on Patterson Road just past Patterson Baptist Church.

17.3   Turn right onto Windrow Road.

17.5   Continue straight, to access Snail Shell Cave Road.

20.0   Turn right onto Old Jackson Ridge Road North.

21.4   Bo Jacks Country Market is on the right, just past the intersection.

21.5   Turn right to continue on Old Jackson Ridge Road North.

22.3   Bear left onto Taylor Road at the T intersection.

24.4   Turn left onto North Lane. (This is a dogleg.)

24.5   Turn right onto Swamp Road.

26.4   Turn right onto Shoemaker Road.

27.9   Turn left at the intersection onto Rocky Glade Road.

29.1   Turn right onto US 41 Alt.

29.8   Turn left onto College Grove Road. The street name becomes Bellenfant Road.

31.2   Turn right onto Horton Highway / US 31A / US 41A beside the Methodist Church.

32.7   Stop at this intersection! Oncoming traffic that is turning left does not stop.

33.4   Turn left onto Cox Road.

36.6   Continue on Cox Road. The rest of the ride is a retrace.

38.6   Turn left onto TN 96 / Murfreesboro Road.

38.7   Turn right onto Wilson Pike / TN 252.

42.3   Caution is advised at the one-way railroad underpass.

43.2   Turn left onto North Chapel Road.

44.4   Turn left into Trinity / Cecil Lewis Park. This is the end of the ride.

RIDE INFORMATION

Local Events/Attractions

Arrington Vineyards: (615) 395-0102; http://www.arringtonvineyards.com. This vineyard has been in business since 2007. It is owned by Kix Brooks of the

Arrington Vineyards Picnic Area

Brooks and Dunn duo, Kip Summers, and John Russell. They sell and ship their own locally grown wines, offer tastings, and host a large outdoor picnic area. They will prepare a special "picnic basket" for you in advance, upon request. They also have music events most weekends on the grounds. You can enjoy the vineyards and wine tasting seven days a week.

Local Eateries

Simply Living Life: https://simply-living-life.com/. Affiliated with Arrington Vineyards, this eatery will prepare a special "picnic basket" for you in advance upon request.

Bo Jacks Country Market is at mile 21.4 on the ride.

Downtown Franklin offers a variety of eating places. It is about 6.5 miles from the start of the ride.

Restrooms

Mile 0.0: There are portable restrooms at Cecil Lewis Park.

Mile 8.0: There are restrooms at Arrington Vineyards.

Moran Road

This flat ride can be done on a Saturday morning, with plenty of time left over for lunch. The route, which centers on the Harpeth River, is one you must see for yourself. In summer, the Harpeth River barely justifies the status of a creek, but during the spring rains, it can become quite a raging torrent. For some reason, pioneers were attracted to it. Some of this history remains, and new residents have added to the bucolic character of the area, mostly building the area into estate farms. The fields, grazing horses, and manicured estates contribute to the charm of this ride. It is easy to access from Nashville.

The ride begins at the Williamson County municipal park across from the Edwin Warner Park office. There are several ball fields there, but the notable activity that has given the park its nickname is flying model airplanes. The Model Airplane Field is at the intersection of Old Hickory Boulevard and Vaughn Road on the east side across from the office of Edwin Warner Park.

Start: The ride begins at the park entrance at Vaughn Road.

Length: 20 miles, loop ride

Approximate riding time: Less than 2 hours

Best bike: Hybrid or road bike

Terrain and trail surface: The terrain is relatively flat. There is one very short climb on this ride, but overall, it is very flat. All the roads are paved, but Old Natchez Trace is rough in some places.

Traffic and hazards: There will be traffic on US 431 / Hillsboro Road / TN 106, but there is a bike lane. Vaughn Road will also be busy.

Things to see: Estate farms

Maps: DeLorme *Tennessee Atlas & Gazetteer*, page 33, C8

Getting there by car: From Nashville, proceed west. Follow US 70 South / Broadway / West End Avenue / Harding Road through the Belle Meade area. At the Y intersection of US 70 South and TN 100, get in the left lane and follow TN 100 about 3 miles to the major intersection at Old Hickory Boulevard. Turn left and proceed 0.6 mile on Old Hickory Boulevard east, until you get to the first traffic light at Vaughn Road, where you'll turn right. Go about 100 yards and turn left into the park entrance. There are several parking lots left and ahead of you to the right, around the Model Airplane Field. **GPS:** N36 03.151' / W86 53.996'

THE RIDE

The ride route begins at Vaughn Road at the parking lot entrance to the Model Airplane Field. Be aware of busy traffic on this section before you go left onto Vaughn Road; it thins out quickly after you pass the residential developments. Make a right at the T intersection onto Sneed Road West at mile 2.0. Just after you cross the Harpeth River, turn left onto Old Natchez Trace at mile 2.5. Turn left onto Moran Road at mile 3.6. Moran Road was formerly known as River Road. Just past the Harpeth River Bridge, the house on the right dates to 1815. It originally faced the river, but around 1908, when the first bridge was built over the river, the house was renovated to face the newly routed and renamed Moran Road.

At the T intersection of US 431 / Hillsboro Road / TN 106, turn right onto US 431 / Hillsboro Road / TN 106, at mile 6.1. Although this is a busy road, there is a bike lane. It begins just after you make the turn. There will be a couple of short sections when the road narrows and the bike lane disappears, but there is ample shoulder, and the traffic has a full turn lane to get around you. You will be on this road about 2 miles.

As you make the turn onto US 431 / Hillsboro Road / TN 106, you ride by River Rest condominiums. The clubhouse on the right, about where the bike lane begins, is the first house in the area built by William Leaton in 1802 as a log cabin. The second owner bought the house in 1846 and expanded it to its current appearance.

You will ride past the Dark Horse Saddlery store. This was the original site of a blacksmith shop operated by Dan Campbell. At the traffic light, turn right onto Berrys Chapel Road at mile 8.7. Berry's Chapel Church of Christ is on the corner at this turn. The congregation originally met in the corner of a school. In 1895, Berry Hamilton donated land at the present site for the church to relocate, and it was named after him.

When you get to the top of the short hill, there is a 90-degree curve. The name of the road changes to Cotton Lane here, at mile 9.3. There is no shoulder on this road. Stay to the right side to allow cars to pass you, especially going

Bike Shops

Cumberland Transit: 2807 West End Ave., Nashville; (615) 321-4069; http://cumberlandtransit.com/cycling/

Gran Fondo: 5133 Harding Rd., Suite A6, Nashville; (615) 354-1090; http://www.granfondocycles.com/

Gran Fondo Trail & Fitness: 5133 Harding Rd., Suite B-1, Nashville; (615) 499-4634; http://www.granfondotrail.com/. (**Note:** You will drive by both Gran Fondos on the way to the ride.)

Mac's Harpeth Bikes: 1100 Hillsboro Rd., Franklin; (615) 472-1002; www.macsharpethbikes.com

MOAB Franklin: 109 Del Rio Pike, Suite 105, Franklin; (615) 807-2035; http://moabbikes.com/

R.B.'s Cyclery: 3078 Maddux Way, #300, Franklin; (615) 567-6633; www.rbscyclery.com

REI: 261 Franklin Rd., Brentwood; (615) 376-4248; www.rei.com

Sun & Ski: 545 Cool Springs Blvd., Franklin; (615) 628-0289; http://www.sunandski.com

Trace Bikes: 8080B TN 100, Nashville; (615) 646-2485; http://tracebikes.com/

up the hills. There will be a three-way intersection at the stop sign where Del Rio Pike begins. At this intersection, turn right onto Del Rio Pike at mile 10.8.

At the T intersection, turn right at mile 12.7 onto TN 46 / Old Hillsboro Road. This is the Forrest Home community. Immediately, turn left onto Old Natchez Trace at mile 12.8. For part of this segment, you will be riding parallel to the Harpeth River. The road will be bumpy in places. There are historic signs describing some of the early history of the area: Montpier, Meeting of the Waters, and White Oak Farm.

When the road separates from the Harpeth River, you will pass Moran Road on the right, at the top of a short hill, at mile 15.9. The remainder of the route is a retrace. Turn right onto Sneed Road at the T intersection at mile 17.0. At mile 17.5 turn left onto Vaughn Road. Turn right into the Model Airplane field parking lot at mile 19.5. This is the end of the ride.

MILES AND DIRECTIONS

0.0 Begin at the parking lot entrance of the Model Airplane Field on Vaughn Road; turn left onto Vaughn Road.

2.0 Turn right at the T intersection onto Sneed Road.

2.5 Turn left onto Old Natchez Trace.

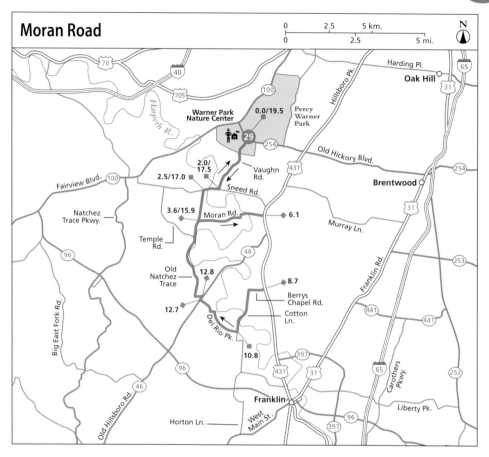

Moran Road

0   2.5   5 km.

0   2.5   5 mi.

N

3.6 Turn left onto Moran Road.

6.1 Turn right at the intersection onto US 431 / Hillsboro Road / TN 106.

8.7 Turn right at the traffic light onto Berrys Chapel Road.

9.3 Street name becomes Cotton Lane at the 90-degree curve.

10.8 At the three-way intersection of Del Rio Pike and Cotton Lane, turn right onto Del Rio Pike.

12.7 At the T intersection of Del Rio Pike and TN 46 South / Old Hillsboro Road, turn right.

12.8 Turn left onto Old Natchez Trace.

15.9 At the top of the hill, Moran Road is on the right. The route is a retrace from here.

Moran Road barn

17.0 Turn right at the T intersection onto Sneed Road.

17.5 Turn left onto Vaughn Road.

19.5 Turn right into the Model Airplane Field parking lot. This is the end of the ride.

RIDE INFORMATION

Local Events/Attractions

You will drive by Percy Warner Park on the way to the ride. One regular event there at the Warner Parks Nature Center is the "Full Moon Pickin' Party." It occurs when there is a full moon, and, unsurprisingly, it centers on music! You can review the schedule by following this link: http://www.nashville.gov/Portals/0/SiteContent/Parks/docs/nature/Warner%20Park%20Nature%20Center/Summer%20Schedule%202013.pdf or just check out Nashville.gov Parks and Recreation site.

Local Eateries

Mile 7.4: There is a wide range of fast-food restaurants and other eateries near the traffic light at Grassland, at the intersection of Battlewood Street and US 431 / Hillsboro Road / TN 106, on both sides of the road.

Restrooms

Mile 0.0 and **19.5:** There are portable and permanent restrooms around the park and ball fields.

Iris City

You can't beat this route if you're looking for a great country-roads ride around west Williamson County at any time of the year. For parts of the ride, you will be in the shade because the tree canopy shades the entire road! From mid-April to June, an added treat is the chance to tour the grounds of Iris City Gardens, a nursery that sells potted iris plants, day lilies, peonies, water lilies, and other perennials. This is all the more special because the Tennessee state flower is the iris. There are short and long options for this ride, but either way, you'll ride by the gardens.

Start: The ride begins in Leiper's Fork at the Hillsboro School on Pinewood Road.

Length: 39 miles (short option, 29 miles), loop

Approximate riding time: 2 to 3 hours

Best bike: Road or hybrid bike

Terrain and trail surface: The terrain is rolling. There are two noteworthy climbs; otherwise, the climbs are not too long or steep. All the roads are paved and rural; some of them even have a yellow centerline.

Traffic and hazards: There is usually some traffic on Leiper's Creek Road. The initial part of the ride on this road is about 1 mile long with a couple of short hills. If you elect to take the short-route return on Pinewood, there is usually traffic, but it is manageable. Once you get to Iris City, it is best to walk your bike around the grounds, because their roads are all gravel and may be difficult to navigate.

Things to see: Many varieties of iris (in season)

Maps: DeLorme *Tennessee Atlas & Gazetteer*, page 33, E7

Getting there by car: The ride begins at the Hillsboro Elementary and Middle School at 5412 Pinewood Road, about 2 miles south of Leiper's Fork. From Nashville, you can follow 21st Avenue South / US 431 / Hillsboro Road / TN 106 south out of town. Then take Old Hillsboro Road / TN 46 to Leiper's Fork. Just past the Leiper's Creek Market / Shell station, turn right on Pinewood Road / TN 46 and then right into Hillsboro School.

Alternatively, from Nashville take Harding Road / US 70 South / TN 1 / Memphis Bristol Highway to TN 100 and follow it to the Natchez Trace Parkway entrance. Take The Trace to the Pinewood Road / TN 46 exit, and then turn right onto Pinewood Road / TN 46 and then left into Hillsboro School. This is a great weekend departure point, but if school is in session, you can always stay on The Trace about 2 more miles and park at the Garrison Creek rest stop; it is only 2.5 miles from the Hillsboro School. **GPS:** N35 53.24' / W87 00.58'

THE RIDE

If you are familiar with the area, the route is a rough circle with I-840 running approximately through the middle. The ride begins at the intersection of the Hillsboro School parking entrance and Pinewood Road / TN 46. Turn left onto Pinewood Road / TN 46 and then turn left onto Leiper's Creek Road at mile 0.2. The next mile is a bit narrow and there is no shoulder, but the locals see a lot of bicycles, so hold your line.

The route follows Leiper's Creek Road through Leiper's Fork; then turn left onto Old State Highway 96 at mile 1.2. There will be one significant climb on the segment, but the descent beginning about mile 6.7 will be worth the trip. The descent takes a slow turn right, then a short left turn, and then a right turn at the bottom. At the bottom of Backbone Ridge, the route follows along the creek.

Bike Shops

Mac's Harpeth Bikes: 1100 Hillsboro Rd., Franklin; (615) 472-1002; www.macsharpeth bikes.com
MOAB Franklin: 109 Del Rio Pike, Suite 105, Franklin; (615) 807-2035; http://moab bikes.com/
R.B.'s Cyclery: 3078 Maddux Way, #300, Franklin; (615) 567-6633; www.rbscyclery .com
REI: 261 Franklin Rd., Brentwood; (615) 376-4248; www.rei.com
Sun & Ski: 545 Cool Springs Blvd., Franklin; (615) 628-0289; http://www.sunandski.com
Trace Bikes: 8080B TN 100, Nashville; (615) 646-2485; http://tracebikes.com/

Entrance to Iris City Gardens

Turn left at the stop sign at mile 9.6 onto Fernvale Road. You will immediately cross a bridge, bearing left onto Caney Fork Road at mile 9.8. You will continue on Caney Fork for about 6 miles. After turning on Deer Ridge you will cross over I-840. When you intersect Pinewood Road you are a few miles west from the starting point.

You will head east on Pinewood Road / TN 46 for a short distance. Only two more turns and Iris City Gardens is on the right at mile 18.7. Even during the off-season, this is an interesting tableau. The interior roads are all gravel, so you may wish to walk your bike, or, at minimum, proceed carefully. As you exit Iris City Gardens, turn right onto Younger Creek Road to continue the route. You will encounter Shoals Branch Road at the next T intersection, at mile 19.4.

At this point, you can choose a shortcut option, with qualification. Pinewood Road is a good road, but there will be more traffic on it than on the long route. However, it is an easier and shorter ride from this point at mile 19.4; it is 9.4 miles back to the start versus 19.7 miles on the long route. If you take the short option, there are three turns to the parking lot. Turn left onto Shoals Branch Road. Proceed 1.4 miles to Pinewood Road and turn right.

Iris City Gardens

Iris City Gardens has been in business for about twenty years, but its history goes back much further. During the 1930s the Nashville Iris Association set a goal to make Nashville famous as "The Iris City." Their influence was substantial in leading the Tennessee legislature to name the iris the state flower in 1933. One of their members, Mr. Williams, was the grandfather of the current owner of Iris City Gardens. He was "an avid hybridizer of tall bearded iris until his death in 1949." In 1993, Macey and Greg McCullough moved four thousand of Mr. Williams' irises to their farm, Iris City Gardens.

Follow Pinewood Road on the relatively easy trek past the I-840 overpass and continue. Turn left into the parking lot at Hillsboro School at mile 28.8. This is the end of ride, shortened by about 10 miles.

Following the long-route option at the T intersection with Shoals Branch Road, turn right onto Shoals Branch Road. There is a nice descent on Shoals Branch Road that has a slow turn to the right. Shortly past this point, at mile 23.6, turn left onto Lick Creek Road; do not cross the bridge. It is a bit confusing here, because you don't want to miss this turn and turn at the second road, about 0.1 mile past the bridge. As you make this left turn, watch for loose gravel in the turn. You will have a short climb ahead, and then the roadbed follows the creek.

You will proceed along the creek; when the road separates from the creek, you will begin the best climb of this ride. You will ascend about 120 feet in 0.6 mile.

After you pass Davis Market, you will turn left on Pinewood Road at the fire station. Hillsboro School is just ahead on the right.

Enjoy Iris City!

MILES AND DIRECTIONS

0.0 Begin at the intersection of Pinewood Road / TN 46 and the school parking lot. Turn left onto Pinewood Road / TN 46.

0.2 Turn left onto Leiper's Creek Road.

1.2 Turn left onto Old State Highway 96.

6.7 Big descent with curves begins here.

9.6 Turn left at the stop sign onto Fernvale Road.

9.8 Bear left onto Caney Fork after crossing the bridge.

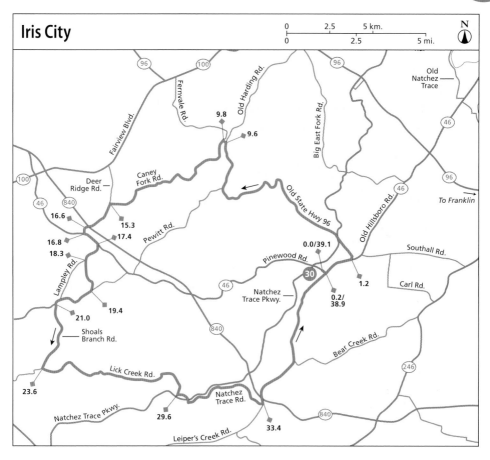

Iris City

15.3 Turn left at the T intersection onto Deer Ridge.

16.6 Deer Ridge becomes Valley Road.

16.8 Turn left at the T intersection onto Pinewood Road / TN 46.

17.4 Turn right onto Lampley Road.

18.3 Bear left at the Y intersection onto Younger Creek Road.

18.7 Iris City is on the right.

19.4 This is the split point for the short option.

The short option is as follows.

19.4 Turn left at the T intersection onto Shoals Branch Road.

20.8 Turn right at the T intersection onto Pinewood Road / TN 46.

28.8 Turn left into the parking lot at Hillsboro School. This is the end of the ride for the short option.

The long option is as follows.

19.4 The long option continues right at the T intersection onto Shoals Branch Road.

21.0 Bear left to continue on Shoals Branch Road.

23.6 Turn left onto Lick Creek Road. Do not cross bridge.

29.6 Turn left at the T intersection onto Natchez Trace Road.

33.4 Turn left at the stop sign onto Leiper's Creek Road.

35.4 Davis Market is on the right.

38.9 Turn left onto Pinewood Road / TN 46.

39.1 Turn right into the Hillsboro School parking lot; this is the end of the ride.

RIDE INFORMATION

Local Events/Attractions

Iris City Gardens: 7675 Younger Creek Rd., Primm Springs; (800) 934-4747; www.iriscitygardens.com. Iris City Gardens is located at mile 18.7 on the ride. This nursery is open to public viewing from approximately mid-April to the end of June. They breed, grow, and ship many varieties of iris everywhere! There is much more information on their website. Even if you are not a gardener, their farm is interesting to view.

Local Eateries

Davis Market is at mile 35.4 in the Boston community.
Leiper's Fork Market is at mile 0.3 on the ride.
Puckett's Grocery is at 4142 Old Hillsboro Road; http://www.leipersfork.net/html/events_.html. They have a restaurant that doubles as a music venue on weekend nights.

Restrooms

There are no public restrooms on the ride.
Mile 18.7: Iris City Gardens has restrooms and water at their offices.

Bowie Nature Park

Bowie Nature Park is a 722-acre nature park in Williamson County, west of Nashville, in Fairview. There are hiking, horseback, and cycling trails throughout the park. Compared to other mountain biking venues in middle Tennessee, this one is relatively easy, and much of the trail is almost dual-track. There are a few hills, but none that are very steep or long. But if you are looking to ride some trails through beautiful woods as a first-time experience, this is the ride. There is a fee for park users who reside in any zip code other than 37062 (Fairview, Tennessee).

The park and all of its trails are very well marked, maintained, and signed. There is even a trash receptacle on one of the trails. There are some trails marked for foot traffic only; horseback trails and cycle trails are shared. There are rules posted as to how cyclists should approach horseback riders. Check out the signs at the restroom building. There are also trail maps available in this same area. Alternatively, you can get one from the website.

Trails are usually closed to cyclists and horseback riders after significant rain. Call Bowie Nature Center at (615) 799-5544, extension 1, to see if trails are open.

Start: The ride begins at the restroom facility adjacent to the bike parking lot.

Length: 5 miles, loop ride. The website identifies 14.5 miles of trails; some are pedestrian-only. There are at least nine different trails, most of which branch from the Perimeter Trail. You can select the ones you like. The Perimeter trail is described in this ride.

Approximate riding time: 1 hour

Best bike: Hybrid or mountain bike

Terrain and trail surface: This is a single-track ride. The trails are generally level to slightly rolling. The surface is maintained in most places with a thin pine-straw layer, except on steeper sections.

Traffic and hazards: The trails are exclusive to pedestrians, horseback riders, and cyclists. The creek crossing may be slick; caution is advised. The trails generally are wide. As with any outside, woodsy area, mosquitoes and poison oak are present.

Things to see: A woodsy park reclaimed from depleted farm land

Maps: DeLorme *Tennessee Atlas & Gazetteer*, page 33, D5. Tennessee Mountain bike map: http://tennesseemountainbike.com/board/trail _maps/fairview-trail-map.jpg

Getting there by car: From Nashville, take I-40 West to the TN 96 exit, exit 182, Fairview/Dickson. There is signage for Bowie Park. Turn right on TN 96 East and go south about 4.5 miles to TN 100 and drive west for 1.3 miles. Alternatively, follow US 70 / Broadway / West End Avenue / Harding Road from Nashville through the Belle Meade area. At the Y intersection of US 70 and TN 100, get in the left lane and follow TN 100 for 18.3 miles. In either case, interstate or secondary roads turn right on Bowie Lake Drive. There is signage. Go straight to the parking, picnic, and restrooms area at the bottom of the hill. There is a sign for bike parking. **GPS:** N35 57.29' / W87 09.34'

Bike Shops

Cumberland Transit: 2807 West End Ave., Nashville; (615) 321-4069; http://cumberlandtransit.com/cycling/
Gran Fondo: 5133 Harding Rd., Suite A6, Nashville; (615) 354-1090; http://www.granfondocycles.com/
Gran Fondo Trail & Fitness: 5133 Harding Rd., Suite B-1, Nashville; (615) 499-4634; http://www.granfondotrail.com/
Mac's Harpeth Bikes: 1100 Hillsboro Rd., Franklin; (615) 472-1002; www.macsharpethbikes.com
MOAB Franklin: 109 Del Rio Pike, Suite 105, Franklin; (615) 807-2035; http://moabbikes.com/
R.B.'s Cyclery: 3078 Maddux Way, #300, Franklin; (615) 567-6633; www.rbscyclery.com
REI: 261 Franklin Rd., Brentwood; (615) 376-4248; www.rei.com
Sun & Ski: 545 Cool Springs Blvd., Franklin; (615) 628-0289; http://www.sunandski.com
Trace Bikes: 8080B TN 100, Nashville; (615) 646-2485; http://tracebikes.com/

Bowie Nature Park entrance

THE RIDE

There are several trails in the park, each one color-coded on the park-provided map. Each one begins and ends at the bike parking lot. There are many combinations of trails you will want to explore on your own.

The Perimeter Trail, red on the park map, is 4.45 miles. Most of the other trails branch off the Perimeter Trail. The Perimeter begins just past the bike parking lot area. This loop will go from west to east. There is a sign directing car traffic to the picnic area. Just past this sign, a trail leads off to the left, adjacent to, but not under, the Tennessee Valley Authority (TVA) power lines. Do not cross the lake to access this trail. There is a trail marker at the edge of the woods, about 50 yards from the start.

This trail generally follows the park boundary. It includes one short climb, a descent, and the creek crossing. The last part of this trail follows the TVA power lines through a field and ends at Shelter #2. Follow the paved road back to the main entrance and turn right to return to the ride start.

Hall Cemetery is on your left at mile 1.8. Private James H. Hall was a veteran of the Confederate Army. You will cross Hickman Creek at mile 3.5. You will reach the paved road at Shelter #2 at mile 4.5. The actual trail per the park website is 4.45 miles to Shelter #2. This is the end of the Perimeter Trail. It is a total of 4.8 miles in a full circle around the park, returning to the bike parking lot. This is the end of the ride.

You can explore all the other trails using the Perimeter Loop Trail. To access the other trails and loops, you will follow the first part of the Perimeter Trail. If you do so, you will see the Dome Road, Dome Loop, Loblolly Loop, and Redbud loop along with some others. Twin Lakes Loop, Sycamore Springs Trail, White Pine Trail, and Bluff Trail are other optional trails.

One advantage of Bowie Park is that you can explore several trails from a single starting point. You can ride for a while and return to the start, then repeat the ride on different trails.

Bowie Nature Park

Bowie Nature Park encompasses more than 700 acres in Williamson County. It is the namesake of Evangeline Bowie. Evangeline, or Van, was born in 1899 and grew up in Nashville. She and her two sisters graduated from medical school during the 1920s and '30s. Only her sister Anna pursued a professional career, practicing medicine at Peabody College. Each sister is honored at the park with a lake in their name: Lake Van, Lake Anna, and Lake Byrd.

Van was charged with finding a suitable place for her younger sister, who suffered from ill health. In 1954, she purchased a 189-acre, worn-out farm in the center of Fairview. Van was noted for her independent thinking, which helped her to develop, with the aid of local experts, a conservation plan to turn the old farm into a usable tree farm. Taking the long view, she terraced the land and slowly planted trees. She ultimately acquired in excess of a thousand acres. Her physician sister and brother financed her ventures. She used some unusual methods along the way, such as paying local schoolchildren to plant trees on her property. Her plan included planting some 500,000 loblolly pine trees!

The old, worn-out farm was transformed into the verdant forest you see today. Van outlived her siblings, and in 1988, she gave 722 acres to the city of Fairview to be used as a nature park. Her eccentricities were legendary—she was an incredible miser, and recycled everything—but her gift to the local community has endeared her to them forever. Van died in 1992.

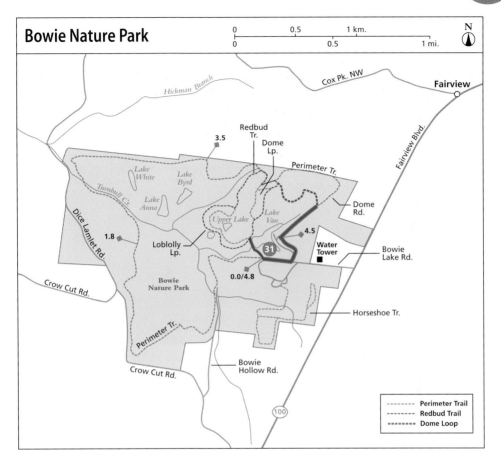

Bowie Nature Park

MILES AND DIRECTIONS

Perimeter Trail (red on the map)

0.0 Begin at the restrooms building. Facing away from this building, turn right, and then bear left onto the Perimeter Trail.

1.8 Hall Cemetery is on the left.

3.5 Cross Hickman Creek.

4.5 Access the paved road at Shelter #2.

4.8 This is the end of the Perimeter Trail ride at the bike parking lot.

Lake Van

RIDE INFORMATION

Local Events/Attractions
Bowie Nature Park: 7211 Bowie Lake Road, Fairview; (615) 799-5544; www
.bowiepark.org. There are a variety of activities at the park, including nature
hikes, kids' classes, and ranger-led educational experiences. The playground
is well-equipped. There is a main picnic area and other places along the trails
with picnic tables.

Local Eateries
There are several local eateries that you will pass in Fairview before the turn
onto Bowie Lake Drive. If you take TN 100 from Nashville, there are several
eateries in Bellevue east of the Natchez Trace Parkway.

Restrooms
Mile 0.0: The restrooms building is in the center of the park services area.
Parking for bikers is adjacent.

Best Bike Rides Nashville

Blazer

The Blazer Ride is a great workout in the middle of Williamson County. It will give you a view of the country around Franklin, east of the Natchez Trace Parkway. For ease of access and location, it begins at the Publix store shopping area at Fieldstone Farms. It passes through two of the old communities in Williamson County: Southall and Bingham. Not much remains today—just a store and church at Southall, and only the critical energy-giving stream at Boyd Mill that once powered the sawmill.

Start: The ride starts at the intersection of Hillsboro Road and Fieldstone Parkway.

Length: 20 miles, loop ride

Approximate riding time: 2 hours or less

Best bike: Road or hybrid bike

Terrain and trail surface: The terrain is definitely rolling. There are not any tough climbs, but there is a regular short hill pattern around this part of Williamson County. The roads are mostly rural. Blazer Road is paved, but a bit rough.

Traffic and hazards: There will be some traffic on Del Rio Pike. There is no shoulder, so ride to the right to allow the car traffic pass. There will also be traffic on Carters Creek Pike, but the shoulder is adequate. As always, watch for debris in the road that may be a problem if you hit it.

Maps: DeLorme *Tennessee Atlas & Gazetteer*, page 33, D8

Getting there by car: From Nashville, head down 21st Avenue South / TN 431 / Hillsboro Road. You are out of the city after you cross Harding Place / Battery Lane. From that point it is about 11 miles to the traffic light at Fieldstone Parkway. Turn left into the parking lot. **GPS:** N35 57.8692833' / W86 53.0046'

Hamilton Place

THE RIDE

The ride mileage counter begins at the intersection of Hillsboro Road and Fieldstone Parkway. Ride beside the bank and head west on Fieldstone Parkway. Turn left onto Cotton Lane at mile 1.0. Stay to the right side of the road to allow cars to pass you, especially going up the hills. There will be a three-way intersection where Del Rio Pike begins at the stop sign, at mile 1.8. You will go straight onto Del Rio Pike. Do you get the feeling that local landowners wanted to "square up" their fields during the early days when the road was surveyed?

At the next three-way intersection, Del Rio Pike goes left, but you will go straight onto Carlisle Lane at mile 3.4. The road will bear right, and you will quickly climb a short hill. Turn left at the top of this grade to continue on Carlisle Lane at mile 3.6. You will cross TN 96 at mile 4.0. Caution is advised, as the traffic is fast on this street.

After you cross TN 96, Carlisle Lane becomes Boyd Mill Pike. At mile 4.7, turn right onto Horton Lane. Follow this to the T intersection and turn right onto West Main Street / TN 246 / Carters Creek Pike at mile 5.8. You can use the shoulder here on the couple of long hills to let car traffic pass. At mile 7.5, bear right at the Southall community onto Southall Road. The Berea Church of Christ is on your right. It was built in 1876 and continues today.

At mile 8.3, turn right onto Blazer Road. The rolling part of the terrain begins in earnest here, and you will begin an ascent as soon as you turn onto Blazer Road. You will stay on Blazer Road up and around the hills and farms until you intersect Boyd Mill Pike at mile 12.0. There is an interesting prominent terrain viewpoint at mile 9.7. At mile 10.6, you will turn right at the intersection with McMillan. If you think the climbs have been difficult, look left just as you make the right turn! Turn right onto Boyd Mill Pike, at mile 12.0.

Follow Boyd Mill Pike through the countryside. At the top of a short climb you pass the Westhaven Golf Club, and at mile 14.1 you will begin a descent; there is a stop sign for Boyd Mill at the bottom of the hill at mile 14.3. It is a little hard to see the oncoming traffic unless you come to a complete stop. You will make a hard left to merge onto TN 96 at mile 14.7, where you will turn right. There is plenty of shoulder here on TN 96. However, you will need to watch traffic and get into the left turn lane at the next street, mile 14.9.

Turn left onto Old Charlotte Pike. The large white Federal-style house on the left at mile 15.6 is known as the Hamilton Place, and dates back to the 1790s. As you make a short climb, there is a T intersection where you have to make a stop at mile 16.4. You will go straight here, but watch for cars from both directions. You are now back on Carlisle Lane. After the descent, the road bears sharply left. There is another three-way intersection at mile 16.6; all directions must stop. You will go straight here to continue onto Del Rio Pike.

Bike Shops

Mac's Harpeth Bikes: 1100 Hillsboro Rd., Franklin; (615) 472-1002; www.macs harpethbikes.com

MOAB Franklin: 109 Del Rio Pike, Suite 105, Franklin; (615) 807-2035; http://moabbikes.com/

R.B.'s Cyclery: 3078 Maddux Way, #300, Franklin; (615) 567-6633; www.rbscyclery.com

REI: 261 Franklin Rd., Brentwood; (615) 376-4248; www.rei.com

Sun & Ski: 545 Cool Springs Blvd., Franklin; (615) 628-0289; http://www.sunandski.com

Trace Bikes: 8080B TN 100, Nashville; (615) 646-2485; http://tracebikes.com/

You are now retracing the route. At mile 18.2, go straight at the stop sign; the street is now Cotton Lane. At mile 19.0 turn right onto Fieldstone Parkway. Go straight across Hillsboro Road at the intersection of Hillsboro Road and Fieldstone Parkway, at mile 20.0; this is the end of the ride. Turn left into the parking lot.

MILES AND DIRECTIONS

0.0   Begin at the intersection of Hillsboro Road and Fieldstone Parkway; head west across Hillsboro Road on Fieldstone Parkway.

1.0   Turn left onto Cotton Lane.

1.8   Continue straight; Cotton Lane becomes Del Rio Pike.

3.4   Continue straight at the three-way intersection onto Carlisle Lane.

3.6   Turn left to continue on Carlisle Lane.

4.0   Cross TN 96; Carlisle Lane becomes Old Boyd Mill Pike.

4.7   Turn right onto Horton Lane.

5.8   Turn right onto West Main Street / TN 246 / Carters Creek Pike.

7.5   Turn right onto Southall Road.

8.3   Turn right onto Blazer Road.

10.6   Turn right at the T intersection with McMillan to continue on Blazer Road.

12.0   Turn right onto Boyd Mill Pike.

14.7   Turn right onto TN 96 and prepare for a left turn at the next intersection.

Boyd's Mill

In 1819, Hendley Stone built a mill on the West Harpeth River. W. A. Boyd purchased the mill from the estate of Stone's son-in-law in 1835. The Boyd family operated the grist- and sawmill until 1900. Power supplied by the river was later supplemented by the addition of a steam engine. Through subsequent owners, it continued to operate until 1922. Then, after its original service, and through years of subsequent owners, it was sold in pieces—except for the foundation stones. In 1988, the Boyd's Mill site was placed on the National Register of Historic Places.

Blazer

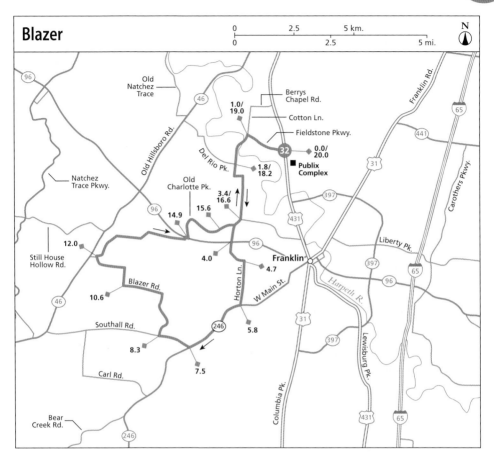

14.9 Turn left onto Old Charlotte Pike.

15.6 Hamilton Place is on your left.

16.4 Go straight onto Carlisle Lane; watch for oncoming traffic.

16.6 Go straight onto Del Rio Pike at the three-way intersection.

18.2 Go straight at the three-way stop onto Cotton Lane.

19.0 Turn right onto Fieldstone Parkway.

20.0 Cross Hillsboro Road. This is the end of the ride.

The Bridge at Bingham

The bridge at Bingham was built in 1874 as a wooden covered bridge. It was replaced in 1930 with an iron structure, which lasted until 1991. A county dump truck filled with gravel and a car both crossing at the same time caused the bridge to collapse. While the new concrete structure—just left of the turn at mile 12.0—is stronger and more efficient, it certainly lacks the charm of its predecessors!

RIDE INFORMATION

Local Events/Attractions

Carnton Plantation: 1345 Carnton Ln., Franklin; www.carnton.org. This plantation was built in 1826 by former Nashville mayor Randal McGavock (1768–1843), a protégé of Andrew Jackson. The McGavock family was prominent in early Tennessee history and politics. Carnton was the site of the Battle of Franklin, November 30, 1864. The mansion and garden have been substantially restored, and various Civil War reenactment events are held here. It also supports a variety of children's educational programs. Carnton was listed in the National Register of Historic Places in 1973, and was donated to the Carnton Association in 1977. Things to see and explore include the Confederate Cemetery, the Gardens, Plantation Guided Tours, the Museum Store, and Carter House.

Local Eateries

There are eating places in the Publix strip mall at the beginning of the ride. The Halfway Market is at mile 7.5. Downtown Franklin offers a variety of eating places. The Five Points area is about 3 miles south from the start of the ride.

Restrooms

There are no public restrooms on the ride.

Trace Loop

This is a good workout ride that combines some of the quiet of the Natchez Trace Parkway with local roads and scenery. The northern part of The Trace is rolling, so you can expect some climbs. However, the ride is relatively short, meaning you can get it in after work during daylight saving time.

There is a little of everything on this ride. Although residential development has transformed this area of Williamson County, significant farming still goes on in the area. This ride will go by some of those farms, as well as some residential developments, to avoid some busy highways. The Trace leg is only 6 miles. If you want to add some miles, it is easy to head south down The Trace for half the miles you want to add, then do a turnaround and join the route at mile 9.8. For example, if you ride south down to the Garrison Creek rest stop, you will add about 14 miles to the ride.

Start: The ride begins at the intersection of Hillsboro Road and Fieldstone Parkway.

Length: 25 miles, loop ride

Approximate riding time: About 2 hours

Best bike: Road or hybrid bike

Terrain and trail surface: The terrain is definitely rolling, with some climbing involved. None of the climbs are extremely steep or long, but there will be several of them. All the roads are paved and generally in good condition.

Traffic and hazards: There will be a couple of places to watch for traffic. The 0.5-mile leg on TN 100 will have traffic, and part of it has no shoulder. Continuing at that point, there will be traffic on Pasquo Road and Union Bridge Road, until you get to the turn at Temple Road. There will be a very limited shoulder on this segment. TN 96 has fast traffic, but there is a wide shoulder. In this case, watch for debris on the shoulder.

Things to see: The Natchez Trace and surrounding countryside

Maps: DeLorme *Tennessee Atlas & Gazetteer*, page 33, D8

Getting there by car: From Nashville, head down 21st Avenue South / TN 431 / Hillsboro Road. You are out of the city after you cross Harding Place / Battery Lane. From that point it is about 11 miles to the traffic light at Fieldstone Parkway. Turn left into the parking lot. **GPS:** N35 57.8692833' / W86 53.0046'

THE RIDE

The ride mileage counter begins at the intersection of Hillsboro Road and Fieldstone Parkway. Ride beside the bank and head west on Fieldstone Parkway. Turn left onto Cotton Lane at mile 1.0. Stay to the right side of the road to allow cars to pass you, especially going up the hills. There will be a three-way intersection at the stop sign where Del Rio Pike begins, at mile 1.8. At this intersection, turn right onto Del Rio Pike.

At the T intersection, turn left at mile 3.7 onto TN 46 / Old Hillsboro Road. This is the Forrest Home community. At mile 4.3, the first road, turn right onto Barrel Springs Hollow Road. This will be a cut-through to eliminate some traffic on TN 46 South and TN 96. You will get to warm up your climbing legs just a bit as you make your way through this subdivision. Turn left at the stop sign onto High Point Ridge at mile 5.4. At mile 6.3, bear left to continue on High Point Ridge Road. By this point in the ride you have climbed about 430 feet. Just ahead, at mile 6.5, turn right onto TN 96 West when you get to the T intersection. There is a wide shoulder that is usually very clean.

There is another climbing opportunity ahead, but you can enjoy the downhill. You will see the Natchez Trace Parkway Bridge as you descend. Turn left onto the entrance access ramp at mile 9.2.

Bike Shops

Mac's Harpeth Bikes: 1100 Hillsboro Rd., Franklin; (615) 472-1002; www.macsharpethbikes.com

MOAB Franklin: 109 Del Rio Pike, Suite 105, Franklin; (615) 807-2035; http://moabbikes.com/

R.B.'s Cyclery: 3078 Maddux Way, #300, Franklin; (615) 567-6633; www.rbscyclery.com

REI: 261 Franklin Rd., Brentwood; (615) 376-4248; www.rei.com

Sun & Ski: 545 Cool Springs Blvd., Franklin; (615) 628-0289; http://www.sunandski.com

Trace Bikes: 8080B TN 100, Nashville; (615) 646-2485; http://tracebikes.com/

Double-arch bridge on Natchez Trace Parkway

This official Natchez Trace Parkway entrance has a map shelter on your right if you want to see a bit more information on The Trace. You have another climb ahead for the next 0.5 mile, but it's a gradual one. You will ascend about 230 feet in this next 0.5 mile. Turn right onto The Trace when you get to the top, at mile 9.8. The sign that indicates "Nashville—6 miles" may be confusing, but it just means that it's 6 miles to the end of The Trace.

If you want to get in some more miles, you can turn left and head south; then, turn around and pick up the route at this TN 96 access ramp. Following the route, you will get a great view of the valley you were riding down a bit earlier as you cross the bridge. You may want to stop at Birdsong Hollow at mile 10.6, when you get across the bridge and get a side view of the double-arch bridge architecture and another perspective of the valley.

At about mile 11.0, there is a turnoff to the right; this is a dead-end road, but it gives you a different view of The Trace as it winds through the country-side. When riding The Trace, there is the impression that you are in the middle of nowhere. This is a great illusion, by design. The Trace averages only 939 feet in width for its entire 444 miles. This spot is unusually wide for The Trace. The Trace is the highest altitude you will see on this ride. At about 860 feet, you are on top of this part of the world!

You will enjoy this long descent as you get to the end of The Trace and follow TN 100 to the right to exit, at mile 14.8. The road will narrow, but you have a short ride until you turn right onto Pasquo Road beside the Pasquo Church of Christ at mile 15.2. If you need bicycle services, Trace Bikes is nearby. At the 90-degree curve, the road becomes Union Bridge; bear left at mile 15.5. Turn right on Temple Road at the traffic light at mile 16.3. Temple Hills Golf course will be on your right.

At the T intersection turn right onto Old Natchez Trace at mile 18.8. At mile 20.2, bear left to continue on Old Natchez Trace. You will pass by one of the early homes of the area, Montpier. It dates to 1822, and was once part of a 12,000-acre farm. At the next T intersection, turn right onto TN 46 South / Old Hillsboro Road at mile 21.2. Immediately, turn left onto Del Rio Pike at mile 21.3. This is now exactly a retrace of the route. Another historical estate, Meeting of the Waters, is on your left. It also dates to the early 1800s.

At the T intersection, at mile 23.2, turn left onto Cotton Lane. Turn right onto Fieldstone Parkway at mile 24.0. Go straight across Hillsboro Road at the intersection of Hillsboro Road and Fieldstone Parkway. This is the end of the ride at mile 25.0; turn left into the parking lot.

MILES AND DIRECTIONS

0.0 Begin at the intersection of Hillsboro Road and Fieldstone Parkway; cross Hillsboro Road, heading west on Fieldstone Parkway.

1.0 Turn left onto Cotton Lane.

1.8 At the three-way intersection of Del Rio Pike and Cotton Lane, turn right onto Del Rio Pike.

3.7 At the T intersection of Del Rio Pike and TN 46 South / Old Hillsboro Road, turn left.

4.3 Turn right onto Barrel Springs Hollow Road.

5.4 Turn left onto High Point Ridge Road at the stop sign.

6.3 Bear left to continue on High Point Ridge Road.

6.5 Turn right at the T intersection onto TN 96 West.

9.2 Turn left onto the Natchez Trace Parkway access road.

9.8 Turn right onto the Natchez Trace Parkway.

10.6 Birdsong Hollow is on your left.

11.0 Interesting viewpoint off the dead-end road on the right.

14.8 Exit the Natchez Trace Parkway, turning right onto TN 100 East.

15.2 Turn right onto Pasquo Road beside the church.

15.5 Go left at the intersection/curve; the road changes to Union Bridge Road.

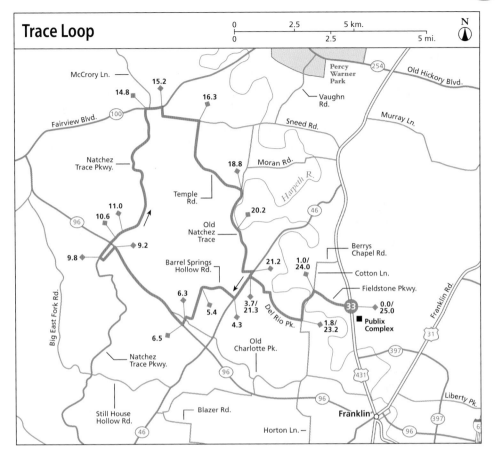

Trace Loop

0   2.5   5 km.

0   2.5   5 mi.

N

16.3 Turn right onto Temple Road at the traffic light.

18.8 Turn right onto Old Natchez Trace at the T intersection.

20.2 Bear left to continue on Old Natchez Trace.

21.2 Turn right onto TN 46 / Old Hillsboro Road at the T intersection.

21.3 Turn left onto Del Rio Pike at the first road.

23.2 Turn left at the three-way intersection onto Cotton Lane.

24.0 Turn right onto Fieldstone Parkway.

25.0 Cross Hillsboro Road; this is the end of ride. Turn left into the parking lot.

Rail fence on the Natchez Trace Parkway

RIDE INFORMATION

Local Events/Attractions

There are many things to enjoy on The Trace, including biking, hiking, horse-back riding, and camping. The National Park Service website is http://www.nps.gov/natr.

Local Eateries

There are places to eat in the shopping area at the Publix center. When you exit the Natchez Trace Parkway at mile 14.8, there is a Shell station and food stop. The most storied eatery near The Trace is Loveless café (www.loveless cafe.com). They feature southern cooking, with an emphasis on country ham and biscuits.

Restrooms

There are no public restrooms on the ride.
Mile 14.8: The Shell station at mile 14.8 has restrooms.

McCrory Lane

The McCrory Lane loop is a great workout in Williamson County. It will give you a view of the county around Franklin, north of the Natchez Trace Parkway. For ease of access and location, it begins at the Publix store shopping area at Fieldstone Farms on US 431 / Hillsboro Road / TN 106, just north of Franklin. This is one of a group of four rides which all depart from the same place (the other three are Trace Loop, Blazer, and Big East Fork). Trace, Blazer, and McCrory are good workout rides and are relatively short, so they work well as an afternoon workout ride.

Start: The ride starts at the intersection of Hillsboro Road and Fieldstone Parkway.

Length: 30 miles, loop ride

Approximate riding time: 2 to 3 hours

Best bike: Road or hybrid bike

Terrain and trail surface: The roads are a mix of urban and rural, with rolling terrain. There are not any tough climbs, but there is a regular short hill pattern around this part of Williamson County. There is a bit of a climb on McCrory Lane as you ascend to Poplar Creek Road.

Traffic and hazards: There will be a couple of places to watch for traffic: first, Pasquo Road and Sneed Road West / Union Bridge Road, after you turn at Temple Road; and second, the 0.5-mile leg on TN 100. There is no shoulder on part of the latter section. TN 96 has fast traffic, but there is a wide shoulder; it's usually clean, but watch for debris.

Maps: DeLorme *Tennessee Atlas & Gazetteer*, page 33, D8

Getting there by car: From Nashville, head down 21st Avenue South / TN 431 / Hillsboro Road. You are out of the city after you cross Harding Place/Battery Lane. From that point it is about 11 miles to the traffic light at Fieldstone Parkway. Turn left into the parking lot. **GPS:** N35 57.8692833' / W86 53.0046'

Alpacas

THE RIDE

The ride mileage counter begins at the intersection of Hillsboro Road and Fieldstone Parkway. Ride beside the bank and head west on Fieldstone Parkway. Turn left onto Cotton Lane at mile 1.0. Stay to the right side of the road to allow cars to pass you, especially going up the hills. There will be a three-way intersection at the stop sign where Del Rio Pike begins, at mile 1.8. At this intersection, turn right onto Del Rio Pike.

At the T intersection, turn right at mile 3.7 onto TN 46 / Old Hillsboro Road. This is the Forrest Home community. Immediately, turn left onto Old Natchez Trace at mile 3.8. For part of this segment, you will be riding parallel to the Harpeth River. Turn left onto Temple Road at mile 6.3. Proceed through this mixed farm and residential area. You will pass the Temple Hills Golf Course on your left. At the traffic light, turn left onto Sneed Road West, at mile 8.7. There will not be a shoulder on this short segment. Keep to the right and let the cars pass as they wish. When you make the 90-degree turn right, the road becomes Pasquo Road at mile 9.6. Turn left at the stop sign onto TN 100 at mile 9.8. There is not much shoulder here, either, and the speed bumps are challenging. If you need bike services, Trace Bikes is a right turn onto TN 100 and about 1 mile east.

There is a Shell station and market at mile 10.1. Turn right at the traffic light immediately past the Shell station at mile 10.2, onto McCrory Lane. There may be some traffic on this leg depending on time of day. You will have a climb of about 250 feet until you get to the four-way intersection with Poplar Creek Road. Turn left onto Poplar Creek Road at mile 11.8. You will enjoy the downhill. This segment remains a farming area.

You will stay on Poplar Creek Road nearly 6 miles until the T intersection. Turn right onto TN 100 at mile 17.1. You may use the shoulder outside the speed bumps, but be aware of any hazards and be prepared to get back into the traffic lane if necessary. This will be a short section. Turn left onto Old Harding Pike at mile 17.7, just past the bridge. This is a shortcut to avoid some traffic. Turn left onto TN 96 East at the T intersection at mile 18.4. The shoulder is wide and usually clear of debris. You will have a bit more than 5 miles on this road. You will pass by the Natchez Trace Parkway access. There will be a bit of a climb here, but you will get it back!

Bike Shops

Mac's Harpeth Bikes: 1100 Hillsboro Rd., Franklin; (615) 472-1002; www.macsharpethbikes.com

MOAB Franklin: 109 Del Rio Pike, Suite 105, Franklin; (615) 807-2035; http://moabbikes.com/

R.B.'s Cyclery: 3078 Maddux Way, #300, Franklin; (615) 567-6633; www.rbscyclery.com

REI: 261 Franklin Rd., Brentwood; (615) 376-4248; www.rei.com

Sun & Ski: 545 Cool Springs Blvd., Franklin; (615) 628-0289; http://www.sunandski.com

Trace Bikes: 8080B TN 100, Nashville; (615) 646-2485; http://tracebikes.com/

Turn left onto High Point Ridge Road at mile 23.9. This is a neighborhood cut-through to avoid some traffic. Just after the turn, you will bear right to continue on High Point Ridge Road. The rolling terrain will provide you with an opportunity to exercise your climbing legs! Turn right at the stop sign onto Barrel Springs Hollow Road at mile 25.0. Proceed to the next T intersection and turn left onto Old Hillsboro Road / TN 46 at mile 26.1. As you can see, horse farms are popular in this area. Turn right at mile 26.7 onto Del Rio Pike. At this point, the ride is a retrace.

Turn left at the three-way intersection onto Cotton Lane at mile 28.6. Turn right onto Fieldstone Parkway at mile 29.4. Cross US 431 / Hillsboro Road / TN 106 at mile 30.4. This is the end of the ride. Turn left into the parking lot.

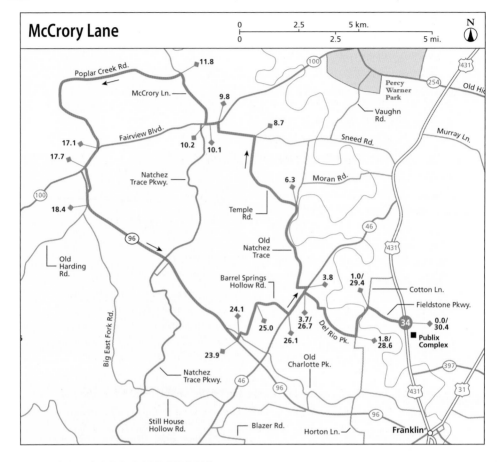

McCrory Lane

MILES AND DIRECTIONS

0.0 Begin the ride at the intersection of Hillsboro Road and Fieldstone Parkway; cross Hillsboro Road heading west on Fieldstone Parkway.

1.0 Turn left onto Cotton Lane.

1.8 At the three-way intersection of Del Rio Pike and Cotton Lane, turn right onto Del Rio Pike.

3.7 At the T intersection of Del Rio Pike and TN 46 South / Old Hillsboro Road, turn right.

3.8 Turn left onto Old Natchez Trace.

6.3 Turn left onto Temple Road.

8.7 At the traffic light, turn left onto Sneed Road West at the intersection of Sneed Road West and Temple Road.

9.6   Having just made a 90-degree curve, the road changes to Pasquo Road.

9.8   At the T intersection of TN 100 West and Pasquo Road, turn left onto TN 100.

10.1   Shell Market is on the right.

10.2   At the traffic light before The Trace, turn right onto McCrory Lane.

11.8   At the stop sign, turn left onto Poplar Creek Road.

17.1   Turn right onto TN 100 West.

17.7   Turn left onto Old Harding Pike.

18.4   Turn left at the T intersection onto TN 96 East.

23.9   Turn left onto High Point Ridge Road.

25.0   Turn right onto Barrel Springs Hollow Road.

26.1   Turn left at the T intersection onto TN 46 South / Old Hillsboro Road.

26.7   Turn right onto Del Rio Pike.

28.6   Turn left at the three-way intersection onto Cotton Lane.

29.4   Turn right onto Fieldstone Parkway.

30.4   This is the end of the ride; as you cross US 431 / Hillsboro Road / TN 106, turn left into the parking lot.

RIDE INFORMATION

Local Events/Attractions

Carter House: 1140 Columbia Ave., Franklin; http://www.battleoffranklintrust.org/carterhouse_history.htm. Carter House played a very important role in the Second Battle of Franklin (November 30, 1864). Prior to the fight, the house was taken over as the headquarters of the 23rd Army Corps commanded by Brigadier General Jacob D. Cox. Today, the house is owned as a historic site by the State of Tennessee. Carnton Plantation is a related Civil War battle site in Franklin. Guided tours are conducted daily. Various reenactments describe the Carter family's role in this battle.

Local Eateries

There are eating places in the Publix strip mall at the beginning of the ride. The Shell station and grocery is at mile 10.1. The most storied eatery near The Trace is Loveless Cafe (www.lovelesscafe.com). They feature southern cooking, with an emphasis on country ham and biscuits. Downtown Franklin offers a variety of eating places. The Five Points area is about 3 miles south from the start of the ride.

Restrooms

There are no public restrooms on the ride.
Mile 10.1: The Shell station and grocery has restrooms.

Big East Fork

Big East Fork is one of those Williamson County rural rides you have to experience yourself. It is not without effort—there is one significant climb and one honorable mention. But once you get over Backbone Ridge (the significant climb), the view down the valley on the other side is fantastic. This is another ride that circles from the Publix shopping area at Fieldstone Farms (see also Blazer, McCrory Lane, Trace Loop).

The route goes out Cotton Lane and Del Rio Pike, then onto Carlisle and Old Charlotte. It goes out Boyd Mill Pike to Old Hillsboro Road / TN 46, then turns onto Waddell Hollow. It makes a circle around Still House Hollow Road and TN 96, then back on Waddell Hollow, returning on the same route. This is another of those rides where you quickly get into a rural area. You will find it pleasant without too much traffic. The combination of traditional farms, horse farms, and country estates keeps the scenery varied and interesting.

Start: The ride starts at the intersection of US 431 / Hillsboro Road / TN 106 and Fieldstone Parkway, about 3 miles north of Franklin.

Length: 34 miles, loop ride (18 miles, short option)

Approximate riding time: 2 to 3 hours

Best bike: Road or hybrid bike

Terrain and trail surface: The terrain is very rolling. Backbone Ridge is a major geologic feature in the area, and the ride goes over it. The streets are all well-maintained paved roads.

Traffic and hazards: There will be some traffic on Del Rio Pike. Be sure to stay to the right going up the hills to allow car traffic to pass. There will be some traffic on TN 96, but it has a wide shoulder. You can ride outside the rumble strip on the shoulder.

Things to see: Big East Fork valley

Maps: DeLorme *Tennessee Atlas & Gazetteer*, page 33, D8

Getting there by car: From Nashville, head down 21st Avenue South / TN 431 / Hillsboro Road. You are out of the city after you cross Harding Place / Battery Lane. From that point it is about 11 miles to the traffic light at Fieldstone Parkway. Turn left into the parking lot. **GPS:** N35 57.8692833' / W86 53.0046'

THE RIDE

The ride mileage counter begins at the intersection of Hillsboro Road and Fieldstone Parkway. Ride beside the bank and head west on Fieldstone Parkway. Turn left at the T intersection with Cotton Lane at mile 1.0. Stay to the right side of the road to allow cars to pass you, especially going up the hills. There will be a three-way intersection where Del Rio Pike begins at the stop sign, at mile 1.8. You continue straight on Del Rio Pike.

At the next three-way intersection, Del Rio Pike goes left, but you will go straight onto Carlisle Lane at mile 3.4. The road will bear right and you will quickly climb a short hill. Continue straight at mile 3.6 onto Old Charlotte Pike.

At mile 5.1, turn right at the intersection with TN 96. There is a wide shoulder on TN 96. Watch for a left turn lane from TN 96. Turn left at mile 5.6 onto Stonewater Boulevard. Boyd Mill Pike is the first street you encounter at mile 5.8; turn right. Turn right at the T intersection with Old Hillsboro Road / TN 46 at mile 8.2. Turn left at the second road, Waddell Hollow, at mile 8.9. Turn left onto Still House Hollow Road at the stop sign, at mile 9.3. If you are thinking maybe the road was named for a still, you are correct. There was once a federally licensed distillery located on Still House Hollow Road—the Boyd & Short Distillery was located near the county poorhouse farm.

Bike Shops

Mac's Harpeth Bikes: 1100 Hillsboro Rd., Franklin; (615) 472-1002; www.macsharpethbikes.com
MOAB Franklin: 109 Del Rio Pike, Suite 105, Franklin; (615) 807-2035; http://moabbikes.com/
R.B.'s Cyclery: 3078 Maddux Way, #300, Franklin; (615) 567-6633; www.rbscyclery.com
REI: 261 Franklin Rd., Brentwood; (615) 376-4248; www.rei.com
Sun & Ski: 545 Cool Springs Blvd., Franklin; (615) 628-0289; http://www.sunandski.com
Trace Bikes: 8080B TN 100, Nashville; (615) 646-2485; http://tracebikes.com/

Big East Fork Valley through the pines

The next 15 miles of the ride are a scenic loop that returns to this point. If you would like to shorten the ride, turn around and retrace the ride back to the start for an approximate 18-mile ride. You can join the ride cues at mile 24.8.

Otherwise, continue on Still House Hollow Road. You won't be able to miss Backbone Ridge. Get ready for an approximate 300-foot ascent in about 1.1 miles. Just at the foot of the ridge is a sign for the Williamson County Poorhouse. You will know when you reach the top because there will be a sign that says "Entering Big East Fork Road." Enjoy the downhill! You will get all of that climbing back as you descend!

Shortly after you begin the descent, you will go under the Natchez Trace Parkway at mile 11.2. Follow Big East Fork Road. It runs beside East Fork Creek most of the way until the next turn. At mile 16.7, turn right at the T intersection onto Old Harding Pike. Turn right when you intersect TN 96 at mile 17.0.

You will pass by the Natchez Trace Parkway entrance at mile 19.6. Continue on TN 96. You will start the second climb over Backbone Ridge, but it is much easier this time. When you reach the top of the hill, prepare for the right turn onto Waddell Hollow Road at mile 21.3; otherwise you will miss it.

Continue on Waddell Hollow Road. There is something a bit disconcerting about Barking Dog Lane, but no worries—you only have to pass by it. Once again you'll get all that climbing back as you enjoy the significant descent. You are back to the intersection with Still House Hollow Road at mile 24.8. From here, the return is a retrace of the outbound route.

Turn right at the T intersection onto Old Hillsboro Road / TN 46 at mile 25.2. Then turn left onto Boyd Mill Pike at mile 25.9. When you pass by Westhaven Golf Club, prepare to stop at the stop sign at the bottom of the hill at mile 28.3. Turn left onto Stonewater Boulevard. At the T intersection with TN 96, turn right, at mile 28.5.

Turn left onto Old Charlotte Pike at mile 29.0. Watch for traffic from all directions at the stop sign at mile 30.5. It is difficult to see traffic coming up the hill on Carlisle Lane. Continue straight at the sign. After the descent, the road bears sharply left. There is another three-way intersection at mile 30.8; all directions must stop.

You will go straight here to continue onto Del Rio Pike. At mile 32.3, go straight at the stop sign; the street is now Cotton Lane. At mile 33.1 turn right onto Fieldstone Parkway. Go straight across Hillsboro Road at the intersection of Hillsboro Road and Fieldstone Parkway. This is the end of the ride at mile 34.1; turn left into the parking lot.

MILES AND DIRECTIONS

0.0 Begin at the intersection of Hillsboro Road and Fieldstone Parkway. Cross Hillsboro Road and head west on Fieldstone Parkway.

1.0 Turn left at the T intersection with Cotton Lane.

1.8 Continue straight at the three way intersection at Del Rio Pike.

Williamson County Poorhouse

The sign at about mile 10.0 for the Williamson County Poorhouse describes the second location in the county of an asylum for the poor. The Tennessee legislature had mandated such places in 1826, and Williamson County selected the first location in 1829. But this second site was selected to meet the county's needs for more acreage and a more centralized location in 1843. At that time, Merrit R. Brown sold 513 acres to the county.

This second location was replaced in 1933 with yet another site that was more central and had better farmland. In 1934, the county sold the 396-acre poorhouse farm in Stillhouse Hollow for $4,250.

The final poorhouse farm on Boyd's Mill Road remained in operation until the last remaining resident was moved to a nursing home in 1958, and then it was sold.

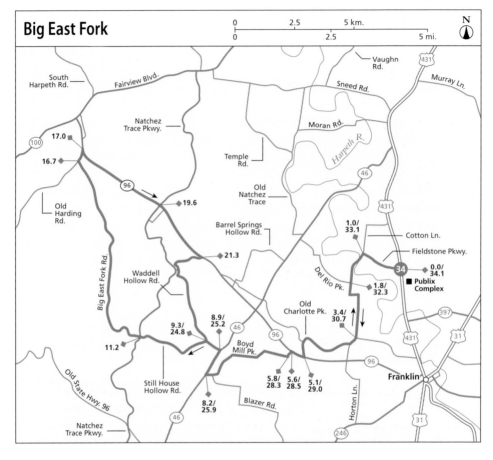

Big East Fork

3.4 Continue straight onto Carlisle Lane at the three-way intersection.

3.6 Continue straight onto Old Charlotte Pike.

5.1 Turn right at the intersection with TN 96.

5.6 Watch for a left turn lane from TN 96. Turn left onto Stonewater Boulevard.

5.8 Turn right on Boyd Mill Pike, the first street.

8.2 Turn right at the T intersection with Old Hillsboro Road / TN 46.

8.9 Turn left onto Waddell Hollow, the second road.

9.3 Turn left onto Still House Hollow Road at the stop sign. This is the short-ride turnaround point. Join the cues at mile 24.8. Short-ride cues are shown in parentheses.

16.7 Turn right at the T intersection with Old Harding Pike.

17.0   Turn right at the intersection with TN 96.

19.6   Pass by, do not turn on, the Natchez Trace Parkway.

21.3   Turn right onto Waddell Hollow Road.

24.8 (9.3)   Continue straight on Waddell Hollow Road at the stop sign.

25.2 (9.7)   Turn right at the T intersection onto Old Hillsboro Road / TN 46.

25.9 (10.4)   Turn left onto Boyd Mill Pike.

28.3 (12.8)   Turn left onto Stonewater Boulevard.

28.5 (13.0)   Turn right onto TN 96.

29.0 (13.5)   Turn left onto Old Charlotte Pike.

30.5 (15.0)   Continue straight on Carlisle Lane at the stop sign.

30.8 (15.3)   Continue straight on Del Rio Pike.

32.3 (16.8)   Continue straight on Cotton Lane.

33.1 (17.6)   Turn right onto Fieldstone Parkway.

34.1 (18.6)   Cross US 431 / Hillsboro Road / TN 106. This is the end of the ride.

RIDE INFORMATION

Local Events/Attractions

Leiper's Fork: Old Hillsboro Road / TN 46, about 5 miles south of the turn at mile 8.2 (and 25.9); http://www.natcheztracetravel.com/natchez-trace-tennessee/leipers-fork-fly-tn.html. Leiper's Fork has long been part of the fabric of Williamson County. There are various things to see and do in the area.

Local Eateries

There are eating places in the Publix strip mall at the beginning of the ride, and downtown Franklin offers a variety of restaurants. The Five Points area is about 3 miles south from the start of the ride.

Restrooms

There are no public restrooms on the ride route.

Bell Buckle

This ride focuses on Bell Buckle and Wartrace, southeast of Nashville. They are both in Tennessee walking horse country. The Tennessee Walking Horse Museum is located in Wartrace. Bell Buckle is the home to the Webb School, a private boarding school.

These communities originated when the railroad was built through the area in the 1850s. In those days, they were staging areas for cattle shipments via rail. As railroad traffic has diminished and roads have improved, these two communities have reinvented themselves as interesting tourist stopovers. Both communities have an old-fashioned store-fronted downtown with interesting shops on the main street, featuring food and local arts and crafts. A particularly intriguing shop in Wartrace is the Dixie Flyer, a model train and toy store.

The ride is flat and has a short option, but it only takes you to Bell Buckle, not Wartrace.

Start: The ride starts at Christiana Elementary School, located at 4701 Shelbyville Pike / US 231 South, Christiana.

Length: 45 miles (short option, 29 miles), loop ride

Approximate riding time: 3 to 4 hours (long option); about 2 ½ hours (short option)

Best bike: Hybrid or road bike

Terrain and trail surface: The terrain is slightly rolling; there are only a few hills. The route is on paved rural roads.

Traffic and hazards: TN 269 is the main road from Christiana to Bell Buckle and Wartrace. There will be some traffic, and there is not much shoulder. Ride on the right and be aware of traffic coming from behind you.

Things to see: Tennessee walking horse country

Maps: DeLorme *Tennessee Atlas & Gazetteer*, page 56, A1

Getting there by car: From Nashville, take I-24 east toward Murfreesboro. From the I-440 East and I-24 East intersection, proceed 28.8 miles and take exit 81, US 231 South / Church Street toward Shelbyville. Follow US 231 South / Church Street 5.6 miles to Christiana Elementary School on Shelbyville Pike / US 231. **GPS:** N35 43.58' / W86 24.41'

THE RIDE

The ride begins from the school parking lot. Exit the parking lot to the back of the school; there is an exit road to the right that leads directly to Parsons Road. Turn left onto Parsons Road at mile 0.1. At mile 1.3 turn right onto Rucker-Christiana Road. Just ahead at the T intersection, turn right to remain on Rucker-Christiana Road at mile 1.4. At the 90-degree turn the road name changes to Lowe-Christiana Road, at mile 1.6. Stay on this road and turn right at the intersection onto Church Street at mile 2.5. At mile 2.9, you will bear left to continue on Main Street. You will pass by Miller Grocery. At the intersection, turn left onto Christiana Road / TN 269 at mile 3.0. Turn right at mile 5.2 to continue on Christiana-Fosterville Road / TN 269/Liberty Pike.

You will continue on this road for about 7 miles until you get to the stop sign for TN 82 in Bell Buckle. There is a slight dogleg in the road as you enter Bell Buckle, but you will continue on Liberty Pike. At the intersection of TN 82, if you are taking the short option, turnaround and retrace the Christiana-Fosterville Road / TN 269 / Liberty Pike route for 3.2 miles until you get to Beechwood Road. Turn right onto Beechwood and rejoin the ride at mile 31.4.

Bike Shops

Murfreesboro Outdoor and Bicycle (MOAB Murfreesboro): 310 North Maple St.; (615) 893-7725; http://moabbikes.com/
Smoopy's Vintage Bicycles: 2042 Lascassas Pike; (615) 410-3928; http://www.smoopysbicycles.com/

If you are doing the long option, turn right at mile 12.9 onto TN 82. There is a slight dogleg here. After you cross the railroad tracks, at mile 13.0, turn left to continue on Fosterville Road / TN 269 / Bell Buckle-Wartrace Road. You will remain on the road for about 6 miles. Just as you enter Wartrace, the Winnette-Ayers Park is on the right at mile 17.8. Turn left at mile 18.1 at the stop sign onto TN 64. Follow TN 64 about 4 miles. Turn left onto Fairfield Road at mile 22.5. Follow Fairfield Road about 4 miles and turn right onto Fosterville Road / TN 269 / Bell Buckle-Wartrace Road at mile 26.7. You will retrace the

Bell Buckle storefronts

route through Bell Buckle. Turn right at mile 28.1, then turn left at mile 28.2 after you cross the tracks.

Turn right onto Beechwood Road at mile 31.4. Just ahead at mile 31.5, bear right to continue on Beechwood Road. At mile 33.6, bear left to continue on Beechwood. At mile 34.5, turn left at the intersection onto Lynch Hill Road. At the T intersection at mile 35.8, turn left onto Christiana Hoovers Gap Road. Bear left at the intersection to continue on Christiana Hoovers Gap Road at mile 38.4. At mile 40.6, turn right onto Lowe-Christiana Road. The street name will change to Miller Johnson Road.

At mile 42.1, turn left to continue on Miller Johnson Road and follow it until you reach the cemetery. Turn right at mile 43.2 onto Rucker-Christiana Road. Turn left onto Parsons Road at mile 43.4. Follow Parsons Road and turn right into the Christiana Elementary School parking lot at mile 44.6. This is the end of the ride at the school at mile 44.7.

MILES AND DIRECTIONS

0.0 Begin at Christiana Middle School. Proceed out the back exit of the school to the right, on the road that leads to Parsons Road.

0.1 Turn left onto Parsons Road.

1.3 Turn right at the T intersection onto Rucker-Christiana Road.

1.4 Turn right at the T intersection to continue on Rucker-Christiana Road.

1.6 The street name becomes Lowe-Christiana Road.

2.5 Turn right at the intersection onto Church Street.

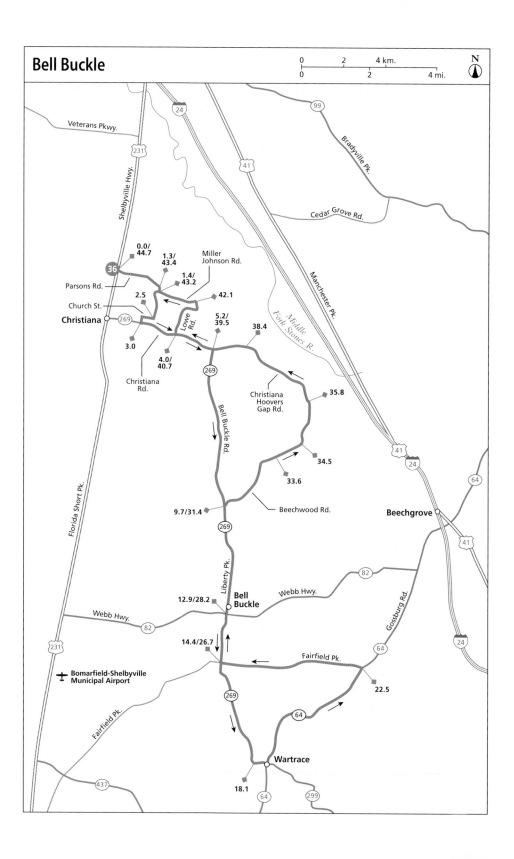

Bell Buckle

0   2   4 km.
0   2   4 mi.

N

Veterans Pkwy.

24

99

231

Bradyville Pk.

41

Cedar Grove Rd.

Shelbyville Hwy.

Manchester Pk.

0.0/
44.7

36

1.3/
43.4

Miller
Johnson Rd.

Parsons Rd.

1.4/
43.2

2.5

42.1

Church St.

Middle
Fork Stones R.

Christiana

269

Lowe
Rd.

5.2/
39.5

38.4

3.0

4.0/
40.7

269

Christiana
Rd.

Christiana
Hoovers
Gap Rd.

35.8

Bell Buckle Rd.

41
24

64

34.5

33.6

Florida Short Pk.

Beechwood Rd.

9.7/31.4

269

Beechgrove

41

82

64

Liberty Pk.

Webb Hwy.

12.9/28.2

Bell
Buckle

Gossburg Rd.

Webb Hwy.

82

14.4/26.7

231

64

24

Bomarfield-Shelbyville
Municipal Airport

Fairfield Pk.

269

22.5

64

Fairfield Pk.

Wartrace

437

18.1

64

299

2.9   Bear left to continue onto Main Street.

3.0   Turn left at the intersection onto Christiana Road / TN 269.

5.2   Turn right onto Christiana-Fosterville Road / TN 269 / Liberty Pike.

9.7   Pass by Beechwood Road on your right.

12.9   This is the turnaround point for the short option. Turn around and retrace the route. When you turn right onto Beechwood Road, you will join the ride at mile 31.4.

The short option mileage is shown in parentheses.

12.9   Turn right at the stop sign onto Bell Buckle Road / TN 82 and cross the railroad tracks for the short dogleg.

13.0   Turn left to continue on Fosterville Road / TN 269 / Bell Buckle-Wartrace Road.

17.8   Winnette-Ayers Park is on the right. You are now in Wartrace.

18.1   Turn left at the stop sign onto TN 64.

22.5   Turn left onto Fairfield Pike.

26.7   Turn right onto Fosterville Road / TN 269 / Bell Buckle-Wartrace Road.

28.1   Turn right onto Bell Buckle Road / TN 82 and cross the railroad tracks.

28.2   Turn left onto Christiana-Fosterville Road / TN 269 / Liberty Pike.

31.4 (16.1)   Turn right onto Beechwood Road.

31.5 (16.2)   Bear right to continue on Beechwood Road.

33.6 (18.3)   Bear left to continue on Beechwood Road.

34.5 (19.2)   Turn left onto Lynch Hill Road.

35.8 (20.5)   Turn left at the T intersection onto Christiana Hoovers Gap Road.

38.4 (23.1)   Bear left at the intersection to continue on Christiana Hoovers Gap Road.

40.6 (25.3)   Turn right onto Christiana-Lowe Road. Street name changes to Miller Johnson Road.

42.1 (26.8)   Turn left to continue onto Miller Johnson Road to the cemetery.

43.2 (27.9)   Turn right onto Rucker-Christiana Road.

43.4 (28.1)   Turn left onto Parsons Road.

44.6 (29.3)   Turn right into Christiana Elementary School parking lot.

44.7 (29.4)   This is the end of the ride.

The Webb School

The Webb School (www.thewebbschool.com) is a private coeducational college preparatory boarding and day school in Bell Buckle. Founded in 1870, it has been called the oldest continuously operating boarding school in the South. Under founder Sawney Webb's leadership, the school has produced more Rhodes Scholars than any other secondary school in the United States. They offer college-preparatory education for grades six through twelve. The school comprises 300 boarding and day students.

The founder stated: "Cultivate in the student a sense of self-reliance by teaching him to think and not merely to accumulate facts—the accumulation of facts being desirable only as furnishing material for thought."

The founder's son and grandson, who founded the Webb School of Knoxville, Tennessee, and the Webb School at Claremont, California, have extended the school's success.

RIDE INFORMATION

Local Events/Attractions

The Bell Buckle Chamber of Commerce (931-389-9663; http://www.bellbuckle chamber.com/) lists seven events through the year. The two major events are the RC Cola and Moon Pie Festival, held in June, and the Webb School Art and Craft Show held in the fall. Locals report that crowds of thousands attend these events.

Local Eateries

You may want to try the Bell Buckle Cafe, 82 Market and Diner, or Trackside Treats and Treasures in Bell Buckle. The Circle 9 Cafe is in Wartrace.

Restrooms

Mile 17.1: There are restrooms at Winnette-Ayers Park in Wartrace.
Mile 18.1: There are portable restrooms at the small park between the street and the railroad.
Mile 18.2: Public restrooms are available behind the Main Street storefront.

Chickasaw Trace

Chickasaw Trace is an 8-mile, single-track mountain bike trail in the Chickasaw Trace Park west of Columbia. The six trails in the park offer a trail for every skill level, all well-marked and -maintained by the Columbia Cycling Club and adopt-a-trail volunteers. There are several well-marked places to exit from a trail.

The pavilion in the parking area has a map of the entire park showing each color-coded trail. This is real single-track riding. There are signs noting the person or group responsible for maintaining each section of the trail. The beginning and end of the trail is plainly marked.

Start: The ride begins beside the pavilion in the parking area.

Length: 8 miles, loop ride

Approximate riding time: 3 hours or less

Best bike: Mountain bike

Terrain and trail surface: This is a single-track ride. Terrain on the ride depends on the trail. The easy and moderate trails are relatively flat. The two advanced trails earn their names with rolling terrain, some climbs, moguls, and tight turns. Except for a few short segments that traverse a field, all the trails are single-track through the woods.

Traffic and hazards: The trails are all through woods and fields. There is only one road crossing near the end of the trail. The two advanced trails are more technical.

Things to see: Very woodsy single-track trail

Maps: DeLorme *Tennessee Atlas & Gazetteer*, page 54, B2. Columbia Cycling map: http://www.columbiacyclingclub.com/mtb_map-2010.pdf

Getting there by car: From Nashville, take I-65 South. From the I-65 South intersection with I-440 West, drive 34.7 miles south toward

Huntsville. Take exit 46; turn right onto TN 412 West / Bear Creek Pike, and proceed for 8.5 miles. Exit right on TN 7 and follow the signs west/north toward Dickson. At the next intersection, turn right to continue on TN 7 north toward Dickson.

Drive 2.9 miles on TN 7 and turn left onto TWC Church Road; there is a sign for Chickasaw Trace Park and the Dump. Go 0.2 mile and turn left onto Mary A. Church Road. In less than 0.1 mile, turn left down a dirt road; there is a sign pointing to mountain bike parking. You will see the Chickasaw Trace pavilion at the bottom of the hill. **GPS:** N35 40.02' / W87 04.55'

THE RIDE

Chickasaw Trace is a single-track mountain bike trail. The six trails vary in difficulty, with one easy, three moderate, and two advanced trails. If you begin at the mountain bike parking area and follow the trails as signed going in a clockwise direction, the difficulty increases for each trail. There are easy-to-spot mile markers on the trail, numbered 1 to 8. (Following the route cue sheet on this ride, these markers consistently registered about 0.3 mile less than the route on this ride.) There are seven well-marked exit points off the trail, with the sign denoting the mileage.

The Creek Trail runs beside Knob Creek. At the beginning, there is an enter sign, just as the trail enters the woods and begins to parallel Knob Creek. At mile 1.2, it intersects the dirt road near the other parking lot. The Duck River is in view. This is the end of the Creek Trail and begins the River Trail.

The River Trail runs generally north, then makes a near 180-degree turn and runs south nearly back to the point where it begins, then generally north and parallel to the other legs. There is an interesting dropout where a bench has been installed with a view of the Duck River. There is a shortcut over to the end of the River Trail at mile 1.6. The 2.0 mile marker is just before the trail turns back to a northerly direction. The River Trail ends at about mile 2.5.

The Ravine Loop begins at mile 2.5. It is not signed, or the sign was missing. It is rated as moderate. This trail completes a loop and ends at mile 3.1.

Bike Shop

The Wheel: 11 Public Sq., Columbia; (931) 381-3225

The Woodland Trail begins at mile 3.1. It is also rated as moderate. At approximately mile 3.5 at the southernmost turn of the Woodland Trail, you

Chickasaw Trace River Trail start

are near the Mary Church Road. There is a water stop here. It is closed in winter. This may be a good exit point for a moderate ride. Approximately, at mile 3.8, there is a shortcut that goes to the Trail of Tears. This trail ends at mile 4.2.

The Trail of Tears begins at mile 4.2. It is a more-technical ride, and rated advanced. At mile 4.7 and 4.8, there is an exit off the Trail of Tears. This can go back to Mary Church Road. There is a trail exit at approximately mile 5.7. There is also a shortcut at mile 5.8. The Trail of Tears ends at approximately mile 6.5.

The Black Hills Trails begins at approximately mile 6.5. It is not signed, or the sign was missing. Although truck traffic is audible on this segment, there is only one place where the dump is visible. The trail is adjacent to JWC Church Road at mile 7.9 and then bears left to loop back to the start. This trail ends at the map pavilion at mile 8.0. This is the end of the ride.

MILES AND DIRECTIONS

0.0 Begin from the Chickasaw Trace pavilion on the trail heading southeast beside Knob Creek.

1.2 The Creek Trail ends at the intersection with the dirt road. The River Trail begins.

1.6 There is a shortcut over to the end of the River Trail.

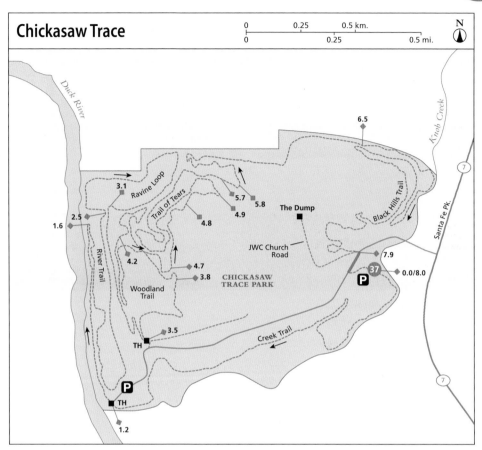

2.5 The River Trail ends. The Ravine Loop begins.

3.1 The Ravine Loop ends. The Woodland Trail begins.

3.5 There is a water stop nearby.

3.8 There is a shortcut to the Trail of Tears here.

4.2 The Woodland Trail ends. The Trail of Tears begins.

4.7 There is an exit off the Trail of Tears here.

5.7 There is a trail exit here.

5.8 There is a trail exit here.

6.5 The Trail of Tears ends. The Black Hills Trail begins.

7.9 There is a view of JWC Church Road here.

8.0 The Black Hills Trail ends at the pavilion. This is the end of the ride.

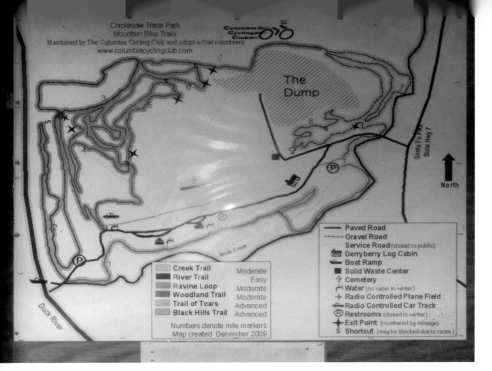

Chickasaw Trace trail map

RIDE INFORMATION

Local Events/Attractions

Columbia: This town has its share of famous citizens, including the eleventh president of the United States, President James K. Polk. President Polk's ancestral home in Columbia is now a museum (http://www.jameskpolk.com/).

Mule Day: Locally, Columbia is most noted for Mule Day (http://www.muleday .com). It began in the 1840s as Breeders Day. Originally a one-day show and auction event, it has evolved into today's four-day celebration of mules, music, arts, crafts, and a flea market, attracting about 200,000 attendees each April.

Local Eateries

There are several eateries when you exit I-65 at exit 46, along with various restaurants in Columbia. At the intersection of US 31 and TN 412, there are eateries north and south on US 31.

Restrooms

The only restroom is located off the trail on Mary Church Road, between the Derryberry Log Cabin and the Duck River. It is closed in winter.

Stones River National Battlefield

The Stones River National Battlefield (SRNB) preserves some of the local history of a key Civil War battle, where the river played a critical role in defining the physical boundaries of the battle. This 570-acre park is maintained by the National Park Service and is located 3 miles northwest of Murfreesboro and 28 miles southeast of Nashville. The park includes the bike trails identified in this ride, which merge into the Stones River Greenway, created by Rutherford County and the City of Murfreesboro.

Fought from December 31, 1862, to January 2, 1863, the Battle of Stones River contributed to the Union's ultimate success in the South. It was the win they needed to get their campaigns moving again and proved that President Lincoln's Emancipation Proclamation of January 1, 1863, was a real step in the process of bringing the nation back together.

One of the interesting sights is the Stones River National Cemetery, a short walk across the street from the visitor center. Approximately 6,100 Union and Confederate dead are interred in the cemetery, most marked by individual headstones. Other key sights in the park detailing the battles of December 31, 1862, and January 2 and 3, 1863, are signed and offer a call-in number to get a narrative for that point.

Start: The ride begins at the Stones River National Battlefield (SRNB) visitor center. The easiest access is to enter the park at 1563 North Thompson Lane, Murfreesboro. The visitor center is located at 3501 Old Nashville Highway, Murfreesboro.

Length: 14 miles (long option) or 9 miles (short option) loop ride

Approximate riding time: 2 hours or less

Best bike: Any bike

Terrain and trail surface: Mostly flat ride on a paved bike path

Traffic and hazards: Part of the ride inside the park is on streets shared with cars. If a bike lane exists, it is well marked on the right side of the street. The bike path exits the park at mile 2.2 and crosses the Old Nashville Highway / West College Street; use caution, as it appears suddenly. There is a short walk at mile 4.1, where signs indicate that no bikes are allowed. Walk your bike on the narrow path up this short hill.

Things to see: Stones River National Battlefield

Maps: DeLorme *Tennessee Atlas & Gazetteer*, page 34, E4. NPS map: http://www.nps.gov/common/commonspot/customcf/apps/maps/showmap.cfm?alphacode=stri&parkname=Stones%20River

Getting there by car: From Nashville, take I-24 East, then take exit 76, Medical Center Parkway. Turn left onto Thompson Lane, then left into the park at the prominent brick facade entrance. Drive through the park to the visitor center, or drive past this entrance and turn left to access the Old Nashville Highway, then turn left into the park at the visitor center. **GPS:** N35 52.50' / W86 26.06'

THE RIDE

The ride begins at the bike trail in front of the visitor center, which has a slightly oblong, circular parking lot in front. Facing away from the visitor center, the paved trail is to the left, running beside the park road. The trail proceeds through a cedar glade, unique to middle Tennessee due to the shallow soil on top of limestone rock formations. These cedar glades provided great cover to the defending Union Army during the battle on December 31, 1863.

At mile 1.1, the sign designating the contributions of the Army of Michigan is displayed. A short walk into the cedar glade gives a realistic feel to the physical barriers both armies had to deal with in this battle. The boys from the Chicago area who had worked in the animal slaughter pens there were heard to say that the human blood ran on the ground here as it had in the slaughterhouses of Chicago—hence, the names given to this little area: "Hog Pen" or "Slaughter Pen." As you leave this area, merge left onto the Park Road.

Bike Shops

Murfreesboro Outdoor and Bicycle (MOAB Murfreesboro): 310 North Maple St., Murfreesboro; (615) 893-7725; http://moabbikes.com/

Smoopy's Vintage Bicycles: 2042 Lascassas Pike, Murfreesboro; (615) 410-3928; http://www.smoopysbicycles.com/

Stones River Michigan marker

Turn right at mile 1.6 onto the "Cotton Field Trail." There is signage for the cotton patch at this turn, also denoted as SRNB Tour Stop 3. Turn right when you intersect the street. Follow the bike lane less than 0.1 mile, then turn left to get back onto the bike trail at mile 1.7. Proceeding on this now-flat, peaceful part of the ride, it's hard to imagine that because of the number of Confederate dead and wounded in this area, it was called "Hell's Half Acre." You will cross the Old Nashville Highway to continue the ride outside the park. Watch for traffic from both directions at this intersection. The Thompson Lane overpass may be confusing, but follow the bike trail; it becomes part of the sidewalk for a short stretch, and then meanders a bit. There is an informative sign about the Stones River Greenway at mile 2.5.

Cross the railroad tracks and follow this trail. As you descend a slight grade, turn left at the trail intersection to go toward McFadden's Farm at mile 2.6. Stop at the river observation point at mile 3.2 and look across the river to the Stones River Country Club clubhouse. This was the site of part of the January 2, 1863, battle. As you reach mile 4.0 there is a sign for a parking lot but continue straight, taking the right fork onto a narrower aggregate concrete sidewalk to reach McFadden's Ford and Farm. Just past the ford there is a sign indicating no bicycles are allowed here. Walk your bike from this point up the short hill to the McFadden's Farm parking lot and monument. This is Tour Stop 6 on the SRNB map. Circle around the parking lot to imagine the way it might have been on the afternoon of January 3, 1863, when 1,800 men were killed or wounded in the space of an hour. Then retrace the route back toward Murfreesboro.

Continue on the Gateway Trail, retracing the route. At mile 6.2 you will intersect the trail that goes back to the park. If you want the shorter 8.8-mile ride, turn right and pick up the route at mile 12.0. Otherwise, as you proceed, there are signs on the trail for the General Bragg Headquarters Site. You will access the boardwalk surface, which will cross the Stones River.

At mile 7.6, take the left fork of the Y intersection to go toward downtown Murfreesboro. You will see signs for the Union depot and fort built on a 200-acre site later in 1863 to house 15,000 troops and supplies for a 65,000-man army. As you cross the railroad tracks at mile 8.5, there is a clear view of the Rutherford County Courthouse. You reach the Cannonsburgh Village at mile 9.1. From this point retrace the route back to the Stones River National Battlefield visitor center.

As you ride onto the boardwalk surface, take a right turn at the Y intersection at mile 10.6 to return to the visitor center. Immediately as you pass the sign to General Bragg Headquarters, turn left at the intersection at mile 12.0 to return to the visitor center. At mile 12.1, cross the railroad tracks, turn right, and continue on the bike trail.

As you retrace the route on the Cotton Field Trail, turn left at mile 12.9 and proceed on the bike lane on the right side. At mile 13.2, at the stop sign and the SRNB Tour Stop 2, turn right and follow the road. There are two places where a separate bike trail runs beside the road—first on the right side, and then on the left side. The road and bike trail lead back to the visitor center. At mile 14.2 you will reach the visitor center; this is the end of the ride.

MILES AND DIRECTIONS

0.0 Go left to begin the bike trail beside the street at the visitor center.

1.1 The Michigan sign denotes one of the key battle areas. Turn left just past this sign and merge onto the street.

1.6 Turn right onto the bike path at the SRNB Tour Stop 3.

1.7 Turn right onto the street and then turn left after about 100 yards, onto the bike trail.

2.5 Cross the railroad tracks and enter the Gateway Trail.

2.6 Turn left to continue on the Gateway Trail.

3.2 The other side of the river from this observation point was a key battle area on January 2, 1863.

4.0 Bear right onto an aggregate concrete sidewalk.

4.6 Turn around at the McFadden Farm and retrace the route. This is SRNB Tour Stop 6.

Stones River National Battlefield

6.2 Continue straight on the Gateway Trail. If you wish to take a shorter route, turn right here and retrace the trail back to the visitor center.

7.6 Take a left turn at the Y intersection on the boardwalk to continue beside the Stones River to downtown Murfreesboro.

8.5 There is a clear view of the Rutherford County Courthouse here.

9.1 Turn around and retrace the route after viewing Cannonsburgh Village.

10.6 Turn right at the Y intersection on the boardwalk to return to the visitor center.

12.0 Turn left to return to the visitor center.

12.1   After crossing the railroad tracks, turn right and continue on the bike trail to return to the visitor center.

12.9   Turn left; follow the bike lane marked on the right side of the street.

13.2   Turn right at SRNB Tour Stop 2 and follow the street and bike trail to return to the visitor center.

14.2   This is the end of the ride at the visitor center.

RIDE INFORMATION

Local Events/Attractions

Cannonsburgh (http://www.murfreesborotn.gov/index.aspx?nid=164) was the earlier name for Murfreesboro. This pioneer town played a significant role in Tennessee history as its capital in the early 1800s. This living history museum depicts life in the village for approximately a century, from the 1830s to the 1930s.

Middle Tennessee State University (http://www.mtsu.edu/) is one of the state's prominent institutions of higher learning, located in Murfreesboro.

Murfreesboro and Rutherford County Greenway: http://www.traillink.com/trail/murfreesboros-stones-river-greenway-system.aspx. This ride only covers part of the greenway. Much more is available and under development.

Oaklands Historic House (http://www.oaklandsmuseum.org/) is one of several sites in the Murfreesboro area that figured prominently in the Civil War. This restored home is open to the public.

Sam Davis Home (http://www.samdavishome.org/) is another historic home located in nearby Smyrna. Several other sites in the area have Civil War significance and detail other Civil War battles. For more information, check out http://www.civilwartraveler.com/WEST/TN/M-Murfreesboro.html.

Stones River National Battlefield (http://www.nps.gov/stri/index.htm) offers various displays, reenactments, and living history events. Interestingly, the park offers a ranger-guided bike tour on Saturday, generally from April through October. Check the website for specific dates and times for this and other events.

Local Eateries

There are various restaurants nearby, including several on Thompson Lane as you leave the park. There are also restaurants in both directions on Old Fort Parkway (TN 96).

Restrooms

Mile 0.0: There are restrooms at the Stones River National Battlefield visitor center.
Mile 9.1: There are restrooms at the Cannonsburgh Village visitor center.

Long Hollow

Sumner County is adjacent to Nashville and Davidson County to the northeast, and offers historic significance and plenty of recreational activities. This ride is a loop in the Goodlettsville and Hendersonville areas that is approximately bisected by TN 174 / Long Hollow Pike. The impoundment of the Cumberland River created by the 1950s construction of Old Hickory Dam has made Hendersonville attractive as a lakeside recreation destination. This area was part of the early settlement of middle Tennessee. Kasper Mansker was one of the early settlers of the area; his home is a tour site at Moss Wright Park in Goodlettsville.

Start: The ride begins at the parking area of the Publix Super Market at Caldwell Square, 460 Long Hollow Pike, in Goodlettsville.

Length: 30 miles, loop ride

Approximate riding time: 2 to 3 hours

Best bike: Road or hybrid bike

Terrain and trail surface: The terrain is a bit rolling in places, but this is generally an easy ride. The route is all paved rural/urban roads.

Traffic and hazards: Most of the traffic will be on TN 174 / Long Hollow Pike, although it is designated as a bike route. The shoulder is wide enough to allow bike riding outside of the rumble strips. All of the other roads do not have shoulders, so be aware of cars passing, especially from behind you.

Maps: DeLorme *Tennessee Atlas & Gazetteer*, page 13, E6

Getting there by car: From Nashville, take I-65 North to the TN 174 / Long Hollow Pike exit, exit 97. Turn right off the ramp and proceed about 0.7 mile to Loretta Drive. Turn left onto Loretta Drive at the traffic light and then make an immediate left into the Caldwell Square shopping area. **GPS:** N36 19.8866333' / W86 41.9380166'

Historic Clark House renovation

THE RIDE

Begin the ride by exiting the Caldwell Square shopping area and turning left onto Loretta Drive. Make a right turn onto Geneva Drive, the first street. Proceed through the subdivision and turn right onto Grace Drive at mile 0.2. Look carefully at the T intersection before making the left turn onto Long Hollow Pike at mile 0.4, because the traffic may be fast. There is an adequate bike lane outside the rumble strips.

Descend the hill and get into the left turn lane when you see the Madison Creek Baptist Church. Turn left onto Madison Creek Road at mile 1.5. Madison Creek Road is a great rural-road ride, well maintained and relatively quiet. The road parallels Madison Creek.

At mile 3.8, turn right onto Hogans Branch Road. At the T intersection, there is a short dogleg. Turn right onto TN 258 / New Hope Road at mile 7.7. Turn left onto Sandy Valley Road at mile 7.9. Proceed on Sandy Valley. At mile 10.1, go straight onto Brinkley Branch at the T intersection with Mount Olivet Road. Proceed on Brinkley Branch and go straight at the next T intersection with Weeping Willow Road at mile 11.0.

At the stop sign, turn left onto Upper Station Camp Creek Road at mile 12.0. At the T intersection, turn right onto Long Hollow Pike at mile 13.8 for a short 0.3 mile. The Station Camp Greenway is on Long Hollow Pike between Upper and Lower Station Camp Creek Roads. You will see the prominent sign on your right. The Clark House is adjacent to the Station Camp Greenway. The first Sumner County Courthouse was built here in 1787. Andrew Jackson appeared in court here. This single-room building has been incorporated within the walls of the present log house.

You will go over Station Camp Creek and turn right at mile 14.1 onto Lower Station Camp Creek Road. There is a store on this corner if you need water or refreshment.

Jenkins Lane is the first road to turn right over Station Camp Creek. Turn right here at mile 15.1. At mile 16.4, turn left at the prominent T intersection onto Anderson Road. Get ready for a short climb. Continue on Anderson Road through several turns and curves. The turn on Jones Lane may be a surprise. At mile 18.1, turn left onto Jones Lane. It is hardly discernible until you get within a few feet of the turn. At mile 19.0, there is a sign directing you to make a right turn to continue on Jones Lane.

At the T intersection, mile 19.8, turn right onto Stop Thirty Road. The road is unmarked. Take care

Bike Shops

Biker's Choice: 709 W. Main St., Hendersonville; (615) 822-2512; http://www.thebikerschoice.com/
Eastside Cycles: 103 South 11th St., Nashville; (615) 469-1079; http://www.eastside-cycles.com/

at the next intersection, Indian Lake Road, because the north-south traffic is not required to stop. You will cross Indian Lake Road at mile 20.5. The next intersection at the traffic light is TN 258 / New Hope Road. Cross TN 258 / New Hope Road at mile 21.7 and turn at the next road. When you turn right onto Goshentown Road at mile 21.8, you can glimpse part of the Hendersonville business district if you look to your left.

You will come to a T intersection with Center Point Road at mile 23.7. Turn right onto Center Point Road. Proceed until you get to the stop sign for Long Hollow Pike. Check carefully for oncoming traffic, because this intersection is on a curve that makes it difficult to see. Turn left onto Long Hollow Pike at mile 25.1. You have an approximate 5-mile return on this bike route.

When you pass Madison Creek Road at mile 28.4, the rest of the route is a retrace. Turn right at the traffic light onto Loretta Drive at mile 29.8, followed by an immediate left into the Caldwell Square shopping center parking lot; this is the end of the ride.

MILES AND DIRECTIONS

0.0   Begin at the intersection of Loretta Drive and the Caldwell Square shopping area. Turn left onto Loretta Drive. Immediately, turn right onto Geneva Drive.

0.2   Turn right onto Grace Drive.

0.4   Turn left onto Long Hollow Pike. Traffic may be fast.

1.5   Turn left onto Madison Creek Road.

3.8   Turn right onto Hogans Branch Road.

7.7   Turn right onto TN 258 South / New Hope Road.

7.9   Turn left onto Sandy Valley Road.

10.1   Continue straight at the T intersection with Mount Olivet Road. The street name is now Brinkley Branch Road.

11.0   Continue straight on Brinkley Branch Road at the intersection with Weeping Willow Road.

12.0   Turn right onto Upper Station Camp Creek Road at the stop sign.

13.8   Turn left onto TN 174 / Long Hollow Pike.

14.1   Turn right onto Lower Station Camp Creek Road. There is a store at this corner.

15.1   Turn right onto Jenkins Lane.

16.4   Turn left onto Anderson Road.

18.1   Turn left onto Jones Lane.

19.0   Turn right to stay on Jones Lane.

19.8   Turn right onto Stop Thirty Road.

20.5   Use caution crossing Indian Lake Road.

21.7   Cross TN 258 / New Hope Road and continue on Old Shackle Island Road.

21.8   Turn right onto Goshentown Road.

23.7   Turn right onto Center Point Road.

25.1   Turn left onto TN 174 West / Long Hollow Pike.

28.4   Pass Madison Creek Road.

29.8   Turn right onto Loretta Drive. Turn left into the Caldwell Square shopping center parking lot. This is the end of the ride.

Long Hollow

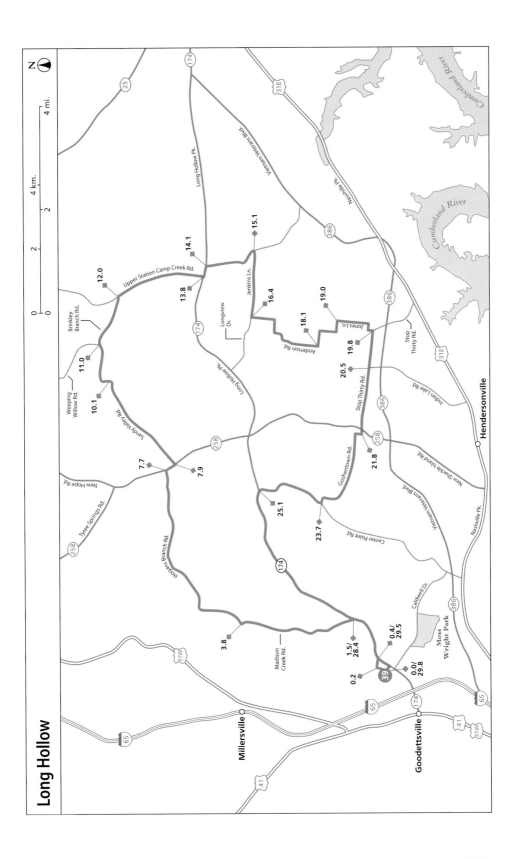

Station Camp Greenway entrance

RIDE INFORMATION

Local Events/Attractions

Moss Wright Park: 745 Caldwell Dr., Goodlettsville; (615) 859-0362; http://www.cityofgoodlettsville.org/index.aspx?nid=147. This municipal park, operated by the City of Goodlettsville, is near the start of the ride. It features baseball, softball, and soccer fields, plus a volleyball court and playground. It is also the home of Historic Mansker's Station, which depicts early Tennessee life from the settlement years of the 1700s. Mansker's Station offers a variety of educational and cultural events each year.

Local Eateries

There are many eateries on Long Hollow Pike around Caldwell Square shopping area. There is also a country store/market at the turn onto Lower Station Camp Creek Road at mile 14.1.

Restrooms

There are no public restrooms on the ride.

Lock 4

Lock 4 is a mountain bike trail with plenty of short hills and rocky segments, located at the end of Lock 4 Road in Gallatin. It is sited on a peninsula of the Cumberland River / Old Hickory Lake. There are four trails marked on the map at the trailhead: green, yellow, orange, and black. The total trail length is 9.6 miles according to the map at the trailhead.

Lock 4 Road is the only road in the area. It separates some of the trails and is the access road to the boat launching area. The trails are marked with the designation "BLT" and a sequential number. The Orange Trail, 5.7 miles, is the intermediate trail. It contains BLT #1 and 4–12. The Yellow Trail, also intermediate, 1.8 miles, is the west side trail. It includes BLT #2, 3, and 4. Lock 4 Road separates the Yellow Trail from the Orange Trail. The Green Trail, 2.1 miles, is the beginner (east side) and time trial course. It includes BLT #14 and 15. On the trail map, trail shortcuts are designated in white.

The Black Trail segments are for advanced riders; for example, such a segment may be marked with a sign depicting an arrow pointing up and the silhouette of a bicycle suddenly pointed down. This means that there is a sudden drop in the trail of about 6 feet. The Black Trail segments are optional!

Start: The ride begins at the parking lot at the trail map shelter.

Length: 7 miles, loop ride (Green Trail, 2 miles; Yellow/Orange Trail, 5 miles)

Approximate riding time: 2 to 3 hours

Best bike: Mountain or hybrid bike

Terrain and trail surface: This is a single-track ride. The terrain is flat in some places and hilly as the trail ascends from the lake. The website calls it more a riding trail than a technical trail. The trail is maintained by the Lock 4 Trailblazers. It is closed when wet.

Traffic and hazards: The trail is a closed mountain bike trail; some segments are converted 4x4 trails. The Black Trails are optional. The ride is on a peninsula formed by Old Hickory Lake, so you won't get lost for very long. It is possible to repeat some segments of the trail if you miss a trail sign.

Things to see: Lots of woods and Old Hickory Lake

Maps: DeLorme *Tennessee Atlas & Gazetteer*, page 13, E8. Nashville Mountain Bike Map: http://www.nashvillemountainbike.com/maps2009/l4map_2005.jpg

Getting there by car: To get to Lock 4, take I-65 North from Nashville. Take Vietnam Veterans Parkway exit, exit 95, and follow Vietnam Veterans Parkway. As you approach Gallatin, take the Highway 109 South exit. Proceed 1.2 miles, then at the traffic light, turn right on Hancock Street, the second exit. Proceed to the T intersection and turn left onto Lock 4 Road. Proceed 3.0 miles. Immediately after you pass Olympic Way, the old silo without a roof marks the parking lot; turn right into the gravel parking lot. There is a small shelter at the trailhead where the trail map is displayed (all references to a map in this ride refer to this trail map). A copy of it is available online at http://www.nashvillemountainbike.com/maps2009/l4map_2005.jpg. There is an option to download a copy. **GPS:** N36 19.982' / W86 28.16'

THE RIDE

The trailhead departs from the parking lot and begins with the Orange Trail. After about 50 feet, an arrow directs you straight for Orange or left for the Green Trail. This ride is divided into two parts: the Green, and the combined Orange and Yellow. It is a bit short of the total 9.6 miles on the map.

The first part of the ride is the Green Trail segment, which actually begins about 50 feet into the woods, on the Orange Trail. Turn left to take the Green Trail. At the end of this segment, you will return to the trailhead.

The shortcuts are not as obvious on the trail as on the map, where they are designated in white. The first shortcut is at 0.2 mile. Make a right turn here to stay on the Green Trail. There is an interesting viewpoint at about 0.5 mile

Bike Shop

Biker's Choice: 709 W. Main St., Hendersonville; (615) 822-2512; http://www.thebikerschoice.com/

as the Cumberland River / Old Hickory Lake comes into view. There is a duck blind here.

At 0.8 mile proceed straight on the trail. This is the other side of the shortcut you encountered at 0.2 mile. At mile 1.0 proceed straight to remain on the trail.

BLT #15 is at mile 1.3. BLT #16 is at mile 1.5. The trailhead and end of the Green Trail is at mile 2.0. This is a chance to take a break if you like. The mile marker readings will continue from mile 2.0 for the next segment.

Old grain bin at Lock 4 trailhead

At this point, you can turn around and take the Orange Trail as previously noted. This time, bear right to stay on the Orange Trail. The Orange Trail is a bit easier to follow. This part of the ride follows the Orange Trail, then crosses Lock 4 Road where it becomes the Yellow Trail at mile 2.6. The trail crosses at an angle, so bear right as you cross the road.

There are four places where you either cross or ride adjacent to Lock 4 Road / Olympic Way. If you have a mechanical problem or need to terminate the ride, it is a short walk to the parking lot. You will ride adjacent to Lock 4 Road at mile 3.1. As you approach mile 3.5, there is a shortcut. Stay straight to remain on the trail. A bit farther along, at mile 3.5, take a left at the Y intersection. This is a segment of the Black Trail, but it is not part of this ride. You will ride adjacent to Lock 4 Road again at mile 3.8.

You will encounter the other side of that shortcut at mile 4.0. Stay straight to remain on the trail. There is a great viewpoint as the trail goes down to the lake at mile 4.5. It is just a little farther to the Lock 4 Road intersection. When you cross Lock 4 Road at mile 4.5, you are reentering the Orange Trail. This was once used for 4-wheel drive trails as you can see at mile 4.8.

From this point, follow the trail. The BLT #7 sign is at mile 5.5. BLT #10 is at mile 6.6. You will encounter BLT #11 at mile 6.9, and BLT #12 at mile 7.2. You will intersect the Green Trail at mile 7.2. Follow the trail to the end of the ride, at mile 7.3.

MILES AND DIRECTIONS

0.0 Begin at the parking lot under the trail map shelter.

0.0 Turn right onto the Green Trail in 42 feet.

0.2 Bear right to remain on the trail.

0.5 This is a great viewpoint as the trail drops down to Old Hickory Lake.

0.8 Continue straight to remain on the trail.

1.0 Continue straight to remain on the trail.

1.3 Pass the BLT #15 sign.

2.0 This is the end of the Green Trail as you return to the parking lot. Turn around and take the Orange Trail.

2.6 Cross Lock 4 Road / Olympic Way and enter the Yellow Trail on the other side of the road.

3.1 Ride adjacent to Lock 4 Road / Olympic Way.

3.5 Continue straight to remain on the trail. Turn left at the Y intersection.

3.8 Ride adjacent to Lock 4 Road / Olympic Way again.

4.0 Continue straight to remain on the trail.

4.5 This is a great viewpoint as the trail opens beside Old Hickory Lake. Cross Lock 4 Road / Olympic Way and reenter the Orange Trial.

4.8 Cross the old 4-wheel drive trail.

5.5 Pass the BLT #7 sign.

6.6 Pass the BLT #10 sign.

6.9 Pass the BLT #11 sign.

7.2 Pass the BLT #12 sign. This is the intersection with the Green Trail.

7.3 Proceed to the parking lot. This is the end of the ride.

The Origins of Old Hickory Lake

Andrew Jackson (March 15, 1767–June 8, 1845) was the seventh president of the United States. Originally from North Carolina, he settled in the middle section of Tennessee near Nashville and built the Hermitage. The Hermitage is preserved today and open as a historic site. Jackson was famous for his battles against the British, especially the Battle of New Orleans in 1815. Although he championed a broad democratic base during his presidency, and supported states' rights, his stands on slavery, Indian removal, and the national bank were unpopular. Jackson's supporters and detractors nicknamed him Old Hickory.

He is the namesake of the Old Hickory Lock and Dam, which was constructed in 1952–54. The backwater created by the impoundment of the Cumberland River near Nashville was named Old Hickory Lake.

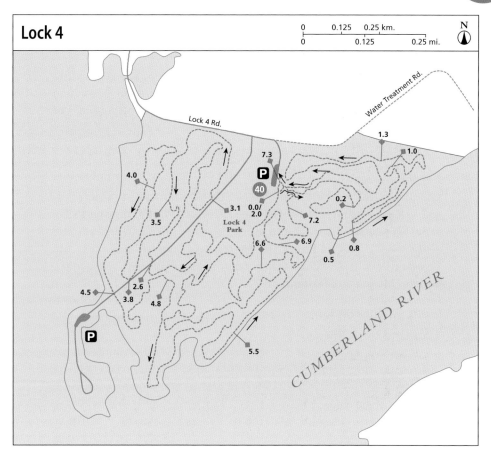

RIDE INFORMATION

Local Events/Attractions

Castalian Springs: 210 Old Highway 25, Castalian Springs; (615) 452-5463; http://www.bledsoeslick.com/wynnewood.htm. This is one of the many interesting historical places to visit in the Gallatin area. This State of Tennessee–owned historic site is located about 7 miles east of Gallatin on Highway 25, a historical corridor. Castalian Springs is the site of an old settlement, part of which is now preserved at Wynnewood, a log house built in 1828. Tours are available, along with historic reenactments.

Cragfont: 200 Cragfont Rd., Castalian Springs; (615) 452-7070; http://www.historiccragfont.org/Historic_Cragfont/Welcome.html. This is another historic house in the area, whose construction actually began in 1798!

Gallatin Museum: 183 West Main St., Gallatin; (615) 452-5648; http://www
.rootsweb.ancestry.com/~tnc13udc/. This museum houses many historic doc-
uments. Trousdale Place, the museum site, is located at the corner of Bledsoe
Street and West Main Street.

Rock Castle: 139 Rock Castle Ln., Hendersonville; (615) 824-0502; http://
www.historicrockcastle.com/. General Daniel Smith, surveyor, Revolutionary War hero, US senator, Indian negotiator, and original owner built this
eighteenth-century home, beginning in 1784. Various eighteenth-century
activities are featured.

Local Eateries

Cherokee Steak House & Marina: 450 Cherokee Dock Rd., Lebanon; (615)
452-1515. To reach this marina, follow Peach Valley Road to the intersection
with Highway 109 South. Turn right on Highway 109 South and go south
across the Cumberland River / Old Hickory Lake. Turn left at the first road,
Cherokee Dock Road, and proceed about 1 mile until you reach the marina.

Gallatin Marina and Restaurant: 727 Marina Rd., Gallatin; (615) 452-9876;
http://www.gallatinmarina.com/restaurant.php. This is the nearest place to
eat from the trail, about 1 mile back on Lock 4 Road at the intersection of Lock
4 Road and Peach Valley Road.

If marinas are not your choice, take Lock 4 Road about 4 miles to the
intersection with Highway 31 East / Gallatin Road / Nashville Pike. Turn left
onto Nashville Pike. There are a variety of eateries and shopping options on
both sides of the road.

Restrooms

There are portable restrooms on Lock 4 Road near Old Hickory Lake. When
you cross or ride adjacent to Lock 4 Road at **miles 2.6, 3.1, 3.8,** or **4.5,** you can
get onto Lock 4 Road and go southwest toward Old Hickory Lake for approximately 0.5 mile.

Appendix A: Bicycling Resources

This list emphasizes venues local to Nashville and middle Tennessee.

Two helpful mountain biking sites identify local and Tennessee mountain bike trails, maps, trail conditions, and much more:
www.nashvillemountainbike.com
http://tennesseemountainbike.com/

These four sites emphasize biking trails, information, and events specific to the Nashville community, including maps, lists of upcoming events where you can meet other cyclists, information on local bike programs for youth, news, and information on local and state laws:
http://www.greenwaysfornashville.org/
http://www.nashville.gov/Parks-and-Recreation.aspx
http://mpw.nashville.gov/IMS/BikeWays/default.aspx
http://www.walkbikenashville.org/

This Tennessee Department of Transportation site has information about biking across the state of Tennessee:
http://www.tdot.state.tn.us/bikeped/

The Tennessee State Parks system promotes cycling in the state parks:
http://www.tn.gov/environment/parks/

The Natchez Trace Parkway begins south of Nashville and is a heavily used cycling venue. If you are interested in overnight cycling on The Trace, this bicycle-friendly site can help with reservations and information:
http://www.natcheztracetravel.com/

BICYCLE CLUBS

Columbia Cycling Club
http://www.columbiacyclingclub.com
This is a club for bicyclists in the Columbia, Tennessee, area.

Harpeth Bike Club
http://www.harpethbikeclub.com
This is a club to promote cycling in the greater Nashville area.

Highland Rimmers Bicycle Club
http://www.host.fptoday.com/restn/hrbc/bikeclub.asp
The Highland Rimmers Bicycle Club, Inc., is a nonprofit corporation chartered by the State of Tennessee whose objects and purposes are to promote the general interests of bicycling in all its phases.

Murfreesboro Bicycle Club
http://www.mborobike.com/
This is a club for bicyclists in the Murfreesboro, Tennessee, area.

Veloteers Bicycle Club
http://www.veloteers.org
This is a bicycle club to promote interest, educate, and encourage fun and safe participation in bicycling of all forms in the greater Nashville area.

There are also various meet-up groups who ride together periodically. They post somewhere in cyberspace, but ride real bikes. Here are two examples:
Sumner County group:
http://sumnerrides.blogspot.com/

Hendersonville area group:
http://fogbees.com/

ORGANIZED RIDES

There are several organized rides in the area. These rides are generally well supported with rest stops, restrooms, a sweep (a last rider who makes sure everyone makes it back to the ride start), and, many times, an on-site mechanic. They are a good way to explore areas you might not want to ride on a first-time basis without support.

Big Hill Challenge

The Veloteers Bicycle Club sponsors the Big Hill Challenge (www.bighill challenge.com) in Wilson County at Watertown. Held in late June, it is a supported tour ride with short and long options and rest stops.

Bike Ride Across Wilson County (BRAWC)

The BRAWC (http://www.wilsoncountyfair.net/special-events/bicycle-ride) is held in Wilson County in Lebanon, Tennessee, as part of the Wilson County Fair, held in August each year. There are both short and long routes, and rest stops are included.

Columbia Cycling Club

The Columbia Cycling Club (www.columbiacyclingclub.com) sponsors seven races throughout the year and one "tour."

Gran Fondo and Femme Fondo

The Gran Fondo bicycle shop (www.grandfondocycles.com) sponsors an annual ride in October in the Leiper's Fork and Natchez Trace Parkway area. It features a post-ride lunch and routes with short and long options. Gran Fondo also sponsors an annual ride for women in September.

Harpeth River Ride

The Harpeth Bike Club sponsors this ride (http://www.harpethriverride.com/) in the Williamson County area. It is well supported, with various route lengths.

Heart of Tennessee 100 (HOT 100)

The Murfreesboro Bike Club (http://www.mborobike.com/) sponsors this ride each August, in the Rutherford County area. It is a popular ride with several route lengths.

Tour de Nash

Walk/Bike Nashville sponsors this ride (www.tourdenash.org) in the metro Davidson County area, in May. It is a popular ride with both short and long routes.

There are other, less-well-known organized rides in the area. Most of them are fund-raisers for worthy causes, generally sponsored by local chapters of a national organization, and are done around the country. They include Ride of Silence and Tour de Cure.

A local charity ride held in the fall is the Hoover Ride for Hope Gran Fondo (www.hooverhope.org). Another locally sponsored, national organization ride is The Cycling for Children Charity Bike Ride, sponsored by the Kiwanis Club of Spring Hill and Thompson's Station (http://www.springhillkiwanis.com/). Yet another is the Gallatin Gran Fondo charity ride, a Lions Club beneficiary event held in September.

Joining a bike club is a great way to meet other people interested in cycling and also gets you on the mailing lists for organized cycling events in this area. Memberships are usually very reasonably priced for individuals or families.

LOCAL BIKE SHOPS

There is a good distribution of bike shops in the middle Tennessee area. This list is intended to include all of them as of the date of this writing. You can check out other resources in the book for possible additions. One good place to check is http://www.walkbikenashville.org/shops.

Biker's Choice
709 W. Main St., Hendersonville; (615) 822-2512
11493 Lebanon Rd., Mt. Juliet; (615) 758-8620
http://www.thebikerschoice.com/
Biker's Choice has been in business since 1989 in Hendersonville. They offer sales, service, repair, and fitting, and include a full warranty—even a money-back guarantee. They sell Specialized, Trek, Haro and Redline BMX, Salsa Adventure Bikes, and Niner mountain bikes.

Cumberland Transit
2807 West End Ave., Nashville; (615) 321-4069; http://cumberlandtransit.com/cycling/
Cumberland Transit has been locally owned and operated since 1971. They are located in the Vanderbilt area of Nashville across from The Parthenon. They are a bike shop / outdoor store with experienced, knowledgeable staff, covering all outdoor activities except skiing. They sell new Specialized, Trek, Felt, and Electra bikes. They will repair any people-powered device on two wheels that you bring in to the store. They rent some bikes, including helmets and locks. They will also accept bikes shipped to them.

Eastside Cycles
103 South 11th St., Nashville; (615) 469-1079; http://www.eastside-cycles.com/
Eastside Cycles is located in East Nashville at Five Points. They are a family-owned, neighborhood-oriented, local shop, and have been in business about six years. They sell new Cannondale, Phat, Kona Electra, Surly, and Giant bicycles. They also rent bikes, including helmets. They will repair any bike. They have a very cool mural on the outside of their building.

Gran Fondo
5133 Harding Rd., Suite A6, Nashville; (615) 354-1090; http://www.granfondo cycles.com/
Gran Fondo is a full-service bike shop for serious bikers. They specialize in drop-bar road bikes; every sale includes a fit. They sell Bianchi, Focus, Lynskey,

Parlee, Pegoretti, and Specialized bikes. They will repair anything, but work on a reservation basis. They offer a beginner class in summer. Their route won *Bicycling* magazine's Top 100 Rides in 2013. This route is available at the store; it is an approximate combination of the Country Store Tour and Leiper's Creek rides in this book.

Gran Fondo Trail & Fitness
5133 Harding Rd., Suite B-1, Nashville; (615) 499-4634; http://www.granfondo trail.com/
Gran Fondo Trail & Fitness is a relatively new shop that is trying to address the need for entry-point and mountain bikes. They have been in business about two years, and share the name only of their sister shop, Gran Fondo. They sell new Specialized and Lynskey road and mountain bikes. They will repair any bike. They have rides from the shop every morning, and welcome riders of all abilities. They also sponsor a beginner ride on Saturday mornings. George and Bryan aim to meet the needs of the person who is just getting into the sport.

Green Fleet Bicycle Shop
1579 Edgehill Ave., Nashville; (615) 379-8687; http://greenfleetbikes.com
Green Fleet is a full-service bike shop in the midtown area. They sell Brompton folding bikes and Linus, Surly, Fuji, and SE bicycles. They will repair any bicycle. They have a fleet of rental bikes (and helmets). They also sell these bikes as used. Green Fleet also has a courier service. If you want one more ride, sign up with these guys for a tour of downtown on a bike! You can bring your own bike if you wish. Their website has full details.

Halcyon Bike Shop
1119 Halcyon Ave., Corner of 12th Ave. S. & Halcyon Ave., Nashville; (615) 730-9344; www.halcyonbike.com
Halcyon is a bit different from most of the other shops, as they only sell used bikes. They are a community bike shop. You can come in and work on your bike using their tools and stands. If you have a question, they will be glad to help you based on availability. You get all that, for no charge, unless they "touch a wrench" on your behalf. Because the only bikes they sell are used bikes, they will sell your bike for you on a consignment basis. They rent mountain bikes and commuter bikes. They are founders of a joint community project with Oasis Center to teach young people how to repair a bike. They also do frame building and repair on steel frames.

Mac's Harpeth Bikes
1100 Hillsboro Rd., Franklin; (615) 472-1002; www.macsharpethbikes.com
Mac's is a local shop near downtown Franklin. They are a full-service shop, including fits, sales, and repairs. They sell Fuji, Haro, Kestrel, Niner, and SE Racing bikes. They also sell used bikes, either based on consignment or from customer trade-ins. They do rent bikes, but only by request. They will repair anything that rolls in the door. They are just down the street from Franklin High School.

MOAB Franklin and Murfreesboro
109 Del Rio Pike, Suite 105, Franklin; (615) 807-2035; http://moabbikes.com/
310 North Maple St., Murfreesboro; (615) 893-7725; http://moabbikes.com
MOAB Bikes is a full-service bike shop with locations in Franklin, Murfreesboro, and Cookeville. They sell Trek, Specialized, Niner, BMC, Yeti, Look, Coinago, Moots, Felt, and Santa Cruz bikes. They also take trade-ins, which they have for sale if you are looking for a used bike. They do have rental bikes, but do not have helmets on a rental basis. They have a passion for helping their customers have a good time on the bike. They also offer weekly rides.

R.B.'s Cyclery, Inc
3078 Maddux Way #300, Franklin; (615) 567-6633; www.rbscyclery.com
R.B.'s is a full-service shop. They sell Cannondale, Felt, Focus, Cervelo, KHS, and Jamis bikes. They do not take trade-ins, but they will sell your bike for you. If you wish to donate your bike to Oasis Center, they will handle it, and give you a 10 percent discount on your new bike (not on sale). Oasis Center offers a variety of services aimed at improving the lives of youth; one such service is training them to work on their own bicycle. They address all level of riders, from beginner to avid; 95% of their sales are to non-racing customers. They also offer shop rides.

REI
261 Franklin Rd., Brentwood; (615) 376-4248; http://rei.com
REI is a nationwide co-op. They offer sporting goods and outdoor equipment, along with a full-service bike shop. They sell Electra, Marin, Raleigh, Cannondale, Novara, Skuut, and Tern bikes. They will repair any bike. They offer member discounts through the co-op.

Ride615
3441 Lebanon Rd. #103, Hermitage; (615) 200-7433; www.ride615.com
Ride615 is a relatively new shop that is trying to address the need for more cycling resources in the Hermitage area. They have been in business about

Appendix A: Bicycling Resources

two years. They sell new Raleigh and Santa Cruz bikes, with more to come. They also rent bikes, including helmets. They will repair any bike. They have Monday/Wednesday rides in summer and Saturday rides in winter, even with trainers if the weather outside is bad. They sponsor meetings and other activities of the Veloteers Bicycle Club. They want to be a bike store, but also a supporter of the cycling community.

Smoopy's Vintage Bicycles
2602 E Mail Street, Murfreesboro; (615) 410-3928; http://www.smoopys bicycles.com/
Smoopy's is a specialty bike shop in Murfreesboro. They specialize in used, cruiser, 3 speed, and vintage road bikes. You can get all kinds of parts and accessories there. They are also a dealer for PureFix and 3G Cruiser bikes.

Sun & Ski
501 Opry Mills Dr., Nashville; (615) 886-4854
545 Cool Springs Blvd., Franklin; (615) 628-0289
http://www.sunandski.com
Sun & Ski is an outdoor store with a full-service bike shop. They sell BMX bikes. They also sell Fujji, Haro, Marin, Orbea, Raleigh, and SE bikes. They do full maintenance and will repair any bike.

Trace Bikes
8080B Hwy. 100, Nashville; (615) 646-2485; http://tracebikes.com/
Trace Bikes is worthy of its name, located about 1.5 miles east of The Trace. They are a local shop that sponsors weekly rides, winter and summer, and a race team. They work often with people who ship their bike in to do a ride down The Trace. They sell new Felt, Trek, and Gary Fisher bikes. They also rent bikes, including helmets. They will repair any bike.

The Wheel
11 Public Square, Columbia; (931) 381-3225; http://thewheelbicycleshop.com
The Wheel has been in business for about forty years. They are a local shop meeting various cycling needs in nearby Columbia. They sell Schwinn, Trailmate, Trek, Cannondale, Eastern, and GT bicycles. They also provide repair services.

Appendix B: Nashville Gems

VISITING MUSIC CITY

Music City has become a convention destination. New convention facilities have been completed, and more are planned for the downtown area. You may be wondering how you can do some riding while you're in Music City. One option is to rent a bike. You should bring your own helmet, riding clothes, water bottle, etc. (although some bike rental shops also rent helmets).

One outstanding bike rental option is Nashville B-cycle (https://nashville.bcycle.com/home.aspx). This is a series of rental stations around the city where you can rent a bike (almost) for free if you return it within an hour. As of this writing, there are twenty-one rental stations around the city (Metro area only). To rent a bike, you need to purchase a twenty-four-hour pass or a seven-day membership. (There are longer membership options available.) Each offers unlimited usage, and the first hour is free. These rental bikes have adjustable seat posts, a basket, automatic lights, and three speeds. This is a great way to see the city or take in a ride or two.

A second way to rent a bike is to go through a bike shop; there are several in the area that rent bikes. Most of them even include a helmet in the rental. Take a look at the Bike Shops section in Appendix A for more information.

If you cannot ride any bike except your own, you can ship it. Again, check out the Bike Shops listing. Almost all of the shops will receive and assemble your bike for you. It is best to call them first for a contact and a recommended shipper.

THE NATCHEZ TRACE PARKWAY

The Natchez Trace Parkway, about 20 miles from downtown Nashville, is a unique treasure in the area, especially for biking. The Trace is a unit of the National Park Service (http://www.nps.gov/natr). It posts a 50 mph speed limit and is closed to commercial traffic. These two factors contribute to its popularity as a great place for biking. On weekends and holidays, you will always meet bikers, but during off-peak times, like weekdays, it can be a quiet place, given its proximity to Nashville. Because of all these things, it attracts both local and regional cycling events.

The Trace is also a popular multiday bike ride venue. It is on one of the Adventure Cycling national routes. There are rest stops at 20- to 50-mile intervals on the entire 444-mile road. The National Park Service does an excellent job of maintaining The Trace. Although its average width is less than 1,000 feet, you still get the feeling that you are riding through an unpopulated area of fields and farmland. There are places to camp along the way, and many people take this self-supported option. There are also bed-and-breakfast venues that are about a day's bike ride apart down the length of The Trace. It is quite customary to encounter "through riders" at the rest stops.

There are many things to enjoy on The Trace, including biking, hiking, horseback riding, and camping. The vendor for information and reservations at B&B sites on The Trace is Natchez Trace B&B Reservation Service (natchez tracetravel.com). Sometimes riders will make reservations and then mail daily clothes and supplies to the B&Bs to avoid packing and carrying for a long trip.

Most riders spend six to ten days to cover the entire Trace. Most bike shops in Nashville will receive bikes shipped in and assemble them for multi-day riders who want to begin their ride from the northern end.

A combination of information from the above reservation site and maps from the National Park Service site can launch your planning process for a multiday ride. You may wish to consult one of several books about The Trace (e.g., F. Lynne Bachleda's *Guide to the Natchez Trace Parkway*). There are various combinations, including two- or three-day rides; for example, Nashville to Tupelo. Regardless of whether it's short or long, you will certainly enjoy your ride on The Trace.

From a sightseeing standpoint, little remains of what used to be the "interstate highway" on The Trace, from Natchez, Mississippi, to Nashville during the period of 1790–1812. A trip down The Trace can challenge your imagination and make you eager to learn more about the early settlers—to see what they saw two centuries ago.

One interesting place on the northern end is Gordon House. Although it is a rather plain two-story brick house, when it was built, it was the first brick house in the area. And, Dolly Gordon, wife of soldier John Gordon, built it! Dolly raised their ten children at this site after the death of her husband.

There are other restorations, exhibits, and places of interest along the entire route: The Trace headquarters in Tupelo has a significant historical exhibit; on the northern end, the Meriwether Lewis historical site has been reconstructed; there are large native Indian mounds in Mississippi; and much more.

Check out The Trace for your next biking adventure!

Ride Index

About the Author

John Doss is a resident of middle Tennessee who has cycled in the area for more than twenty years. He cycles independently, and is also a regular rider with the local Harpeth Bike Club. John appreciates the easy access and shorter routes that can be covered after work or on a weekend morning, and he also enjoys multiday bike tours. He has ridden bike tours in Virginia and North Carolina on the Blue Ridge Parkway, and in Georgia and Tennessee, but the Bike Ride Across Tennessee is his favorite. John enjoys riding on the Natchez Trace Parkway, meeting cyclists from other states and countries who are "riding through." He is a member of the Harpeth Bike Club, the League of American Bicyclists, and the Adventure Cycling Association.